About Island Press

Island Press is the only nonprofit organization in the United States whose principal purpose is the publication of books on environmental issues and natural resource management. We provide solutions-oriented information to professionals, public officials, business and community leaders, and concerned citizens who are shaping responses to environmental problems.

In 1994, Island Press celebrated its tenth anniversary as the leading provider of timely and practical books that take a multidisciplinary approach to critical environmental concerns. Our growing list of titles reflects our commitment to bringing the best of an expanding body of literature to the environmental community throughout North America and the world.

Support for Island Press is provided by The Geraldine R. Dodge Foundation, The Energy Foundation, The Ford Foundation, The George Gund Foundation, William and Flora Hewlett Foundation, The John D. and Catherine T. MacArthur Foundation, The Andrew W. Mellon Foundation, The Joyce Mertz-Gilmore Foundation, The New-Land Foundation, The Pew Charitable Trusts, The Rockefeller Brothers Fund, The Tides Foundation, Turner Foundation, Inc., The Rockefeller Philanthropic Collaborative, Inc., and individual donors.

Collaborative Planning for Wetlands and Wildlife

Collaborative Planning for Wetlands and Wildlife

ISSUES AND EXAMPLES

Edited by Douglas R. Porter and David A. Salvesen

ISLAND PRESS
Washington, D.C. • Covelo, California

Library of Congress Cataloging in Publication Data

Collaborative planning for wetlands and wildlife: issues and examples
/editors, Douglas R. Porter and David A. Salvesen
    p.   cm.
  Includes bibliographical references and index.
  ISBN 1-55963-287-9 (paper)
    1. Wetland conservation—United States—Planning.   2. Wildlife
conservation—United States—Planning.   I. Porter, Douglas R.
II. Salvesen, David.
QH76.C65   1995   94-30143
333.91′816′0973—dc20   CIP

Contents

Foreword

This book grew out of a series of policy dialogues initiated by Lindell L. Marsh in 1986 through the Federal Policy Council of the Urban Land Institute, based in Washington, D.C. Known as the Federal Permitting Working Group, the group brought together federal agency officials, congressional staff, conservationists, developers, academicians, state and local officials, and private planners and attorneys to discuss ways in which federal permitting processes for wetlands and endangered species protection worked and did not work. Meeting two or three times a year over several years, the group eventually was cosponsored by the Environmental Law Institute and was co-chaired by Lindell Marsh and myself. The group still meets periodically, now cosponsored by the Environmental Law Institute and the Growth Management Institute.

The group's discussions typically centered on issues within a particular geographic area or region that was experiencing substantial pressures for development and for conservation of wetlands or endangered species habitat.

Out of these meetings emerged a consensus that the permit-by-permit, ad hoc approach to wetlands and habitat conservation often does not produce optimum results for either development or conservation interests. Adding to the dilemma, federal permit processes usually are poorly integrated with state and local permit processes.

The Federal Permitting Working Group began to take a closer look at comprehensive, rational approaches to accommodating development while protecting wetlands and sensitive wildlife habitats. It brought in state and local officials, as well as federal regional officials, to describe efforts "in the field." To provide additional information on the subject, the Environmental Protection Agency (EPA) funded four case studies prepared jointly by the Environmental Law Institute and the Urban Land Institute. The case studies attempted to define success factors in planning efforts involving multiple layers of government and a variety of private interests. The discussions and case studies furnished the core and *raison d'être* of this book.

I have been impressed by the success of collaborative, area-wide approaches, but even those successes illustrate the need for policy direction and funding commitments from federal agencies at the top, especially the U.S. Army Corps of Engineers and EPA. Furthermore, it is clear that links to state and local planning and management efforts need to be strengthened, so that the end product of an area-wide planning and implementation program can assure both conservation interests and the development community that participation in such programs results in certainty and timeliness for all parties.

Florida has supported collaborative planning focused on specific issues since the enactment of its first series of growth management laws in 1972, specifically with the Environmental Land and Water Management Act and its provisions for designating areas of critical state concern. A 1979 amendment led to the establishment of a number of resource planning and management committees charged with involving all relevant interests in crafting and implementing an area-wide resource management plan. While not without problems, as the East Everglades case study suggests, these collaborative efforts have improved our capacities for balancing growth and environmental concerns—for achieving sustainable development in local as well as global terms.

John DeGrove

Director, Florida Atlantic University/Florida International University Joint Center for Environmental and Urban Problems, Fort Lauderdale, Florida

Introduction

David A. Salvesen and Douglas R. Porter

In many parts of the country, particularly in the Southwest and Southeast, shy, diminutive creatures such as the least Bell's vireo, the Stephens' kangaroo rat, the Mission blue butterfly, and the Key Largo woodrat have practically become household words. These rare animals gained instant notoriety for temporarily or permanently stopping development in its tracks. Similarly, all across the country, the presence of wetlands has prevented, delayed, or rerouted development, moving developers to search for dry land for their projects.

Conflicts between development and environmental protection are not new and likely will become increasingly common as urban communities continue to expand into exurban and rural areas. These conflicts become particularly acute in areas that are rich in wetlands or endangered species and that also have strong real estate markets—areas like Austin, Texas; San Diego, California; Orlando, Florida; and Lindhurst, New Jersey. While federal laws and some state laws protect wetlands and endangered species habitats, they also allow some development to occur in these environmentally sensitive areas. For example, one of the purposes of the Clean Water Act (CWA) is to protect wetlands by regulating dredging and filling of wetlands. Each year, the U.S. Army Corps of Engineers (Corps)—the permitting agency—reviews about 10,000 applications for dredge-and-fill permits, all on a case-by-case basis, and regularly approves the vast majority of them, usually with some conditions for mitigation of adverse environmental impacts.

In addition, even the Endangered Species Act (ESA), one of the strictest land use laws in the nation, allows development to occur under certain conditions in habitats of endangered species.

Environmentalists and developers have charged that the existing federal and state regulatory programs neither adequately protect wetlands and endangered species nor guide urban growth in a rational, consistent manner. Environmentalists have long complained that the case-by-case permitting

1

process causes "death by one thousand cuts" of environmentally sensitive areas. While each individual development project may only minimally impact a particular wetland, cumulative impacts over time become significant as each project gradually reduces an entire wetland or habitat ecosystem.

Developers, on the other hand, chafe under a system of interminable delays, inconsistent decisions, and different objectives and guidance from one level of government to the next. Little coordination exists among federal, state, and local resource agencies, and developers must endure separate, often redundant, and sometimes conflicting review and permitting processes. Federal agencies typically respond only to development proposals currently before them and lack the authority, funding, or will to develop comprehensive policies and standards to reconcile conservation and development objectives. Under such programs, regulators cannot anticipate future conflicts and take steps to avoid them.

The problem of overlapping local, state, and federal permitting authority was cited over a decade ago in a report by the federal Office of Coastal Zone Management: "Developers may obtain all necessary state and local permits only to have a project denied by federal agencies. Often this occurs after specific sites have been selected, land acquired, local permits obtained, and large sums of money invested in engineering drawings, site investigations, and environmental analysis."[1] In addition, applicants often get mixed signals from government policies. For example, local zoning maps may designate wetland or endangered species habitat areas for residential development. Developers may be falsely encouraged to build there, only to have federal agencies belatedly tell them otherwise.

The failure of existing regulatory programs to reconcile conflicts between development and environmental protection led policymakers in several jurisdictions, particularly those with a prevalence of wetlands or endangered species habitat, to initiate collaborative planning efforts to address such conflicts within a coordinated, consensus-building framework. Working with all affected interests, including developers, environmentalists, and regulators, the communities sought to develop comprehensive plans that balanced development with environmental protection in special areas, ensuring that critical natural resources would not be gradually degraded and providing a more predictable permitting process. Only a handful of such plans exist so far; many of them are described in this book.

Collaborative, Area-wide Planning

The concept of collaborative, area-wide planning, like regional planning, was born out of the need to address problems with greater than local significance.

Area-wide planning differs from traditional regional planning, however, in its focus on conflicts between development and protection of natural resources in a specific geographic area, such as a watershed, estuary, or endangered species habitat. Typically, also, the areas encompass a number of land ownerships and several local jurisdictions.

Several models already exist for large-scale resource management. For example, the Pinelands Commission, comprising state, federal, and local representatives, guides development in the Pinelands National Reserve—an ecologically unique area encompassing approximately one million acres in southern New Jersey. The reserve contains a core preservation area, where strict land use controls apply, and an outer protection area, with less rigid controls in force. Similarly, the Adirondack Park Agency guides land use in roughly six million acres in northern New York.

Area-wide plans, however, typically apply to much smaller areas, usually a few hundred or few thousand acres. They generally focus on only one or two resources, such as wetlands or endangered species. But probably the most important distinction is the way the plans are developed. Area-wide planning is a collaborative, often voluntary, ad hoc process that brings developers, environmentalists, and government regulators to the negotiating table to balance natural resource protection with development for a particular area.

Typically, such planning efforts occur in areas where intense development pressures collide with strong interests in protecting an imperiled natural resource, like wetlands. The plans generally set aside high-value resource areas for preservation and identify areas where development may readily occur. For example, in Austin, Texas, an ad hoc coalition of developers, public officials, and environmentalists has been working to identify and preserve suitable habitat for a number of endangered species, including the golden-cheeked warbler and the black-capped vireo, and to earmark areas for development in advance of permit applications. By providing assurances to all parties, the plan can help avoid future land use conflicts and reduce permit processing time as well.

Ideally, collaborative, area-wide plans offer something for everybody. Developers gain greater predictability, reduced regulatory burdens, and a streamlined permit process. Moreover, such plans offer developers certain economies of scale: the cost of conducting environmental studies and of acquiring sensitive lands to preserve can be spread among many developers. Environmentalists receive greater assurance that environmentally valuable natural areas will be protected in perpetuity and that individual development projects will not ultimately consume an entire ecosystem. And federal agencies reduce the number of individual permits they must process.

With so much to gain, why haven't regulatory agencies and the private sector enthusiastically embraced and promoted collaborative planning? Because, unfortunately, planning consumes large amounts of time and talent, and for the most part, no institutional mechanism exists to fund the necessary studies, countless meetings, and negotiations, or to develop and implement a plan. Instead, the process relies primarily on voluntary contributions of both money and time.

Moreover, no guarantee exists that the process will result in long-term benefits or in definite regulatory products. Collaborative planning may end in stalemate, with no agreement on levels of preservation or development. Furthermore, collaborative, area-wide plans involve trade-offs and compromises—for example, allowing development in degraded wetlands in exchange for preserving pristine wetlands—but some agencies and conservationists simply cannot bring themselves to label any environmental resources as expendable.

One of the first examples of collaborative, area-wide planning occurred in 1975 in Grays Harbor, Washington, where a planning group of local, state, and federal government agency representatives developed an estuary management plan for the region. The protracted and rather inconclusive planning process in Grays Harbor has been considered ultimately unsuccessful, however, primarily because two of the main groups that would be affected by the plan, developers and environmentalists, were not officially involved in the planning process.

Federal Planning Mechanisms to Support Collaborative Planning

Federal agencies such as EPA, the Corps, and the U.S. Fish and Wildlife Service (USFWS) have three main planning devices at their disposal to support collaborative, area-wide planning: advance identification, special area management plans, and habitat conservation plans. Under Section 230.80 of the EPA 404(b)(1) guidelines, the EPA and the Corps may carry out studies and, in advance of permit applications, designate wetlands as suitable or unsuitable for disposal of dredged or fill material. Advance notice of where fills should or should not occur guides developers in their site selections and also should minimize conflicts between the Corps and EPA.

The 1980 amendments to the Coastal Zone Management Act allow the Corps, in conjunction with federal, state, and local resource agencies, to develop a comprehensive plan—called a special area management plan (SAMP)—to provide both natural resource protection and reasonable coastal-dependent development in a specific geographic area. The plan contains a comprehensive statement of policies and criteria to guide land use.

Finally, under the Endangered Species Act, the USFWS can approve plans, called habitat conservation plans, that allow some development to occur in endangered species habitat if the development will not substantially reduce the survivability of a species.

All three area-wide planning mechanisms attempt to balance conservation with development in a way that reduces future conflicts, provides predictability, and protects important ecological areas. Recently the EPA, the Corps, and the private sector have shown much greater interest in moving away from the case-by-case permit process, as evidenced by the increase in the number of SAMPs, advance identification plans, and habitat conservation plans. However, although a number of such plans have been completed, few guidelines exist to assist the planning process, and there is no record indicating successes and failures of those efforts.

Building on Experience

This book begins to build a record and suggest guidelines for more effective planning for wetlands and wildlife protection. Although the examples illustrated in this book are not intended to serve as infallible models of collaborative, area-wide planning—this is not a how-to book—the studies demonstrate how different communities have creatively reconciled the often competing goals of development and environmental protection. The plans they developed and their experiences in developing them offer valuable insights for other communities facing similar dilemmas. In addition, the issues and problems encountered in their experiences have important implications for future actions of state and federal agencies.

The book begins with Lindell Marsh and Peter Lallas's penetrating analysis of the limitations of traditional regulatory approaches and their detailed elucidation of approaches to and benefits of collaborative planning efforts, which they term focused, special-area planning.

Next, Timothy Beatley presents a comprehensive overview of the current state of habitat conservation planning; he argues for a multi-species approach that integrates conservation plans with local planning efforts. Chapters 4 and 5 describe multi-species habitat planning for a large region around Austin, Texas, and efforts of three counties in Southern California to provide a multi-species planning framework for habitat conservation plans, respectively.

The next seven chapters describe specific planning efforts involving wetlands as the key issue, including two in large, complex regions, Chesapeake Bay and the Columbia River estuary, and five focused on smaller but significant areas. In two of the smaller planning efforts, Chiwaukee Prairie and Anchorage, advance identification of wetlands played an important role in the plans, and in one, the Hackensack Meadowlands, a special area management plan was a key element of the planning process. The final chapter draws conclusions about these experiences and defines the obstacles that remain to be overcome.

Throughout, the book attempts to answer the questions asked by regulators, environmentalists, and developers who seek practical alternatives to the existing case-by-case permitting process: Will wetlands and wildlife have greater protection and will developers have greater certainty under collaborative, area-wide plans than with the case-by-case process? Why have some efforts failed miserably while others worked admirably? What are the requisites for success? What potential funding sources might be tapped? Finally, the book offers valuable lessons learned from past and ongoing area-wide planning efforts.

NOTE

1. H. Grant Dehart and Michael Glazer, "Improved Coordination for Planning and Permitting in Special Areas: A Report to the President for the Federal Coastal Program Review," U.S. Office of Coastal Zone Management, National Oceanic and Atmospheric Administration, 1980, p. 18.

Focused, Special-Area Conservation Planning: An Approach to Reconciling Development and Environmental Protection

*Lindell L. Marsh and Peter L. Lallas**

E D I T O R S '   S U M M A R Y

Traditional project-by-project, "command and control" approaches to ensuring environmental protection in urbanizing areas have addressed issues in a fragmented manner, promoted conflict among the interests involved, allocated costs of development and environmental protection inadequately, and resulted in questionable outcomes. Marsh and Lallas argue that environmental protection can be reconciled with development objectives better if collaborative area-wide planning processes are employed to address conflicting interests and concerns. They describe some mechanisms for this type of planning that are available through state and federal environmental rules and regulations. Although focused approaches to special-area planning are not problem-free, wider use of these and similar mechanisms promises improved, more long-lasting results than the more common project-focused review process.

Background

During the past several years, the use of focused special-area conservation plans to resolve conflicts between development and environmental conservation interests has won an increasing number of proponents.[1] Such plans seek to focus on specific needs, such as wildlife conservation, in the broader context

---

*The views expressed by Mr. Lallas in this chapter are his personally and do not necessarily reflect the views of his employer, the Environmental Protection Agency, or the U.S. Government.

of competing concerns, such as urbanization and timber production, in a defined subregional area. The plans generally include prescriptions and standards, as well as assurances that the plans will be implemented. Also, the plans may limit impacts on the other concerns, assuring a reconciliation between competing concerns. The plans are designed and carried out by local interests and agencies, working together in a special planning process.

The focused process and resulting plan remain subject to all existing regulatory rules and requirements and are intended to support their implementation and increase their effectiveness. Nevertheless, in its focus on specific issues, inclusion of diverse interests, and collaborative planning approach, the process differs in important ways from more traditional approaches to land use governance.

The Traditional Paradigm in Land Use Regulation

Historically, planning and development of privately owned lands generally has been delegated to the private sector and carried out on a project-by-project basis, with public review occurring primarily at the local level. The public review process, which evolved from early English judicial procedures, traditionally has been characterized by the presentation of privately initiated and prepared project proposals before judge-like panels, with the public and others cast as critics or supporters of the proposals.

Before the 1960s, the environmental impacts of proposed development activities generally received little attention in land use reviews. This approach has changed significantly in the past 20 years. As a result of growing concern with environmental impacts, the U.S. Congress and state legislatures have enacted a series of laws that broaden public review and impose stricter regional, state, and federal levels of agency review over proposed land use activities.[2] In the same period, the field of administrative law has undergone a virtual revolution with the articulation of new requirements for agencies to carry out these new legislative mandates. The courts also have assumed an active role in these developments and in ensuring that administrative agencies adequately carry out legislative and regulatory mandates.

These and other reforms have been important in limiting the environmental damage of development activities. The Endangered Species Act, for example, has been critical to the preservation of several individual species. Similarly, laws encouraging protection of wetlands have saved countless wetlands from dredging and filling activities. Nevertheless, widespread, irreversible adverse impacts on the environment continue to occur, on a local, regional/national, and—increasingly—global scale. For example, threatened or endangered plants and animals exist in every one of California's 58 counties. Nationwide, recent counts indicate that over 750 animal and plant species of the United States are listed as endangered or threatened, and 3,930 species are waiting to be listed.

At the same time, the decision-making process for protecting the environment frequently is inefficient and results in an inadequate and inequitable allocation of the costs of achieving preservation objectives. Further, the result imposed can cause very high economic costs for affected individuals or entities.

One source of these problems appears to be the degree to which the process relies on the traditional regulatory paradigm of land use governance, based on public-sector reviews of private-sector proposals, and its inability to transcend the limitations of this approach. The reforms and changes of recent years, while revolutionary in many senses, have not displaced this traditional paradigm. They have focused instead on strengthening public-sector reviews. Both the Clean Air Act and the Clean Water Act, for example, include detailed top-down types of regulations to be applied during the review stage of proposed land use activities. The protective provisions of the Endangered Species Act also focus on public agency reviews and restrictions on proposed actions or development activities.

As discussed in more detail below, this proposal/review approach tends to (1) address issues in a fragmented and incomplete manner, (2) promote conflict and discourage cooperative and trusting relationships within the constituency involved, (3) allocate the costs of development and environmental protection inadequately and inequitably, (4) fail to provide certainty to the various interests, and (5) result in unnecessary losses and costs to the broader constituency.

Fragmentation

The reconciliation of development and wildlife and habitat conservation often involves concerns that span space (geographical distances), systems (ecosystems and human-made systems), and time (impacts of past activities, effects on future generations), as well as several levels of policy (local, regional, and national). The traditional proposal/review paradigm fragments or isolates the evaluation of these concerns in a number of ways.

PROJECT-BY-PROJECT ORIENTATION

The proposal/review model generally narrows the focus of land use governance decisions to individual development projects. This traditional approach evolved as a complement to the predominant land use ethic of incoming settlers in the early years of this nation, which generally favored rapid settlement of lands and virtually unrestrained exploitation of the once astonishingly abundant wildlife and resources. It also may have reflected a vision that the lands, wildlife, and resources were inexhaustible, and that the impacts of human activities therefore were isolated and relatively confined. But the evidence suggests that the development activities of these earlier times took an enormous toll on habitat and wildlife.

The variety of public environmental review requirements and environmental protection laws adopted in recent years reflects a change in this earlier ethic and attitude. These laws, among other things, evince a growing recognition that any apparent dividing lines between individual land projects or uses and their impacts on wildlife and the environment which may once have existed have all but disappeared—dissolved by changes in population, expanding development, and the continuous growth in the scale and impact of human activities.

Nevertheless, many of these recently adopted laws have maintained the project-by-project orientation of the traditional system. The environmental impact statement requirements of NEPA, for example, apply to "major federal actions," often in a project-specific context, and parallel state statutes adopt a similar project-by-project focus. The protective provisions of the federal Endangered Species Act also focus in large measure on restricting individual project activities. The Clean Water Act Section 404 regulatory program pertains to project-related discharge of dredged or fill material into navigable waters. Frequently, the projects under consideration are isolated development proposals, with the timing of the review process determined by private objectives rather than concerns for wildlife and wetlands protection.

The traditional approach generally separates the review of concurrent or future activities in adjacent areas, even though such areas may be connected ecologically or in other ways to a project site. As a consequence, conservation concerns are not addressed in an integrated fashion but are considered in the more narrow context of the individual project. The protection of the California desert tortoise exemplifies the failure of the traditional approach. The tortoise's historic range extends over a large portion of southeastern California, southern Nevada, and western Arizona. It has proved virtually impossible to resolve protection issues over the specie's entire range as individual projects are proposed and reviewed in and around Clark County, Nevada, for example. How much habitat will be left when projects are completed? How secure is that habitat? Are there other projects that can be anticipated in the future which will impact the habitat? Who will take care of the remaining habitat? Where will the funding come from?

DIVIDED JURISDICTION AND SEPARATED STAGES OF REVIEW

The traditional project review process is further fragmented at the institutional level, because of the division of review responsibilities and potential benefits and harms (of individual projects) among a variety of governmental authorities. This division occurs both horizontally (i.e., among neighboring political jurisdictions) and vertically (i.e., local, regional, state, and national authorities).

Horizontal separation of authority over individual project decisions creates discontinuities in addressing conservation concerns. Local jurisdictional/political boundaries often do not coincide with the locus of environmental effects of land use activities. At the same time, the potential economic benefits of a particular activity (e.g., the creation of a tax-revenue base) may be concentrated in the authority with primary project jurisdiction. These factors create a lack of accountability for interjurisdictional "spillover" impacts and a potentially significant imbalance among neighboring jurisdictions in the distribution of fiscal benefits versus environmental impacts of particular activities. The difficulties are compounded by the fact that little cooperation may occur among neighboring jurisdictions in project decisions.

The local/nonlocal division of jurisdictional authority (the vertical division) has led to its own set of problems, in part because responsible authorities often carry out their project reviews in separate and sequential stages— that is, local, regional, state, and national (as appropriate). Under current practice, for example, where regional, state, and/or federal regulatory approvals are required for a particular land use proposal, the responsible agencies frequently become involved only *after* local approvals have been granted. Frequently, only minimum levels of coordination exist among these stages of review.

Furthermore, where the issues involved are broader than the geographical limits of the local municipality, the local permitting agency often will simply approve a project, leaving resolution of broader issues to state and federal agencies. Although the existing regulatory framework clearly contemplates that local planning decisions must take into account the broader concerns and mandates of federal or state agencies, local authorities may be frustrated by extremely technical issues that may extend beyond project and even municipal boundaries. The desert tortoise, for example, is threatened not only by the loss of habitat due to development but also by habitat destruction from off-road vehicles and fires. How can a single project or a single municipality be expected to shoulder the burden of such an issue?

The consequence is that the current system often fails to consider environmental values in the early planning stages of potential land use activities (i.e., proactively), the point at which adjustments to these activities are most easily made. In such a situation, all sides lose. State and federal agencies may be faced with a locally approved project that does not adequately consider environmental concerns. As such concerns are factored into the design of the project at later stages, conservation interests or the public may believe that regulatory requirements have been ignored or squeezed in as an afterthought. On the other hand, the project proponent may consider that project changes made after local planning approvals were won have significantly altered the project and dashed its objectives. Clearly, a mechanism is needed to coordinate land use planning between agencies and across political boundaries.

RELIANCE ON COMMAND-AND-CONTROL OR TOP-DOWN REGULATIONS

The traditional approach tends to rely in large measure on restrictive, targeted, mandatory regulations handed down from federal and state agencies, uncoordinated with other types of intervention measures such as land conservancies, acquisition and management programs, area-wide planning techniques, and creative funding mechanisms. While provisions for the latter types of measures are found in existing law, frequently they are difficult to apply within a particular agency's regulatory process. Land acquisition to address impacts arising from several individual projects governed by separate regulatory review processes, for example, requires extraordinary cross-jurisdictional efforts. In addition, under a simple regulatory approach, even if a project is denied, a subsequent proposal for the same area may soon be attempted. As a result, the regulatory action often is limited to a simple approval or disapproval of a project (or, as a variant, to imposition of project-specific conditions) as the means to carry out environmental protection policies.

This is not intended to suggest that command-and-control/top-down regulations have not played a significant role in protecting wildlife, wetlands, and other environmental resources. However, they are inadequate, by themselves, to achieve the full purposes of the laws and to promote a fair reconciliation between these purposes and the interests of development. Regulatory imperatives alone may not, for example, offer adequate opportunity to perform scientific studies at the appropriate ecological level or to address economic losses that may occur through enforcement of such regulations.

For development interests and others, the result is a limited range of options available to reconcile environmental protection interests with development plans or other economic activities in a manner that respects both sets of objectives. For conservation interests, the patchwork of protection and/or mitigation measures that results from this type of regulation conflicts philosophically with an ecosystem approach to conservation.

LIMITED SCOPE OF REGULATIONS

The traditional system also often sharply limits the scope of regulation of land use activities. For example, the permit program under Section 404(b)(1) of the Clean Water Act covers the discharge of dredged or fill materials in navigable waters, including wetlands. The program does not extend, however, to activities in immediately adjacent uplands. As a result, the water quality, specific riparian habitat, and wildlife values of the wetlands that the regulations seek to protect may be destroyed by development in adjacent uplands (which, for example, isolates the wetlands) that lie beyond the regulatory framework.

Similar concerns arise in the protection of habitat and wildlife. The protective provisions of the federal Endangered Species Act generally do not apply to species that are rapidly approaching the status of "threatened" or "endangered" species. The act also is not focused on curbing gradual and expanding impacts that threaten biodiversity within large ecosystems.

The fragmentation of issues in a decision-making process may serve important purposes in an analytical process and is a basic concept of Western thought. At the same time, such fragmentation may inhibit the ability of a process to address basic relationships among the fragmented concerns. The historic process has tended to address isolated concerns (project by project, direct impacts), but often not the bigger picture (ecosystems, impacts over time, indirect impacts). It is reactive (separated stages of review, top-down) and not proactive (integrated decision-making process, use of horizontal non-regulatory intervention approaches).

The results are often detrimental for all interests. Long-term, coordinated measures for conservation at the ecosystem level often are not implemented and fragmentation of habitat and other environmental resources continues to occur. The consequences of fragmentation can be severe: some observers view the fragmentation of wildlife habitat as the single most important cause of species extinction today.[3] At the same time, the costs to society from increased development expenses, job losses, and land price inflation may be very significant. For individual land developers, costs increase as time is lost in the regulatory process, as substantial mitigation is required due to inefficient and perhaps inequitable project-by-project measures, and as risks associated with a more chaotic decision-making system increase.

Conflicts between Interests

The dynamics of the traditional project-by-project regulatory process tend to promote conflict and emotion-laden decisions. At the local level, participants in the process come before a relatively removed and often unsophisticated quasi-judicial panel, prepared for an intense and often brief argument with parties who may have conflicting interests. Project proponents frequently have a significant investment in the project by the time of the local review decision. To the extent that other levels of agency review occur later, costs or investments in a project may be even higher.

In this sense, the traditional paradigm resembles a forest fire moving across the landscape. All attention is focused at the fireline as each project comes up for public review. The clash of values is at its highest flash point; cool, well-thought-out, and even-handed decisions are often the exception. From the developer's perspective, the land is likely to be at its highest value (i.e., prepared for development and intended use). The conservation interests, on the other hand, may consider that the proposal that is already formulated has failed to take into account increasingly urgent environmental protection requirements and is positioned to go forward as is or not at all. Under such conditions, flexibility and options are all too often reduced on all sides.

The resulting conflict builds neither trust nor a cooperative spirit among the interests involved. This loss transcends the individual project decision and tends to prevent the interests from working together on solutions that might solve the underlying concerns, including solutions that may require broad efforts at the state and federal levels over time. Repetition of these encounters simply reinforces hostility and aggravates the situation. The problem is that the society has difficulty seeing the effects of this continued behavior.

Allocation and Internalization of Costs

The traditional process also makes it difficult to allocate the burdens of environmental protection adequately and equitably among the responsible interests. For example, the impacts of unregulated development generally are externalized as costs to environmental quality. Under existing regulations, for instance, the costs of unregulated development in upland areas (e.g., the isolation of wetland areas) may fall on adjacent wetlands or the ecosystem as a whole. In other cases, regulations may be skewed to cover large-scale, regionally significant projects but may allow small projects to proceed unregulated. These externalities may occur intergenerationally, from past generations to the present, and from the present to the future.

Developers want a level playing field; to the extent possible, costs should be spread equitably among the development interests. Cost sharing would assure that none would enjoy a competitive advantage (though even in this case some might continue to argue that such costs will be passed along to the ultimate user and tend to inflate the price of existing development). Conservation interests and others generally concur on the importance of achieving an equitable allocation of the costs of these impacts (based on the "polluter pays" principle and other concepts), both on grounds of equity and in order to prevent undue cost-based incentives for activities that create adverse impacts.

The equitable and adequate allocation of the burdens of conservation will continue to be the subject of significant legislative and judicial action. Who should bear the costs? The regulated developer? Those impacting the habitat (regulated and unregulated)? New development? What about previous development that has impacted the environment? Is there a state role? A federal role?

Cost issues continue to be contested in adjudications on takings, in the continuing struggle to reconcile visions of public and private interests in the rights and uses of property. In the land use area, one trend of recent cases has been to tolerate increased use by local authorities of exactions on individual developers. As pointed out in the later section on the takings issue, the courts traditionally have ruled that a taking shall be found only where a property owner is left with no viable economic use of the land. Recent decisions by the U.S. Supreme Court suggest that future courts may be increasingly willing to review the equitable allocation of environmental protection costs.

Predictability and Assurances

The traditional land use process is characterized by uncertainty and broad levels of administrative discretion, notwithstanding the significant level of detail contained in a variety of environmental protection statutes and regulations. Local agencies, as well as trustee or wildlife agencies, have a wide degree of latitude in deciding the fate of specific projects within the limits of their jurisdictional competence. The project review process contains many steps involving a variety of differently focused agencies, often with little or no coordination among them. Changes in the political landscape can be abrupt and can alter the prospects of an individual project quickly; as the approval process is protracted, this factor can become a fearful specter, one that has been characterized as "death by a thousand cuts."

For land development interests, the system has been viewed as a multiple-veto process with high transaction costs, varied and often conflicting and confusing objectives among the different agencies involved, and few mechanisms to reconcile those objectives. Developers share the fear that the rules of the game may change even after an initial approval is obtained. The attendant uncertainty is multiplied with a large-scale or phased project, particularly where major infrastructure must be constructed during an early stage.

Conservation interests, on the other hand, often find it difficult to monitor and participate effectively in a multiphase permitting process, and they also often face the prospect that if a development proposal is defeated, it may be replaced with yet another proposal or series of proposals in the future, each with the uncertain prospect of approval or denial. Developers and conservationists appear to share a common interest in increased predictability and long-term assurances.

A New Paradigm: Focused, Special-Area Conservation Plans

The current system offers a significantly stronger legal basis for environmental protection than the pre-1970 system, but environmental problems continue to grow and the inadequacies of the traditional process are increasingly apparent. Accordingly, there appears to be a common basis among conservation and development interests, as well as the public generally, for addressing the shortcomings of the system and for making it more effective in reconciling development and wildlife concerns.

At the international level, an evolving concept that reflects this element of common interest is "sustainable development," a concept that became the overarching theme and objection of the Earth Summit held in Rio de Janeiro in 1992. The idea is premised on the view that environmental protection and economic development are not separate challenges. It also reflects broad public and international support for both the objectives of environmental protection and economic development. The question, therefore, is not which policy to favor but how to effect the reconciliation.

There are indications that the traditional "command-and-control" regulatory paradigm may be changing to answer this question and other concerns within the present system. One change is the use of focused, special-area planning efforts as a supplement to existing regulatory processes. Historically, special protection and regulation for specific geographic areas within the United States has been limited largely to specially designated public lands, such as national parks, national forests, wildlife refuges, wild and scenic rivers, and wilderness areas. In recent years, however, a number of governmental authorities and private parties and organizations have further explored the establishment of new types of special areas and special-area programs, as an adjunct to the traditional land use process, for privately owned and generally nondesignated lands. The types of programs that have been established at regional, state, and interstate levels are discussed below.

Governance by a Special Regulatory Authority or Commission

One type of special-area program is based on the establishment of a commission or authority to regulate certain activities (e.g., land use development) within an area of special environmental concern. Generally, this category of special area includes

- Programs that rely in large part on command-and-control or top-down regulations (e.g., in California, the San Francisco Bay Conservation and Development Commission, the California Coastal Commission, and the California Tahoe Regional Planning Agency and its sister agency, the California-Nevada Tahoe Regional Planning Agency)

- Programs that include regulations as well as public acquisition and ownership (e.g., programs for the Hackensack Meadowlands, New Jersey Pinelands, and Adirondack Park)

- Programs that involve the establishment of a federal/state agency to plan for and regulate certain activities to address regional concerns (e.g., river-basin authorities)

Ad Hoc Resource Management Plans

A more flexible, ad hoc approach to the governance of special areas is provided under laws such as the Florida Environmental Land and Water Management Act (FL. Stat. 380.05) and the federal Coastal Zone Management Act of 1972 (16 U.S.C.A. sections 1451-1464). These statutory schemes contemplate the establishment of special area management plans (SAMPs) on an ad hoc basis to provide for the governance of areas of special significance that may be designated from time to time. The Florida act requires the preparation of state, regional, and local comprehensive plans to regulate development activities, with special plans for areas of critical concern. In addition, it provides for the development of resource management plans with respect to areas designated on an ad hoc basis.

The Coastal Zone Management Act provides for the federal government to assist the coastal states to develop a management program and SAMP for the land and water resources of coast lines. Federal assistance is conditioned on a number of factors, including findings by the federal government that the management program is in accordance with federal rules and regulations, and that the program makes provisions for procedures to designate specific areas for the purpose of preserving or restoring them for their conservation, recreational, ecological, or aesthetic values (16 U.S.C.A. section 1455).

The SAMP provides for regulations as well as other measures to attain their objectives. The prototype under the federal act was the planning process to reconcile future development and wetlands conservation in Grays Harbor, Washington. Under the Florida legislation, a number of plans have been completed, including the plans for the East Everglades described in Chapter 11.

A geographically broader variation of the SAMP approach is reflected in the estuaries program of the National Oceanic and Atmospheric Administration (NOAA) that has included, for example, the interstate efforts to conserve natural resources within the Columbia River estuary and the Chesapeake Bay, described in Chapters 6 and 9, respectively. Other, similar ad hoc efforts include the Maine Bay program, which includes interstate participation as well as participation by Nova Scotia and New Brunswick, Canada. These efforts reflect cooperation by public agencies at local, regional, state, national, and international levels to focus upon environmental concerns within a commonly shared geographic area.

The Environmental Protection Agency also recently has emphasized the use of a place-based approach in carrying out its mission. The Summary of the new Five-Year Strategic Plan of the Agency, published by EPA in July 1994, highlights, among others, the guiding principle of "ecosystem protection," and states:

> Because EPA has concentrated on issuing permits, establishing pollutant limits, and setting national standards, as required by law, the Agency has not paid enough attention to the overall environmental health of specific ecosystems. In short, EPA has been *program-driven* rather than *place-driven*.
>
> EPA must collaborate with other federal, tribal, state and local agencies, as well as private partners, to achieve the ultimate goal of healthy, sustainable ecosystems. The Agency will act to solve integrated environmental problems through a place-driven framework of ecosystem protection in close partnership with others ...

The Summary states that EPA "...will enlist the support of a spectrum of participants in priority-setting and decisionmaking processes." It adds that EPA will, working with appropriate partners, identify stressed or threatened ecosystems, define environmental indicators and goals, develop and implement joint action plans on the basis of sound science, measure progress and adapt management approaches to new information, and identify support and tools that can be offered at the national level.

Habitat Conservation Plans
A third type of approach that evolved during the 1980s is the use of habitat conservation plans (HCPs) under the federal Endangered Species Act (16 U.S.C.A. Section 15399(a)). Habitat conservation plans are extensively described in the next chapter.

Negotiation and Study Mechanisms
At a different level, a number of efforts in recent years have focused on land use and environmental issues outside the traditional regulatory processes and the courts. These efforts have taken various forms: negotiations roundtables, study groups, task forces, and mediation efforts. They have addressed a range of concerns, including habitat and species protection, protection or allocation of water supplies, air quality impacts from offshore oil drilling, or simply the resolution of environmental concerns regarding a specific project.

In some cases, these efforts are difficult to distinguish from the focused planning processes outlined above. Generally, however, they are more project- or issue-oriented and result in reports and recommendations, whereas focused planning involves a relatively fuller plan with the kinds of assurances provided by, for example, a habitat conservation plan or special area management plan. Occasionally, the distinction may be simply that the process used is characterized as environmental mediation or negotiation rather than planning; in fact, the approach employed and the solutions posited may be very similar.

Relationships of Special-Area Programs to Existing Regulations

A common element of all special-area approaches is their focus on a specific concern, such as the reconciliation of development and wildlife and habitat conservation, within a specified geographic area. The area may be identified in the context of a more general planning/regulatory framework. Accordingly, these approaches have been characterized as focused or focal-point planning efforts, in contrast to comprehensive planning, which focuses broadly on all land use planning issues within a given area.

The focused, special-area approach may be adopted as a complement to a jurisdiction's comprehensive regulatory/planning framework. Indeed, this approach offers a potentially significant means to implement the requirements and criteria of such a larger framework, through a process of cooperative reconciliation of focal issues among the concerned interests. In addition, because fiscal planning has tended to be addressed separately from land use planning, the special-area approach may provide a bridge between general and fiscal plans and between policy and implementation.

In turn, the existence of an enforceable, comprehensive regulatory or planning framework provides an incentive for the effective use of the area-wide approach to resolve competing land use concerns. A similar concern to develop a more comprehensive policy and planning framework for the regulation and management of activities on public lands helped lead to adoption of the Federal Land Policy and Management Act of 1976 (43 U.S.C.A. Sections 1701–1784). Under these circumstances, the special-area process could provide a means to achieve both effective local community participation and implementation of broader, nonlocal requirements in land use governance decisions. Ideally, the area-wide process could be used to transcend the tension between the local community and state or federal officials.

There is a significant distinction, however, between approaches that involve the establishment of regulatory commissions for specific areas such as the coastal zone commissions and those involving ad hoc special area/habitat conservation planning processes. The ad hoc processes generally depend less on specific regulations to address the focal concerns and rely more on informal dialogue and the formation of a package of measures which may range from regulations, to contractual assurances, to conveyances and taxes and assessments. Further, there is also a distinction between those planning processes and roundtables or study groups in that the planning processes tend to be more implementation-oriented and to result in an action plan.

The focused planning approach may also help to promote the purposes of the National Environmental Policy Act and similar environmental review processes adopted at the state level. They call for the exploration, analysis, and narrowing of reasonable alternatives to develop a plan that reconciles the various concerns. If properly prepared, this type of analysis can provide the type of road map that the courts have required increasingly in their review of land use regulatory decisions. The potential close fit between a special-area process and the requirements of NEPA is reflected in the study of special area management planning in New Jersey's Hackensack Meadowlands, described in Chapter 7.

Elements of Focused Special-Area Planning

Special-area programs may operate on a formal regulatory basis or on a more ad hoc, informal basis as already discussed. The ad hoc processes generally are conducted in coordination with other regulatory and public review processes and are designed to bring together the constituency of interests concerned with a specific bundle of issues. The objective is to reconcile the interests through development of a plan and specific implementing measures (normally extending beyond regulation), as well as through assurances that the plan will be honored.

The Plan

Focused, special-area plans represent a significant departure from the historic regulatory paradigm. These plans may include conservation, management, monitoring, and funding elements, in addition to specific regulatory guidelines. The recently developed habitat conservation plan for the Stephens' kangaroo rat in Riverside County, California, for example, provides funding for acquisition, management, maintenance, and other purposes through a per acre impact fee on all new development, and it may include the use of an assessment district under recently passed state legislation. It is anticipated that other conservation plans in Southern California may follow the same approach.

One advantage of these types of plans is that they are not constrained by individual project boundaries or defined regulatory limits. The plan can address, for example, the specific needs for protection as part of a broader ecological community, together with broader land use and development concerns relating to the focal issues. The plan could address an issue relating to the need for a road, or the impacts of activities in unregulated areas (e.g., adjacent uplands), which may traditionally be beyond the scope of existing regulations but which are determined to have sufficient indirect impacts.

For example, the region-wide process to develop a plan to protect the California gnatcatcher and coastal sage scrub habitat commenced before the gnatcatcher was listed as "threatened" under the Endangered Species Act, and before it was formally protected under Section 7 or Section 9 of the act. The basic objective of the process was to support efforts to protect the gnatcatcher and the sage scrub habitat before further irreversible actions were taken, and to reconcile other affected interests with this basic objective. The goal was to provide for immediate and long-term protection and conservation of habitat whether or not the gnatcatcher was formally listed by the U.S. Fish and Wildlife Service (USFWS).

The Process

The special-area planning process differs from the traditional project-by-project, adversarial approach. The process is convened by a lead agency, such as the principal land use authority, an association of governments, a state or federal environmental protection or wildlife agency, or a specially designated agency. Several agencies and interests also may combine to perform this function. The habitat conservation planning process involving the Stephens' kangaroo rat in Riverside County, for example, has been led jointly by the county, several cities within the county, and, for purposes of the environmental review and permit decision processes, the USFWS. Chapters 8, 10, and 11, describing experiences in the Chiwaukee wetlands, Anchorage, and the East Everglades, respectively, also illustrate the possibilities of participation by affected constituents in the special-area planning process.

The process is intended to provide a forum for the entire constituency of interests in the focal issues. The members of this constituency are essentially self-defined, on the basis of their specific interests in the issues that are focused upon. A central concern of the process, therefore, is to ensure that the entire constituency is included.

One way to address this concern is for the lead agency and/or other participants in the process to provide public notice of the existence and progress of a special-area program before the initiation of formal public review, and to organize meetings of both a smaller core group and the larger general public group as part of the overall program. The process may take on a tiered form, with meetings of a steering committee, working group, and public review group. This tiered review process is readily compatible with the scoping or review process contemplated by the NEPA and many of its state-level counterparts. It readily accommodates refinement of plan alternatives and impacts through the use of scoping reports and, subsequently, draft environmental impact statements or reports.

Various types of incentives may be employed to achieve and sustain adequate commitment of participants to a special-area planning process. As noted above, the existence of an enforceable regulatory/planning framework offers one type of incentive. In such a context, a firm commitment by a local agency and appropriate state and federal agencies to the preparation and adoption of a plan as part of their regulatory program usually is sufficient inducement to provide the necessary level of continued participation. (Timothy Beatley, in Chapter 3, refers to these types of incentives as a kind of "balance of terror" which discourages participants from exiting a process.)

While it would appear that the various concerned interests would (or should) appreciate the value of long-term resolution of conflicts between conservation or other environmental values and development, the reality is that our culture and society/economy tends to focus on short-term objectives and tends not to support long-term planning efforts. This cultural bias, together with the historic lack of assurances available with the implementation of an adopted plan (such as those provided by a dedication of land in perpetuity or a development agreement), and problems of trust among various concerned interests, has not encouraged participation in such planning efforts. Accordingly, without a regulatory backdrop to such a broader planning program or increased assurances that a plan once adopted will be honored, there may be insufficient incentive on the part of the various interests to participate.

Timing is an important consideration. Once commenced, the process sometimes takes on a life of its own, stagnating with endless meetings and few commitments. Accordingly, it is important to establish a time schedule at the outset for the completion of the plan, with appropriate milestones that will be strictly observed.

The habitat conservation plan/special-area management plan processes often benefit from the engagement of a facilitator who is neutral, well-respected, and familiar with the issues and regulatory process. The facilitator assists in managing the meetings, overseeing the technical work, and assisting the group in resolving particularly difficult issues. The facilitator may be engaged, paid, and supervised by the lead agency but should be viewed as responsible to the working group or constituency of interests as a whole.

The development of comprehensive and reliable technical (e.g., biological) data often is of central importance to a special-area planning process. Such data forms the essential foundation for determining potential measures to reconcile competing interests in a special-area plan. Often, the charge is given to the facilitator to assemble, as part of the "facilitation team," consultants who will assist in analyzing various issues.

Whether decisions should be made by majority vote or consensus is often a question. If the majority vote approach is used, individual accountability is high; at the same time, however, the various interests become very concerned with the exact composition of the working group. Further, significant energy will be devoted to procedures for establishing the group and monitoring and controlling participation. An alternative model is to view the process as a "scoping" process, with self-selected participation. Under this approach, the composition of the group may vary from issue to issue, and decisions are made by consensus rather than by vote.

The consensus decision-making methodology assumes that the function of the group is to scope the issues involved with the formal decisionmakers who have the authority and responsibility for making final determinations. Thus, the facilitator/staff convenes the working group and scopes both the alternatives and impacts of the particular issue or proposal, normally using a draft discussion paper or report. The views of the working group are reflected in the revision of the paper/report and the alternatives are refined and normally narrowed, although sometimes additional alternatives are suggested. Often unanimous agreement on particular points and alternatives is achieved (in part because the working group normally does not wish to relinquish its power, which is based on its ability to come to consensus, to the formal decisionmaker). Of course, where the working group is unable to reach consensus, the formal decisionmaker is required to decide.

Interestingly, in contrast to the hostility and lack of trust promoted by the project-by-project review paradigm, this scoping/consensus process often increases understanding and trust among the participants, with consensus becoming the rule over time. Nevertheless, the process can break down in the face of difficult issues, as described in the chapters on the East Everglades, Bolsa Chica, and Anchorage.

Provision of Assurances

The provision of assurances to the entire constituency of interests that the plan will be honored is vital. Conservation agencies and organizations, for example, generally desire that full and adequate provision be made to protect the environmental values in question, such as water quality and wildlife habitat, and that an effective conservation or management program be established. In cases involving wildlife habitat, the first concern may be addressed by the establishment of conserved habitat, pursuant to conveyances in fee or easement to a public agency or approved nonprofit organization. Further assurances can include the designation of a trusted habitat operator, establishment of a specific program to maintain, restore, and monitor the conserved habitat, and long-term assured funding.

Development interests generally are concerned that agreed-upon compensation for lands reserved for conservation purposes will be secured or that mitigation requirements will not be increased later. These concerns may be addressed by a multiagency agreement that accompanies and provides for the implementation of the plan. For example, the habitat conservation plan for the Stephens' kangaroo rat in Riverside County, California, plan permits a take on 4,400 acres of occupied habitat (or 20 percent of total habitat, whichever is less) in a two-year period on the basis of a specific allocation formula administered by the locally involved agencies. The timing of development is tied to the acquisition of habitat through a set of concurrency requirements.

Other examples of assurances are described in Chapter 8, which notes the importance of assuring compensation to Chiwaukee Prairie landowners for rezoned lands; Chapter 10, which describes concerns over vague assurances in Anchorage; and Chapter 11, regarding land acquisition in the East Everglades. Timothy Beatley's review of habitat conservation plans in Chapter 3 describes techniques that were used to provide assurances in a number of recent habitat conservation planning processes.

Agency and Public Reviews

The plan and related decisions remain subject to normal regulatory approval requirements, including procedural requirements (e.g., those under environmental review statutes requiring the preparation of environmental statements, reports, and studies) as well as substantive environmental protection provisions and requirements of administrative procedure.

The focused, special-area approach, nevertheless, supplements the formal regulatory review process by developing a broader array of implementation measures that extend beyond those normally applicable under a project-by-project review approach. Further, the approach permits the participants, within the strictures of the law, to assist in coordinating the multiagency review process and the required preparation of underlying reports and analyses. This is a role usually denied to the conservation organizations and not generally available to an agency concerning the regulatory process of another agency. For example, the various studies and conclusions of a focused planning process may be used in the preparation by the USFWS of a recovery plan that may allow reclassification of a listed species to a threatened or nonlisted status, or in connection with an alternatives analysis or mitigation program prepared in compliance with the Section 404(b)(1) permit program.

If properly designed, the planning process may also be used as a scoping procedure in the preparation of required environmental documentation pursuant to environmental review requirements, during which issues are reviewed, evaluated, and narrowed. The draft plan, together with the draft environmental impact statement/report and other documents, can then be circulated for formal public comment. This predictably will strengthen compliance by the various agencies with constitutional and statutory procedures.

The preparation of scoping reports can be very helpful in the process of preparing the draft plan and impact statement. These reports can be designed and circulated to provide for appropriate input from the constituency of interests as well as the public at large, and to document the decisions made in the consideration and narrowing of issues.

Special Issues and Concerns

The recent use of focused, special-area planning processes generally has been directed at two specific types of environmental concerns: wetlands protection and endangered species. The processes have tended to focus on a specific environmental interest or value already protected by regulatory permit requirements (i.e., a listed endangered species or a wetland area). Relatively less attention has been given to adjacent and unregulated land areas, to responsibility for previously generated impacts, or to interests that are, for example, threatened but not specifically protected by law or regulation.

One of the benefits of the focused, special-area approach is that these broader concerns can be addressed. The regulatory process can be designed to focus instead on the conservation of the entire community of species living within the habitat and ecosystem of the listed species. Alternately, such an approach might be used to establish a plan for an entire drainage system or watershed, or to protect and restore wildlife corridors or landscape linkages in support of habitat or ecosystem values and, more broadly, efforts to maintain and restore biodiversity.

The ability to address such broad concerns in an ad hoc process depends to some extent on the existence of a more comprehensive, coherent, and enforceable regulatory or planning framework, or an equivalent incentive system (e.g., a common desire for long-range planning), to ensure area-wide cooperation. It is no accident that previous and current area-wide processes are focused principally on wildlife and wetlands issues, where a strong federal regulatory hammer already is in place. In such a context, as the Columbia River estuary plan illustrates, the special-area planning approach may help to elevate efforts to protect wetlands and wildlife to the ecosystem level, and to support the implementation of regionally established priorities to reconcile environmental concerns with development.

Protecting or Co-opting the Public Interest

One potential concern with the focused, special-area process is to ensure that the public interest is not co-opted by various interested parties. The special-area approach offers a more informal decision-making process than the current system. Furthermore, the direction of the process may depend to a greater degree on input from private participants—including participants with a significant power of the purse over the proceedings—than does the traditional approach. As a result, the area-wide planning process could be used to circumvent or supplant other efforts of citizens or agencies to address land use issues, such as voter initiatives or local public hearings, or effective enforcement of existing laws. However, recent habitat conservation plan documents have suggested that a major reason for pursuing a Section 10(a) permit is the practical difficulty experienced by the USFWS in enforcing Section 9 protections in areas where diverse land ownership and high development pressures exist.

One important means to address these concerns is to ensure that the special-area process remains closely linked with, and an adjunct to, the formal regulatory review process (procedurally as well as substantively) and is not used to constrain or avoid other efforts. The use of a tiered review process, and the distribution of drafts of the plan being developed as part of a public scoping process, may be useful to allay concerns.

The responsible agencies must enforce their conservation mandates faithfully in the context of a special-area process, even in cases where the process appears to be deviating from the fulfillment of these purposes. Furthermore, the entire constituency of interests must be fully and adequately represented in the process, including those who speak for constituencies susceptible to exclusion in such an informal decision-making setting. This concern is reinforced by apparent inequalities in staff time and financial resources between volunteer organizations and well-funded business enterprises with cadres of professional consultants.

Finally, the special-area process should not be overly institutionalized; such a move might simply reproduce, in a different form, weaknesses of the present system, such as inadequate government enforcement policy and excessive influence over decisions by the parties with the greatest resources. Where developers seek only to circumvent the existing regulatory system, the area-wide process can only fail. But, where participants seek to reconcile interests in an integrated, efficient, and equitable manner not possible through traditional means, on the basis of common interests, then the public (and the environment) as well as individual parties may have much to gain.

The Takings Issue

The issue of regulatory takings continues to be widely litigated. In the last few years, the U.S. Supreme Court issued several important decisions in this area, including its 1987 trilogy of cases,[4] *Lucas v. South Carolina Coastal Council* in 1992 (described in the accompanying box), and *Dolan v. City of Tigard* in 1994.

Because the area-wide planning process incorporates the use of program elements beyond command-and-control regulations, it provides important flexibility in considering specific concerns relating to both conservation and development. Thus, there is a greater probability that common interests among the various parties can be reasonably accommodated. If such interests are not accommodated fully, the articulation of the rationale for conservation and development provided by the plan and process may be used to identify the public interest and nexus in the measures called for by the plan, in keeping with standards for takings articulated in cases such as *Nollan* and *Lucas*.

Further, because of the complexity of the multiagency special-area plan process, the takings issue deserves full attention. The process itself may make visible and explicit the inherent tension between private and public interests in privately owned lands. It may clearly frame the question of whether or in what circumstances a landowner should be compensated when a plan provides that a tract of privately owned land must be preserved or restored as wetlands or habitat of an endangered species. The process can also provide means to lessen the impacts of a plan on a particular landowner by such methods as land exchanges or transfers of development interests. By making the effects more visible, the special-area process can allow a finer balancing and more adequate and equitable allocation of the burden of impacts.

As the issue of the allocation of the burdens of governance programs becomes more visible, it is likely that the courts and the legislatures will become more concerned about questions of adequate allocation and fair sharing of burdens. In this regard, the heightened scrutiny standard suggested by *Nollan* and *Tigard* will apply not only to the nexus between a development condition and the impacts of development but also to the relative weight of the burden imposed on the individual landowner under that condition.

When Is a Taking a Taking?

The Lucas Case

Property owners have long been concerned about regulations that sharply reduce opportunities for development and thus decrease real or potential land values. Although courts have long held that overly strict regulations may be interpreted as a taking of property that requires compensation under the Constitution's Fifth Amendment, the point at which reasonable restrictions become too restrictive has proven difficult to define. In 1992, the U.S. Supreme Court again tried to resolve the issue in deciding *Lucas v. South Carolina Coastal Council.*

David Lucas, a building contractor, paid $975,000 in 1986 for two beachfront lots in Isle of Palms, South Carolina. In 1988, Hurricane Hugo passed right across the Isle of Palms, causing substantial damage and loss of beach sand. Soon thereafter, the South Carolina legislature enacted the Beachfront Management Act, which prohibited further development on the beachfront, including Lucas's property. Lucas sued the South Carolina Coastal Council, the enforcement agency for the law, claiming that the law amounted to a regulatory taking of his property, for which he should be compensated.

The trial court agreed and awarded Lucas $1.2 million in compensation. After the South Carolina Supreme Court overturned this decision, Lucas took his complaint to the U.S. Supreme Court. The issue before the court was a classic question: How and when should public interests outweigh private property rights in making development decisions? Lucas claimed that his property had lost all value due to the coastal act; the state countered that development determined to be harmful to a public interest can be prohibited without compensation.

In 1980, in *Agins v. Tiburon,* the court ruled that a regulation can effect a taking if it "does not substantially advance legitimate state interests" or if it "denies an owner economically viable use of his land." Yet, U.S. courts usually uphold governments' use of the police power to restrain or prohibit land uses that will harm public health, safety, and general welfare. In the *Lucas* case, however, the U.S. Supreme Court decided that the South Carolina Supreme Court "was too quick to conclude" that this case involved prohibition of harmful or noxious uses of property and that the public interest demanded that Lucas sacrifice his investment and all future use of the property.

The *Lucas* case, at bottom, appears to apply to the relatively rare circumstance of property owners deprived of *all* value of their properties by regulations. But *Lucas* demonstrates the Court's increasing inclination to scrutinize public actions more carefully, as it did in the *Nollan* case (when it scolded the California Coastal Commission for inadequately linking an exaction to a stated public purpose) and in the more recent decision in 1994 in the case of *Dolan v. City of Tigard* (when it required the public agency to demonstrate that the burden of bikeway and flood control exactions on a permit applicant were "roughly proportional").

A collaborative planning process, therefore, may go far toward providing an answer to long-term debates regarding the takings issue. That is, it may provide a way to balance and reconcile—effectively, adequately, and specifically—the interests of the owner and the public in a specific area of land.

Funding

A focused, special-area planning process generally presents several critical funding needs: funding for the process; funding for acquisition of lands to be protected; funding for operation, maintenance, and monitoring activities; and (potentially) funding to support individuals or others affected by the process or existing regulations.

Typically, the sources of funding are unique to the particular planning process. In past or ongoing cases, development interests often have funded much of the process, either directly or through locally assessed impact fees. In some cases, state or federal funds have been obtained, to date through specific federal and state legislative action.

Sources for acquisition funds have included the federal Land and Water Conservation Fund and refuge acquisition funding, land exchanges among Bureau of Land Management lands, state bond financing, land exactions, and development impact fees. The operation and maintenance of conservation areas may be funded by landowner assessments (e.g., through covenants, conditions, and restrictions covering the specific development project), benefit assessments, or special taxes. In some cases, where a long-term funding mechanism has been established, affected landowners have established a trust fund to provide for start-up operations.

Historically, however, funding has been scarce for the operation and maintenance of the lands to be conserved. In turn, the lack of such funding has discouraged local agencies from agreeing to manage conserved lands. As a result, in many cases it has been difficult to find a responsible operator for the lands to be conserved and thereby to establish the conservation program. In addition, the traditional regulatory system generally has failed to make funds available for economic conversion programs and/or compensation for workers and families whose economic circumstances may be affected by regulatory programs or protective measures. As in the cases of coal miners in West Virginia and loggers in the Pacific Northwest, such programs may be a critical element in helping affected communities make the necessary short- and long-range adjustments to achieve more sustainable patterns of economic activities.

A focused conservation planning process can draw on many sources and participants to develop an effective funding strategy for these varied purposes. The combination of landowners, public agencies, and conservationists often provides a significant political force that can be effective in obtaining state and federal funding. Funding issues are discussed in detail in the next chapter and the East Everglades case study of Chapter 11.

Interagency Cooperation

The focused planning process offers an important opportunity and forum for cooperation among various agencies that have responsibility over the environmental and land use interests at issue in a particular setting, as well as at the appropriate level geographically, ecologically, and financially. Indeed, the process itself generally is predicated on the existence of these types of cooperative efforts.

Evolving Institutional Concepts

The land use decision-making process increasingly is asked to bridge the gap between individual project proposals and broader environmental impacts. The evolving demands on this process reflect growing concern with the scale of human impacts on the environment and with the relationship of these effects to economic conditions and development. These concerns have led, in part, to the development of relatively new norms or principles to address the basic underlying problems, including concepts of sustainable development, intergenerational equity, and protection of biodiversity.

The emerging concept of sustainable development suggests the need "to meet the needs and aspirations of the present without compromising the ability of those to meet the future."[5] With reference to the related concept of intergenerational equity, Professor Edith Brown Weiss suggests that the global environmental crisis requires us to develop the "intertemporal dimension of international law to relate the present to the future." To achieve this, ". . . we must anticipate the legal norms that are needed to bring about justice between our generation and future generations."[6]

The renewed emphasis on the need to protect biodiversity as a guiding principle in environmental conservation calls for the increased integration of goals of biological diversity into the land use and planning framework as a fundamental component to improved conservation and the reconciliation of wildlife and habitat concerns with development.

The paradigm of focused, special-area planning can assist in addressing these broader concerns and in building the programmatic bridges that relate individual projects to these geographically and temporally broader horizons. The process could facilitate the use of coordinated and proactive measures to address the interrelated interests of development and environment. The protection of wetlands and wildlife habitat, and the reconciliation of these interests, does not have to be limited to an ability to say yes or no to an individual project proposal, as is so frequently the case in the present paradigm.

Effectiveness of Focused, Special-Area Planning

The focused, special-area planning process resolves the shortcomings in the traditional land use paradigm. In particular, the special area-wide approach may have the effects described below.

- *Reduce Fragmentation* The focused, special-area approach, combined with a broader, coherent, and enforceable regulatory or planning framework—or equivalent incentives—offers a potentially significant means to help reduce the fragmentation of the traditional process. Environmental concerns throughout an entire ecosystem can be addressed comprehensively, taking into consideration past and future, direct and indirect impacts in a manner that relies not only upon regulation but also other proactive measures such as funding, comprehensive research, conservation or management programs, and compensatory programs for individuals or families affected by conservation plans.

- *Promote Cooperation, Not Conflict* The focused, special-area approach offers a forum in which varied interests can evaluate and resolve potential conflicts early in the land use decision process, taking into account issues on the appropriate systemic, geographic, and temporal scales. By comparison with the traditional project-by-project, proposal/review process, this approach can improve flexibility in the decision process and thereby promote improved cooperation and trust among the diverse interests.

- *Achieve a More Equitable and Adequate Allocation of Costs* The process offers the potential for a more adequate and equitable allocation of the costs of development impacts on environmental qualities and features. Approaches can be fashioned to allocate costs to past activities and/or to otherwise unregulated activities that may indirectly generate adverse impacts that presently are externalized for others (or the environment) to bear.

- *Provide Improved Predictability and Assurances* Finally, the process offers the opportunity to provide early and timely assurances—in the form of agreements, conveyances, and regulations—to all interests (conservation as well as development) and the public that the plan will be honored. The nature of these assurances has, however, varied considerably and is determined by the measures established during the process.

The trend toward focused, special-area conservation planning will make it easier to discuss and resolve conflicts early in the land use process, when options still may exist for all interests to be served. More important, these processes may provide one means to help us to live up to our own ideals, to protect the environment and provide for our economic well-being—to provide for "sustainable development" now and for the future.

It is not enough simply to state that a good balance between these objectives is desirable. All of us concerned with public institutions and these varying and common interests need to explore reforms that may help to achieve such a balance. The use of collaborative approaches such as focused, special-area conservation planning, which combine regulatory and proactive implementation measures, may help realize this balance.

NOTES

1. See, for example, *Managing Land Use Conflicts: Case Studies in Special Area Management*, edited by David Brower and D. Carol, Durham, NC: Duke University Press, 1987; L. Marsh, "Focal Point Planning," Chapter 28A in *Zoning and Land Use Controls*, Vol. 5, edited by P. Rohan, New York: Mathew Bender, 1987; M. Bean, *Reconciling Conflicts Under the Endangered Species Act*, Washington, D.C.: World Wildlife Fund, 1991; R. Thornton, "Searching for Consensus and Predictability: Habitat Conservation Planning Under the Endangered Species Act of 1973," *Environmental Law*, Vol. 21, Portland, Oregon: Lewis and Clark School of Law, 1991; T. Beatley, *Habitat Conservation Planning; Endangered Species and Urban Growth*, Austin, Texas: University of Texas Press, 1994.

2. Federal legislation providing for stricter environmental review of land use activities has included the National Environmental Policy Act of 1969, 42 U.S.C.A. §§ 4321-4347(1977, Supp. 1990) (NEPA); the Endangered Species Act, 42 U.S.C.A. §§ 1531-1542; the Clean Air Act 42 U.S.C.A. §§ 7401-7642; and the Federal Water Pollution Control Act 33 U.S.C.A. §§ 1251-1265, 1281-1376 (as amended by the Clean Water Act of 1977) (1986, Supp. 1990). Individual states have adopted similar types of environmental review or protection requirements. For further discussion, see L. Marsh and P. Lallas, "Wildlife and Habitat Protection," Chapter 24 in *Environmental Law Practice Guide*, Vol. 2, edited by M. Gerrard, New York: Mathew Bender, 1993. Many local and regional authorities have also significantly strengthened project review requirements and local land use control measures.

3. T. Lietzel, "Species Protection and Management Decisions in an Uncertain World," in *The Preservation of Species*, edited by B. Norton, College Park, Maryland: Institute for Philosophy and Public Policy, 1986, p. 247.

4. *Keystone Bituminous Coal Association v. DeBenedictis*, 480 U.S. 470 (1987); *First English Evangelical Lutheran Church of Glendale v. County of Los Angeles*, 482 U.S. 304 (1987); and *Nollan v. California Coastal Commission*, 483 U.S. 825 (1987).

5. *Our Common Future, Report of the World Commission on Environment and Development*, New York: Oxford University Press, 1987. See also the Rio Declaration and Agenda 21, adopted at the United Nations Conference on Environment and Development, Rio de Janeiro, June 1992.

6. Edith Brown Weiss, *In Fairness to Future Generations: International Law, Common Patrimony, and Intergenerational Equity,* Irvington-on-Hudson, New York: Transnational Publications, 1989.

Preserving Biodiversity through the Use of Habitat Conservation Plans

Timothy Beatley

E D I T O R S '   S U M M A R Y

Based on an examination of dozens of regional habitat conservation plans (HCPs) either completed or under way, and drawing from extensive interviews with those involved with the process, Beatley offers some keen insights and observations about HCPs and provides a number of recommendations for improving the process.

While citing the benefits of HCPs, such as providing a mechanism to resolve conflicts between development and protection of endangered species habitat, addressing such conflicts in a comprehensive rather than piecemeal fashion, and providing a mechanism to raise money to acquire habitat, Beatley questions the efficacy of some HCPs. In a few HCPs, for example, the target species fared poorly, with the majority of their remaining habitat earmarked for development. Others were left stranded on islands of habitat, cut off from other habitat areas.

Beatley examines critical issues and raises a number of questions, such as who should develop and implement HCPs, how much habitat should be preserved to ensure the survivability of a species, and who pays? Given the uncertainties, limitations, and costs of HCPs, Beatley suggests that local planners should reduce the need for HCPs by recognizing species conservation needs and steering development away from biologically rich areas.

Habitat Conservation Plans under the Endangered Species Act[1]

Most experts agree that planet Earth is undergoing a period of unprecedented species extinction and may lose as much as one-quarter of all species by the early part of the next century. The United States tends to view the problem of species loss as primarily one that occurs somewhere else—from the loss of rainforests in Central and South America to illegal poaching in Africa. Unfortunately, dramatic species loss is also an American problem. More than 750 species of flora and fauna in the United States are listed as endangered or threatened under the federal Endangered Species Act (ESA), and several thousand species are candidates for listing, many of which may eventually be listed.

The Endangered Species Act is the cornerstone of the federal effort to protect biodiversity in this country. Enacted in 1973, and reauthorized most recently in the fall of 1988, the act sets forth a strong national mandate to protect and manage endangered species and their habitats. Once species are placed on the federal endangered species list, ESA provides them with special protection. A major protective element of the Act, Section 9, prohibits a "take" of species listed as endangered. For species listed as threatened, although a take is not absolutely prohibited, the U.S. Fish and Wildlife Service (USFWS) generally determines a prohibition on taking. The term *take* is defined broadly in the act as "to harass, harm, pursue, hunt, shoot, wound, kill, trap, capture, or collect, or attempt to engage in any such conduct" (ESA, Section 3(19)).

Criminal and civil penalties are available under the act for individuals who violate these provisions. Section 9 has been particularly problematic for land developers who wish to undertake projects where listed species might be located. Clearly, land development activities such as grading, land clearance, and construction will often result in a taking of listed species.

One option for developers who are faced with this situation is to utilize Section 10 of the act, which permits the USFWS, the primary agency in charge of enforcing ESA, to issue an incidental take permit following the successful completion of a habitat conservation plan (popularly referred to as an HCP). According to Section 10(a)(2)(A) of the ESA, an HCP must specify at a minimum the following:

- The impact that will result from the taking

- The steps that will be taken to minimize and mitigate such impacts and the funding that will be available to implement these steps

- The alternative actions to the taking that were considered by the applicant and the reasons why such alternatives were not chosen

- Such other measures that the Secretary of the Interior may require as being necessary or appropriate for the purposes of the plan

This section also stipulates that an HCP may be approved and an incidental take permit may be issued only if the following conditions are satisfied:

- The taking will be incidental to an otherwise lawful activity

- The applicant will, to the maximum extent practicable, minimize and mitigate the impacts of such a taking

- The applicant will ensure that adequate funding for the plan will be provided

- The taking will not appreciably reduce the likelihood of the survival and recovery of the species in the wild

Since ESA was amended in 1982 to allow the issuance of incidental take permits, over 75 HCPs have been completed or are under way (the majority in the latter category).[2] This chapter provides a description and overview of several different HCP planning efforts and provides a preliminary evaluation of the success and effectiveness of the HCP mechanism as used to date. Much of the information and analysis presented here is the result of extensive personal interviews conducted by the author with key participants involved in the HCPs described and discussed here. Technical reports and papers, and the HCPs themselves, also have been used extensively.[3]

This chapter focuses on "regional" HCPs, that is, plans which cover a fairly large geographical area and usually involve numerous property owners and a variety of different governmental jurisdictions and interest groups (for example, Coachella Valley and San Bruno Mountain) as distinguished from HCPs prepared for individual private projects and properties. So far, relatively few regional HCPs have been completed. A number of such regional plans are currently under way, however, and sufficient experience exists to come to some tentative conclusions about how this process is functioning.

HCPs prepared by a single landowner, then, have not been addressed in this chapter. For instance, one landowner in North Key Largo, Florida, was able to secure a Section 10(a) permit to clear and develop his land in exchange for undertaking certain on-site mitigation (e.g., including the construction of several nests for endangered cotton mouse and woodrats). A number of such individual plans have been prepared.

A regional HCP offers considerable advantage over a case-by-case, property-by-property approach. It permits a comprehensive analysis of species and habitat conservation needs and generally permits the setting aside of larger, more ecologically viable habitat areas. By comparison, the mitigation requirements imposed under a case-by-case project review are often of marginal utility in promoting the protection and survival of endangered species.

Overview and Comparison of Habitat Conservation Plans

The first HCP was prepared for San Bruno Mountain, California. One of the last remaining large tracts of open space in the San Francisco Bay Area, it was slated for development in the early 1970s by Visitacion Associates. Some 8,500 residential units and 2 million square feet of office and commercial space were initially proposed for the mountain. After substantial opposition to the project emerged, a compromise was reached that substantially reduced the size of the project. Subsequently, however, the mountain was found to be home to several species of rare butterflies, including the federally listed Mission blue butterfly. Because development of the mountain would certainly have resulted in the loss of some butterflies, in one life stage or another, environmentalists argued that such development was prohibited under ESA. The developers, also concerned about their liability under ESA, sought some mechanism that would permit development of the mountain to proceed, while ensuring long-term protection for the butterflies.

What resulted was a unique management plan, developed after extensive biological study of the butterflies and their habitat needs, that identified areas of the mountain that would be set aside in perpetuity. The plan was developed jointly by the developer, environmentalists, local government officials, and other interests; it resulted in the setting aside of some 87 percent of the butterfly habitat. The San Bruno Mountain plan was viewed by many involved as such a successful mechanism for resolving urban development/endangered species conflicts that ESA was amended in 1982 to specifically permit the preparation of such plans. The San Bruno Mountain plan then became the first HCP to receive a 10(a) permit under these new provisions.

Since the San Bruno Mountain HCP was approved and ESA amended, a number of regional HCPs have been initiated. Table 3.1 presents brief profiles of ten of the regional HCPs that have been completed or are in progress. The table provides a quick comparison of the differences or similarities between major regional HCPs. The discussion that follows compares the HCPs according to certain features and characteristics, including the type and number of species addressed, the organization and structure of the HCP process, and the types of implementation and management measures incorporated, among others.

Process and Methodology

Like the San Bruno and Coachella Valley plans, many HCPs have gone through, or are going through, fairly similar processes. Typically, a steering committee, comprised of key stakeholders in the community or region, is formed to guide and oversee the preparation of the plan. HCP committees are quite similar in their general makeup and usually include representatives of the real estate and development community, the environmental community, the local governments involved, and state and federal resource agencies (e.g., state wildlife agencies, USFWS, federal Bureau of Land Management). Table

3.1 lists the primary groups participating on HCP steering committees. In addition to the steering committee, which usually acts as the official policy-making body, HCPs often involve a technical or biological committee consisting of experts on the species of concern, as well as other individuals who may have special technical expertise. Much of the background work on the HCP, and the nuts and bolts of the conservation measures included in the HCP, is undertaken by such technical committees. In addition, a private consultant is typically hired by the steering committee to collect necessary data and to prepare the plan and the accompanying environmental review documentation (e.g., state environmental impacts reports in the case of California or federal environmental impact statements). A few consultants have prepared the bulk of the regional HCPs so far. (Thomas Reid Associates of Palo Alto California, for example, has prepared or is in the process of preparing at least six of the California HCPs; Regional Environmental Consultants of San Diego is responsible for three of the largest HCPs currently in progress.)

While each of the HCPs has gone through or is going through a similar kind of process and methodology, they differ in a number of respects. The HCPs vary, for instance, according to who is given responsibility for organizing and coordinating the process. In some instances, like the San Diego HCP, a regional government coordinates the process (San Diego Association of Governments or "SANDAG"); in other cases a single jurisdiction such as a local planning department coordinates.

Despite the general similarities in the types of groups and interests involved in HCPs (i.e., real estate and development interests, environmental and conservation interests, local governments, etc.) there is also substantial variation, depending on the specific local and regional circumstances. Because the individuals and groups that have a stake in HCPs varies from place to place, the composition of HCP steering committees varies as well. While oil and gas representatives have a special stake in the Kern County, California, HCP, they had no interest in most other HCPs. Off-road vehicle users have a clear interest in being involved in the Clark County, Nevada, desert tortoise HCP, and sand and gravel miners have a keen interest in the San Diego HCP for the least Bell's vireo (many of their operations are located in riparian areas).

Differences are also apparent in the methodologies of the different HCPs. The San Diego HCP, for instance, has employed a two-tiered approach, preparing a range-wide comprehensive species management plan and then more detailed HCPs for four river basins (due to landowner opposition, one of these river basin HCPs was later abandoned, and another converted to a set of policy guidelines; only two were submitted to USFWS for approval).

Moreover, the organizational structure accompanying the process is different. The San Diego HCP has a large 30-member task force overseeing the

TABLE 3.1 Overview of Selected Regional Habitat Conservation Plans Completed or in Progress[a]

Selected regional habitat conservation plans	Status	Size of study area	Primary species of concern	Primary conservation tools/strategy	Development mitigation fee?	Other funding sources	Amount of protected/conserved habitat	Percentage of existing local habitat protected	Key participants
1. San Bruno Mountain HCP (San Mateo County, CA)	Completed; 10(a) permit issued	3,800 acres	• Mission blue butterfly • Callippe silverspot butterfly	• Habitat set aside/clustered development • Habitat restoration • Construction management	Annual mitigation fee ($20 per year per unit for residential; $10 per 1000 sq. ft for commercial per year)	Land donation as condition of development	2,700 acres	87%	• Visitacion and other landowners/developers • San Mateo County • Surrounding local governments (e.g., South San Francisco, Daly City, Brisbane) • Save San Bruno Mountain Committee
2. Coachella Valley HCP (Riverside County, CA)	Completed; 10(a) permit issued	250 sq. miles; 127 sq. miles of occupiable habitat	• Coachella Valley fringe-toed lizard	• Fee simple acquisition of habitat • Three lizard preserves • Habitat restoration and management • Research program	$600 per acre	• Federal Land and Water Conservation Fund • BLM land trades • The Nature Conservancy • California Wildlife Commission	16,000 acres in preserves (8000 acres of blow-sand habitat)	10–15%	• Sunrise Development Corporation • California Nature Conservancy • Coachella Valley Association of Governments (CVAG) (nine cities) • Coachella Valley Ecological Reserve Foundation • Bureau of Land Management
3. North Key Largo HCP (Monroe County, FL)	Original plan never adopted; new versions under consideration	12,000 acre island; 12 mile segment of island; 2,100 acres of hardwood hammock	• Schaus swallowtail butterfly • Key Largo cottonmouse • Key Largo woodrat • American crocodile	• Zoning and TDR • Land acquisition (by state) • Development clustered into five development nodes • Restrictions on hammock clearance • Exotic plant control and removal • Road removal and other habitat restoration	$2500 per unit development fee; annual mitigation fee ($2.00 per overnight accommodations unit per night; $2.00 per week for residential units	Special $98,000 appropriation to fund preparation of HCP, with matching funds from private interests, and state and local government	Projected 1,773 acres (hardwood hammock)	84%	• Florida Audubon Society • Landowners • Monroe County

Plan	Status	Area	Species	Mitigation measures	Cost	Funding	Projected acres	Projected replacement	Parties involved
4. Metro Bakersfield HCP (CA)	Completed; awaiting approval by USFWS	405 sq. miles	• San Joaquin kit fox • Blunt-nosed leopard lizard • Tipton kangaroo-rat • San Joaquin antelope ground squirrel • Bakersfield beavertail cactus	• Restoration of state-owned water back (back to habitat) • Some additional fee-simple acquisition • Hand excavation of kit fox dens required	$680 per acre		Projected 15,000 acres	Projected replacement of habitat: three acres for each acre that is destroyed	• City of Bakersfield • Kern County • Major developers/Building Industry Association • The Nature Conservancy • Sierra Club
5. San Diego HCP (CA)	In progress (two riparian plans submitted to USFWS)	About 20,000 acres of riparian habitat in four river basins; about 5,000 acres of existing vireo habitat	• Least Bell's vireo	• Land dedication/habitat restoration through project-by-project mitigation • Habitat buffers and local land use control (proposed HCP overlay zone) • Cowbird management • Habitat creation/restoration	None yet; mitigation requirements established on project-by-project basis	• Matching funds from state legislature for HCP study • Possible special riparian assessment district to fund long-term management	Projected minimum of 9,000 acres of vireo habitat (15,000–22,000 acres of riparian habitat overall)	140% (projected 40% increase in vireo habitat; small increase perhaps in riparian area, but main increase in vireo habitat through increasing ratio of vireo to riparian habitat)	• San Diego Association of Governments • Development community • Sierra Club • Audubon Society • County League of Women Voters • U.S. Army Corps of Engineers

table continues

Table 3.1 (continued)

Selected regional habitat conservation plans	Status	Size of study area	Primary species of concern	Primary conservation tools/strategy	Development mitigation fee?	Other funding sources	Amount of protected/conserved habitat	Percentage of existing local habitat protected	Key participants
6. Balcones Canyonlands Conservation Plan (Austin, TX)	In progress	990 sq. miles in Travis County	• Black-capped vireo • Golden-cheeked warbler • Texas amorpha • Canyon mock-orange • Bracted twist-flower • Tooth Cave pseudoscorpion • Tooth Cave ground beetle • Kretschmarr Cave mold beetle • Bee Creek Cave harvestman	• Habitat acquisition; system of preserves • Land use controls through city's comprehensive watersheds ordinance • Cowbird control	None yet; proposed fee of $3,000 per acre of habitat; $300 per gross acre	• Local bond measure proposed • Utility surcharge • Percentage of CIP improvements	Proposed 29,160 acres	—	• Texas Nature Conservancy • Sierra Club • Audubon Society • Earth First! • City of Austin as well as Travis, Williamson, Hays and Burnet counties • Texas General Land Office • Texas Capital Area Builders Association
7. Clark County HCP (NV)	In progress	7,800 sq. miles; 5 million acres of tortoise habitat	• Mojave Desert tortoise	• Large blocks of BLM land will be set aside as tortoise preserves • Compensation will likely be needed for cattle grazers, miners, and other users of these lands • Three-year short-term HCP approved	$250 per acre ($550 per acre in Las Vegas Valley under short-term HCP)	• Possibly proceeds of BLM land sales • Funds from several lawsuit settlements will be used for habitat acquisition and research • Revenue from state bond referendum	800,000 to 1 million acres of BLM land; grazing rights to 400,000 acres have already been secured	—	• The Nature Conservancy • Bureau of Land Management • Southern Nevada Homebuilders Association • Clark County and cities • Resource users, including cattle ranchers, miners, and ORV users • Environmental Defense Fund

8. Eastern Riverside County HCP (CA)	In progress	Approximately 22,000 acres in ten study areas over an area of approximately 100,000 acres	Stephens' kangaroo rat	• Short-term HCP approved • Land acquisition; system of preserves	$1,950 per acre; maximum $1,000 per residential unit; solid waste tipping fees	Estimated 10,000–15,000 acres	Estimated 50%	• Riverside County and incorporated towns • Sierra Club • Bureau of Land Management • Building Industry Association • The Nature Conservancy
9. Kern County Valley Floor HCP (CA)	In progress	3,200 square miles	• San Joaquin kit fox • Blunt-nosed leopard lizard • Giant kangaroo rat • Buena Vista lake shrew	• System of protected land (otherwise too early in process)	None yet, except those collected under Metro-Bakersfield	• California Division of Oil and Gas	Too early in process	Too early in process	• Oil and gas industry • Farm Bureau • The Nature Conservancy • Development community • BLM California Energy Commission • Audubon Society
10. Marina HCP (CA)	In progress	626 acres	• Smith's blue butterfly • Black legless lizard	• Development will be restricted to designated areas • Remaining conserved habitat will be deeded to a conservation group	None	• California Coastal Conservancy and landowner split cost of HCP study • Room tax being considered to fund long-term habitat maintenance/restoration	Projected 485 acres	—	• Landowners (sand mining companies) • California Department of Parks • Regional Park Authority • Marina City

[a] U.S. Fish and Wildlife Service has played or is playing a key role in each HCP and is consequently not listed here; the same applies to state wildlife departments.

preparation of the comprehensive species management plan and the broader process, with individual advisory committees overseeing the preparation of the more detailed river basin HCPs. The comprehensive species management plan analyzed the range-wide needs of the vireo and set a goal of establishing 5,000 breeding pairs of vireos (there are currently as few as 350 breeding pairs) and at least 9,000 acres of vireo habitat (15,000 to 20,000 acres of riparian habitat overall).

The river basin HCPs contain more specific plans for acquiring, regulating, and managing habitat areas and generally for achieving these broader breeding pair and habitat conservation goals. As another example of such methodological and structural differences, the Sand City and Marina HCPs have incorporated an extra planning layer because they are being prepared in combination with revisions to their "LCPs"—local coastal plans required by law in California. This has necessitated consideration of issues not particularly germane to species conservation, such as coastal erosion, beach access, and coastal view protection, and has made the process more difficult.

Most HCPs are issued for 30 years. The Section 10(a) permits for both the San Bruno Mountain and Coachella Valley HCPs were issued by USFWS for periods of 30 years but are revocable if the plans are not carried out successfully. Some variation exists; the Metro-Bakersfield HCP, for example, will cover only a 20-year period.

Number and Types of Protected Species

One of the more obvious ways in which HCPs differ is in the number and types of species addressed. Species of concern include reptiles and amphibians, such as the threatened Coachella Valley fringe-toed lizard in the case of the Coachella Valley HCP, the American crocodile in the North Key Largo HCP, the desert tortoise in the Clark County HCP, the San Joaquin blunt-nosed leopard lizard in the Kern County HCP, and several species of salamanders in the Balcones Canyonlands Conservation Plan.

Endangered rodents are heavily represented, including several species of kangaroo rat (the Stephens' kangaroo rat in Riverside County, the Morro Bay kangaroo rat, and the giant kangaroo rat in Kern County), the Key Largo woodrat and cotton mouse (North Key Largo HCP), the San Joaquin antelope ground squirrel (the Metro-Bakersfield and Kern County HCPs), and the Buena Vista lake shrew.

Endangered butterflies have been a major focus of at least four regional HCPs (the Mission blue and callippe silverspot in San Bruno; the Smith's blue butterfly in the Marina and Sand City HCPs; the Schaus swallowtail in North Key Largo). Several of the major regional HCPs have focused heavily upon endangered songbird species, including the least Bell's vireo (San Diego HCP)

Expanding agricultural development usurps the least Bell's vireo's habitat in Southern California.

and the black-capped vireo and golden-cheeked warbler (the Austin HCP). One regional HCP, the Balcones Canyonlands Conservation Plan, addressed non-butterfly invertebrates (specifically six cave-adapted invertebrates). At least three regional HCPs have considered plant species (the Balcones Canyonlands Conservation Plan, Metro-Bakersfield, and Kern County HCPs).

HCPs for larger mammals have been fewer in number, although the endangered San Joaquin kit fox is a primary focus of the Metro-Bakersfield HCP.

Different species of concern in turn imply different biological factors and characteristics that need to be considered. Some species, like the desert tortoise, have wide ranges, while others have very narrow ranges. Some species are migratory, such as songbird species like the least Bell's vireo and golden-cheeked warbler, while others are not. These different biological characteristics in turn imply a variety of differences in necessary management and conservation measures.

Interestingly, these differences may also affect the relative importance given to conservation efforts by public officials and the general public. While ESA does not differentiate in the relative importance of listed species, it is considerably easier to gain public sympathy for conservation efforts for species that are cute and cuddly (e.g., the San Joaquin kit fox) than for a rodent or lizard or cave invertebrate that may be repulsive to most people. (This is consistent with survey research done on this subject.)[4]

It may be difficult to raise acquisition monies locally to preserve a species of rat or to convince local officials that they should enact tough management measures to preserve a spider. In the Coachella Valley, for example, local officials initially were troubled by the notion of spending large amounts of money to protect a lizard. In the words of one local councilman: "I don't get extremely emotional about the fringe-toed lizard. I really don't care if it stays or leaves . . . . I don't know whether its endangered or not. I wear lizard boots, so there . . ."[5] It is clear that without the legal force of ESA such conservation and protection efforts would be difficult or impossible to sell locally.

There are, of course, strong arguments for protecting biodiversity. Native flora and fauna represent a tremendous biological storehouse from which considerable medicinal, scientific, and commercial benefits can be obtained. Maintaining biodiversity for aesthetic and recreational reasons has become increasingly important, as well, as more and more people become interested in viewing and experiencing other forms of life (witness the increasing popularity of so-called "ecotourism"). Protecting species and their habitats also means protecting the integrity and sustainability of the ecological systems upon which humans rely.

In addition to these more anthropocentric arguments, deeper ethical concerns are increasingly expressed about the loss of species. Many believe that we need not justify preservation of species in narrow instrumental terms (i.e., because they have value to humans), but that other forms of life have inherent worth and intrinsic value and a right to exist irrespective of the value placed on them by *Homo sapiens*.[6] These biocentric views are still quite foreign to most citizens and public officials involved in habitat conservation planning, who are more likely to be persuaded of the importance of species conservation by arguments stressing the economic, environmental, and other benefits to humans.

Types of Threats

Types of threats to species of concern vary among the habitat conservation plans. For instance, in the Coachella Valley, the primary threats are the direct loss of blow-sand habitat (areas of unstable wind-blown sand) due to private urban and resort development (such as the Palm Valley Country Club, which in effect led to the initiation of the HCP) and indirect degradation of habitat due to sand shielding. For the desert tortoise, not only is direct loss of habitat from development a problem, but a host of other threats must be addressed, including respiratory disease, off-road vehicles, overgrazing, and raven predation. For the least Bell's vireo in San Diego, the primary threats have been from public projects such as state highways, flood control projects, bridges, and

TABLE 3.2   Public and Private Projects in the HCP Study Area

	Sweetwater	San Diego	San Luis Rey	Santa Ana
Flood control	• Channelization projects	• Channelization projects	• Corps project for single and double levees	• Corps "Mainstem" project in three-county area
Transportation	• Construction on State Highways 125, 94, and 54 • Construction of Guajolote Road	• Construction on State Highways 52, 125, and 67 • Extension of Jackson and Princess View Drives • Extension of light rail (trolley) • River crossings in Santee and Lakeside	• Construction of State Highway 76 bypass • Construction of replacement for Bonsalt Bridge	• Bike trails on Riverside County park land
Recreation	• Sweetwater Regional Park • Equestrian trails • Golf courses • Water sports at reservoir	• Mission Trails, Mast, and Cactus Parks • Equestrian trails • Golf courses • Fishing at Hollins Lake		• Facilities at Prado Dam
Residential, commercial, and industrial uses	• Build-out of planned community • Destination resorts • Sand mining • Rural residential	• Industrial and commercial redevelopment • Santee Town Center (commercial) • Sand mining	• Rock and gravel extraction • Others to be determined	
Water storage and provision	• Expansion of reservoir storage capacity • Urban Runoff Division System	• Continued use of El Capitan Reservoir		• Corps proposal to raise dam 30 feet • Increase storage above dam • Increase flow into spreading basins

Source: San Diego Association of Governments.

dams. This is illustrated by Table 3.2, which lists the types of projects planned or under construction in each of the four different river basins. For San Bruno Mountain, butterflies were endangered in large part because of the gradual replacement of native grasslands (and host plants such as lupine) with brush and other nonnative vegetation.

Size of Planning Areas

Habitat conservation plans also differ considerably in the size of their planning areas, again in large degree as a result of biological differences in the

The desert tortoise feels right at home in the arid, barren-looking landscape of Clark County, Nevada (*top*). This same area, however, faces strong real estate development pressure (*bottom*).

species of concern. Planning areas range in size from 550 acres for the Marina HCP to the 3,200 square mile valley floor HCP being prepared by Kern County. The latter clearly assumes a larger, more regional context, while others have sought a more localized approach.

A related issue is the extent to which HCPs are able to consider and address a number of different species of concern. HCPs such as Kern County's and Austin's are clearly more regional in nature, largely because they must simultaneously consider and protect multiple species.

HCPs have been limited in the number of species which they consider. The Coachella Valley HCP, for instance, was focused primarily on the habitat and conservation needs of a single species—the Coachella Valley fringe-toed lizard. Similarly, the San Diego HCP for the least Bell's vireo and the Clark County HCP for the desert tortoise are essentially single-species approaches, although these types of HCPs may incidentally protect other species of concern. With its emphasis on single species, the federal Endangered Species Act is probably largely responsible for this orientation.

Many of the more recently initiated HCPs, such as Kern County's and the Balcones Canyonlands Conservation Plan, have attempted to take a much more comprehensive biological focus, looking not just at federally listed species but also at state-listed species, federal candidate species, and other species of concern. There is an increasing recognition by both conservationists and developers that it makes more sense, economically and technically, to deal with multiple species in a comprehensive management framework (e.g., looking at areas of overlapping habitat, comprehensive acquisition schemes) than to address one species at the risk of being faced with additional listings at a later date.

Implementation and Management

Variations in the nature of threats to species of concern, as well as other geographical, biological, and institutional factors, require differences in the conservation and management strategies adopted by HCPs. All of the HCPs share the basic, central strategy of identifying and protecting certain designated habitat conservation areas. How this is accomplished, however, can be quite different. The Coachella Valley HCP, for instance, focused on acquisition of large privately owned lands. With the help of The Nature Conservancy, three preserves, encompassing a total of more than 16,000 acres, were set up for the fringe-toed lizard. The largest of these preserves, the Coachella Valley Preserve, encompasses approximately 13,000 acres, the bulk of which was purchased from a single landowner, Cathton Investments Inc. The two small "satellite" preserves were comprised primarily of Bureau of Land Management (BLM) property. The principal strategy of HCPs such as Coachella

Valley is to purchase fee-simple rights to habitat areas and to set these areas aside in perpetuity as habitat preserves.

Other HCPs have taken different approaches to establishing habitat preserves. The original North Key Largo HCP of 1986 set aside hardwood hammocks through a somewhat different means: relying heavily on the use of the local jurisdiction's zoning powers in combination with a plan to allow the transfer of development rights to designated development nodes. While the plan incorporated a two-year waiting period that provided a window of time for the state to purchase habitat lands, after a certain date (August 1, 1988) the plan was to allow development only in designated development nodes, restricting (by way of a conserved habitat zoning category) any development outside of these areas (approximately 84 percent of the habitat).

The plan permitted a maximum of 3,500 dwelling units in the development nodes, with this maximum density achievable only through the transfer of density from the conserved habitat. Additional restrictions were also placed on the extent of hammock clearance permissible even in development nodes. The plan specified that developers and landowners would not be permitted to clear more than 20 percent of high-quality hardwood hammock unless one of the following four mitigation actions was taken:

1. Preservation in perpetuity through transfer of 200 acres of mangrove wetland in the conserved habitat to public ownership for each additional acre cleared

2. Preservation in perpetuity through transfer of four acres of hardwood hammock in the conserved habitat to public ownership for each additional acre cleared, and the extinguishment of the development rights for eight dwelling units appurtenant to the land

3. Preservation in perpetuity and replanting of hardwood hammock on three acres of successional habitat (returning to hardwood hammock) for each additional acre cleared

4. Preservation in perpetuity, replanting of hardwood hammock, and provision of at least three and no more than six rubble piles of four cubic yards of either rock or logs on two acres of scarified land for each additional acre cleared

While the North Key Largo plan was never officially adopted (several more recent versions are currently being considered by Monroe County), in concept it would have relied to a considerable degree on the protective elements of the local zoning ordinance. North Key Largo did utilize the two-year window to acquire the fee-simple rights to much of the hardwood hammock habitat.

Coachella Valley–style, fee-simple habitat acquisition appears to be the most frequently employed conservation strategy.

In some cases, habitat is preserved not through off-site purchases but by setting aside land already owned by developers or other parties to the HCP. For instance, in the San Bruno Mountain and the Marina HCPs, it has been possible to direct development onto particular parts of a private site—that is, to cluster future development in ways which set aside conserved habitat areas. Figure 3.1 presents the plan diagram from the San Bruno Mountain HCP, with small shaded areas representing developable portions of the mountain. In the case of the Marina HCP, the majority of the habitat of the Smith's blue butterfly is owned by three sand mining companies. The proposed plan would involve, much like San Bruno, restricting future development to certain designated development "bubbles" to place the remainder of the land (some 485 of the 626 acres) in conserved habitat. These conserved areas likely will be deeded over to a public agency or a private conservation group.

HCPs also differ in the extent to which public land, usually federal, is involved, and this in turn influences the strategy for conserving habitat. For instance, in the Clark County desert tortoise HCP, the vast majority (approximately 90 percent) of remaining habitat in the planning area is owned by the federal Bureau of Land Management (BLM). Consequently, acquisition of private land largely will be unnecessary. What will be necessary, however, are

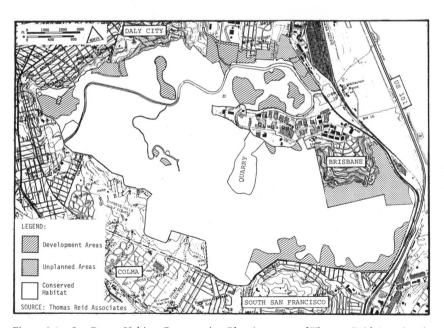

Figure 3.1   San Bruno Habitat Conservation Plan (courtesy of Thomas Reid Associates).

actions to modify the uses of these publicly owned lands. Where necessary, compensation will be provided to individuals and groups who have certain rights or vested interests to use these areas (primarily miners, cattle grazers, and off-road vehicle enthusiasts). Indeed, under the short-term HCP, some 400,000 acres of BLM habitat has already been protected through acquisitions of grazing rights.

Other HCPs have attempted to find creative ways to utilize federal or state lands for conserved habitat areas. For instance, in the Coachella Valley, a considerable portion of the land in the largest preserve was acquired through BLM land trades—that is, The Nature Conservancy (TNC) would first purchase preserve lands, which would then be swapped for BLM lands in other areas. BLM became an owner of land in the preserve, and TNC would sell its newly acquired BLM lands to recoup its original acquisition costs.

As another example of creative habitat conservation, the Metro-Bakersfield HCP currently is planning to restore kit fox habitat by converting agricultural lands back to native grasslands, in combination with a state water banking program. The state Department of Water Resources purchased some 20,000 acres of farmland southwest of the city that will become the Kern Water Bank, used by the state to replenish regional groundwater supplies. The HCP likely will propose inclusion of some additional lands but envisions converting a significant acreage of agricultural land in the water bank back to grassland habitat. The Metro-Bakersfield HCP will probably also propose restoring and adding to city-owned acreage located along the Kern River. This river habitat will serve as an important migration corridor linking kit fox populations to the north and south.

Thus while HCPs tend to share the general strategy of setting aside conserved habitat, the specifics of how this is done vary depending upon unique local circumstances.

In addition to setting aside habitat, each HCP typically includes a variety of other implementation actions. Most HCPs, for instance, incorporate a program for habitat management and restoration as well as additional biological research and monitoring. In the North Key Largo HCP, for example, restoration and management activities included controlling and removing exotic plants and domestic pets; eliminating aerial application of insecticides (for mosquito control); removing roads and bridges to restore historic water regimes and to minimize human intrusion (e.g., closing and roadbed removal for old 905); introducing host species (e.g., periodic burns to promote torchwood and wildlime—plants upon which female Schaus swallowtail butterflies lay their eggs); and modifying canal banks to provide nesting sites and habitat for the American crocodile, among others.

As another example, a major component of the restoration and management of butterfly habitat in the San Bruno Mountains was strict construction management practices for development that occurs on the mountain (e.g., fencing of habitat areas, close monitoring of grading and other construction activities) and restoration and replanting of native grasslands.

Certain threats to species of concern may require special conservation techniques beyond habitat preserves. In the San Diego HCP, for example, an important component of long-term management may be programs to control the brownheaded cowbird, a species with a parasitic effect on the least Bell's vireo (depositing its eggs in vireo nests which in turn displaces young vireos). A cowbird control program is already under way in Austin and was to be an important management strategy in the Balcones Canyonlands Conservation Plan. Similar programs to control the expansion and propagation of raven populations, which prey on young desert tortoises, may prove to be an important component of any desert tortoise conservation program. In other HCPs, however, control of such competitor and predator species may be unnecessary.

An important issue that must be addressed in any HCP process is the entity assigned responsibilities for implementing the plan. There is considerable variation among HCPs. In the Coachella Valley HCP, this issue was resolved by assigning major responsibilities to TNC, which manages the funds generated by the mitigation fees collected by the local governments and assumes the primary habitat management responsibilities for the preserve system (under a management agreement between TNC, BLM, USFWS, and the state of California). In the San Bruno Mountain HCP, the San Mateo County planning department takes the lead on implementation and long-term management responsibilities.

Funding of HCPs

The HCP mechanism requires funding at several points. Funding is required initially to undertake the necessary biological and planning studies, to conduct the HCP process, and to prepare the plan and resulting environmental review documentation (e.g., environmental impact reports). In most cases, however, the major funding requirements are for acquisition and preservation of habitat areas. Funds also are needed for long-term management and restoration activities. Most HCPs are employing some combination of federal, state, local, and private funding. Approximately $10 million was secured from the federal Land and Water Conservation Fund to purchase preserve lands in the Coachella Valley, while most of the money for the Kern County HCP was provided by the California Division of Oil and Gas. Table 3.3 shows the projected distribution of funding for the Coachella Valley fringe-toed lizard preserves.

TABLE 3.3   Projected Distribution of Funding
for Coachella Valley Fringe-Toed Lizard Preserves

Funding sources	$ Million
Federal	
Land and Water Conservation Funds	10.0
BLM land exchange (cash value)	5.0
State Wildlife Conservation Board	1.0
The Nature Conservancy	2.0
Developer mitigation fees	7.0
Total	25.0

Source: Coachella Valley Fringe-toed Lizard Habitat Conservation Plan,
June 1985.

Moreover, the California Coastal Conservancy has provided funds, on a 50-50 cost-sharing basis, for the Marina and Sand City HCPs. Private funding for planning, acquisition, and management has also been important. The Nature Conservancy, in particular, has played an instrumental role in this regard in several of the HCPs, including supplying much of the start-up and biological background funding for the Balcones Canyonlands Conservation Plan.

Most HCPs have used or are using some form of development mitigation fee assessed on new development located in habitat areas. These one-time assessments are basically a form of impact fee assessed on a per-acre basis and usually are collected at the time a parcel is graded. Fees are normally tied to some delineated habitat area or mitigation fee zone. Figure 3.2, for instance, depicts the mitigation fee zone for the Coachella Valley HCP, which is intended to correspond roughly to the range of the fringe-toed lizard. In the Metro-Bakersfield HCP, fees are assessed for any new development anywhere in the metropolitan area except for:

- Additions, remodelings, or reconstructions totaling not more than half of the square footage of preexisting development

- Commercial farming or related farm accessory structures, oil field development, or development within the Downtown Redevelopment Agency project boundary

- Development of any parcel of less than one-half gross acre where at least half of the adjacent parcels have been developed prior to September 23, 1987

In most cases, mitigation fees are established on an interim basis, even before an HCP is completed, to provide funds for biological and planning studies and the HCP process itself. Once the HCP is adopted, the fee becomes a long-term source of funding for future management and acquisition. The amount of the fee varies considerably among HCPs, ranging from a low of $250 per acre in Clark County, Nevada (desert tortoise HCP; $550 per acre within the short-term permit take area) to a high of $1,950 per acre in Riverside County for the Stephens' kangaroo rat HCP. At least one HCP, San Bruno Mountain, imposes an annual mitigation fee ($20 per dwelling unit per year; $10 per 1,000 square feet per year for commercial development) and the North Key Largo HCP envisioned a similar annual fee (e.g., $2 per week per residential unit; $2 per overnight accommodation unit per night), though such a fee was never adopted. So far, development mitigation fees have been the major source of local funding and there are currently no HCPs funded through broader community-wide taxation or revenues (e.g., a jurisdiction-wide sales tax or *ad valorem* assessment).

The imposition of development fees generally is deemed to be an equitable way to raise funds for HCPs because development in habitat areas is creating the need for conservation measures. Critics of the heavy use of fees argue that past development also caused the need for HCPs, and consequently broader community measures (e.g., property taxes) ought to be employed. Passing these costs along to future homeowners and residents through mitigation fees, however, is clearly more politically acceptable than taxing existing residents (and voters).

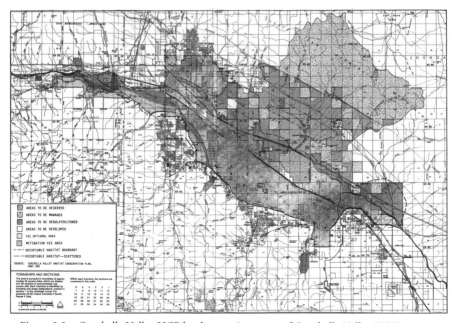

Figure 3.2   Coachella Valley HCP land status (courtesy of Coachella Valley HCP).

Evaluating the Success of Habitat Conservation Plans

Because relatively few regional habitat conservation plans have been completed and approved by USFWS, it may be premature to draw conclusions about their effectiveness. Nonetheless, based on the limited number of HCPs completed or under way, some tentative conclusions can be drawn. The following observations are based on field visits and personal interviews with participants involved in many of the completed or ongoing plans.

First, on the positive side, HCPs have been responsible for setting aside considerable amounts of natural habitat. In the Coachella Valley, for instance, nearly 17,000 acres of desert habitat have been protected in three different fringe-toed lizard preserves. Within these preserves, some 8,000 acres of lizard habitat (blow-sand habitat) have been protected in perpetuity. The San Bruno Mountain HCP has preserved the vast majority—nearly 90 percent—of butterfly habitat (some 2,700 acres). Under its short-term permit, the Clark County desert tortoise habitat planning process has already protected about 400,000 acres of habitat through acquisition of grazing rights. Even in places like North Key Largo, where the HCP was never officially adopted or approved by USFWS, the HCP clearly served as a catalyst for public acquisition of substantial amounts of natural hardwood hammock habitat using money from the state's Conservation and Recreation Lands program. Furthermore, although the San Diego River HCP prepared for the least Bell's vireo (one of four river basin plans) has yet to be formally adopted, it has influenced the design and review of several highway and bridge projects, such as the extension of State Highway 52 across the San Diego River.

Furthermore, HCP processes, even where plans have yet to be completed or approved, are generating revenue and funds necessary to undertake management activities and biological research that would not be undertaken otherwise. For instance, in the Coachella Valley HCP, revenues generated from the plan (from developer mitigation fees) are being used to undertake a variety of management and research activities, including fencing off certain areas to keep off-road vehicles away from lizard habitat, dismantling windbreaks that interrupt natural blow-sand movement, and conducting an annual lizard count that ultimately will enhance understanding of the ecology and population dynamics of the species.

As mentioned previously, funds generated from the San Bruno Mountain HCP (annual mitigation fees) are being used to restore native grasslands essential for butterfly survival. These native grasslands had been declining for many years through infiltration of nonnative vegetation. In both cases, it appears that the species of concern would have been in jeopardy even if the habitat was left undeveloped. The funding and management activities resulting from the HCPs clearly have had positive effects.

Furthermore, it appears that HCPs have provided a badly needed pressure-release valve under the ESA, adding flexibility to the act, and promoting compromise and negotiated settlements between the development and environmental communities, rather than confrontation and litigation. The HCP concept acknowledges that some degree of development and human use of species habitat may not be inconsistent with the conservation and survival of threatened or endangered species. And, in some instances, some degree of development may have a positive impact, it can be argued, if it serves to generate funds to be used for habitat restoration and conservation that would otherwise not be available.

It is remarkable how well the HCP process seems to have functioned and is functioning in many places, given the potential volatility of the mixture of community factions and stakeholders typically involved. While there has been considerable acrimony in many of the HCP processes, normally warring factions have come together to accomplish common conservation goals. As a result, developers have recognized the need to preserve endangered species habitat, while members of the environmental community have acknowledged that much can be accomplished through collaboration and pursuit of common interests and that the HCP process can be used to garner financial and political resources that would otherwise not be available. Many of the HCP participants characterize the HCP process as a "win-win" process. (Some participants are, of course, quite critical of the HCP process for reasons discussed below.)

To be sure, environmental and development communities have stayed at the bargaining table, and have remained as good faith participants in these processes, because they have seen it in their best interests to do so. Several HCP participants have described the situation as a kind of "balance of terror," in which each side would experience a certain liability if they walked away from the process. From the development community's perspective, HCPs represent an efficient solution to a major development obstacle. The alternatives would be either to expend considerable time and expense in legal fights, or to attempt to deal with the endangered species problem on a fairly inefficient site-by-site, project-by-project basis, or both. The development community also has clearly seen the HCP process as a way to spread the costs of habitat conservation to the broader public. And while some members of the environmental community support HCPs primarily as a means of marshalling financial and political support for the establishment of habitat preserves, they also recognize the political difficulties that USFWS has in shutting down development in habitat areas, and the likely political fallout that would result if such actions were taken. Despite the accomplishments and positive outcomes of HCPs, the picture is not entirely rosy, as discussed below.

The Adequacy of Habitat Conservation Measures

One of the main unanswered questions about HCPs is whether the extent and nature of conservation measures contained in the plans are sufficient to adequately protect the endangered or threatened species involved, and indeed sufficient to ensure the protection of overall biodiversity. For example, what level of habitat conservation is required, or what level of species protection is actually demanded under Section 10(a)? How much habitat loss is acceptable? Recall that ESA states that a Section 10(a) permit can be issued and incidental take allowed only where the taking "will not appreciably reduce the likelihood of the survival and recovery of the species in the wild."

Considerable variation exists among HCPs in determining the amount of habitat conservation necessary or desirable. At least three different approaches can be identified. One approach might be described as the "minimal survival" position, where only the minimum amount of habitat needed to protect a species is set aside. The actual extent of loss of existing habitat or range is less important. In this approach, the key question is what is the minimum number and size of preserves to be set aside? The answer often is determined through consultation with leading biological experts and a USFWS recovery team, where one exists.

The Coachella Valley HCP is perhaps the best example of this approach in that while the preserves were large enough to sustain the species, in the opinion of many biological experts (including the USFWS recovery team), they only protect about 10 percent of the habitat that existed at the time the plan was prepared. Granted that much of the habitat was already undergoing degradation due to sand shielding, it is difficult to imagine how an 85 to 90 percent reduction in the existing habitat of a listed species could satisfy the Section 10(a) criteria contained in ESA. Moreover, many of the wildlife scientists who signed off on the plan expressed concern in interviews about the long-term prospects for the lizard. Many of those HCP participants described the plan as a "gamble." However, many participants also stated that what was accomplished in terms of habitat conservation was certainly better than nothing and probably the best deal that could have been struck.

Concerns about the extent of habitat loss are further reinforced by the dramatic population swings exhibited by the lizard populations in the three preserves in recent years. Lizard populations are prone to "wild yearly fluctua-

The fringe-toed lizard's habitat is threatened by desert development in the Southwest.

tions," closely tied, it appears, to precipitation patterns, though this is not understood very well. Some members of the Coachella Valley HCP Steering Committee have criticized the plan because it essentially "gave up" on large areas of potentially occupiable habitat. While much of this land has been undergoing degradation due to sand shielding, no serious consideration was given to such options as removing existing sand shields (such as the Southern Pacific railroad windbreaks, which are estimated to be a major cause of sand shielding and habitat degradation). For many of these reasons the Coachella Valley plan has been the most heavily criticized of the HCP efforts to date. One reviewer concluded that HCPs

> . . . can only be described as doing, under the guise of an "incidental take," great violence to the concepts of recovery and survival. Taking a "threatened" species, with a range already reduced by one-half, and permitting it to be reduced to less than one-quarter of its remaining range, makes its reclassification as "endangered" certain. Even if the biological evaluation is correct and adequate preserves will remain to prevent extinction, the fringe-toed lizard probably will warrant reclassification as an endangered species in the near future.[7]

A second approach exhibited in several of the HCPs might be characterized as the "mitigation ratio" position, where the amount of habitat protected, restored, or created is in some sense directly related to the amount of habitat destroyed or lost. Such mitigation ratios are employed in a variety of environmental laws. For example, if a developer is allowed to fill an acre of wetland, then he or she will often be required to create, restore, or protect an acre somewhere else in exchange. This "no net loss" concept is appealing from an equity standpoint. Those who are responsible for destroying or degrading habitat ought to be required to compensate for these impacts in some way.

The mitigation ratio concept has been used extensively in wildlife habitat issues. The California Department of Fish and Game, for instance, has required mitigation for habitat loss on as much as a 5-to-1 ratio (under the California Endangered Species Act). Mitigation ratios greater than 1:1 are generally intended to compensate for the inherent riskiness of allowing natural habitat to be replaced with newly created or rehabilitated habitat.

Several HCPs appear to have the concept of a mitigation ratio as their underlying philosophy. The Metro-Bakersfield HCP is a notable example, in that a goal of the plan is to restore/protect three acres of kit fox habitat for each acre of natural habitat destroyed. (The mitigation ratio for "open" or agricultural lands is one-for-one.) Similarly, the San Diego HCP for the least Bell's vireo HCP emphasizes mitigation on a project-by-project basis. Obviously, this mitigation ratio approach will be more difficult to apply where restoration or re-creation of habitat is difficult or impossible (e.g., it may be completely impossible to re-create desert blow-sand habitat). In maintaining or even expanding the existing habitat of threatened or endangered species, the results of this type of strategy seem more consistent with the Section 10(a) standards contained in ESA.

A third approach might be described as the "minimal footprint" position, where the consumption of habitat areas used for development or other destructive uses is minimized. For instance, the San Bruno Mountain plan minimizes destruction of habitat by development and thus sets aside some 90 percent of butterfly habitat. This is an attractive strategy from a biological and conservation standpoint but obviously will be less desirable to developers and others who wish to maximize their economic use of habitat lands. And, due to constitutional limits on the extent to which land can be restricted or regulated before such actions constitute government "takings" (requiring compensation), the determination of the minimum footprint is closely related to allowing landowners or developers a reasonable economic return on their investment.

A related concern is whether the conserved habitat areas that are being set aside will be viable over the long term. In many cases, HCPs will create habitat islands that eventually will be surrounded by development and that are not connected to nor relate very well to the broader natural landscape. One has to wonder about the long-term viability of areas like the "east dunes" in Sand City—a small habitat island that inevitably will be surrounded by intensive human uses. In Coachella Valley, the long-term viability of the lizard preserve system, particularly the two satellite preserves, is anything but assured. Already, incompatible land uses adjacent to the Coachella Valley preserves, such as the recent proposals to construct a racetrack adjacent to the Whitewater floodplain preserve as well as flood control and other activities, threaten the survivability of the lizard. These isolated preserves should be linked through protected corridors of habitat or landscape "linkages."

The Metro-Bakersfield HCP is encouraging in this regard, with its efforts to tie together conserved habitat areas and to protect a contiguous corridor along the Kern River. Furthermore, stringent controls on adjacent uses and activities would help to ensure the viability of habitat preserves.

Even the largest and most protected preserve, of course, may have difficulty ensuring species preservation. For migrating species, such as the least Bell's vireo or the black-capped vireo, survival also depends on protection of sufficient wintering habitat, which is beyond the control of a local HCP. In addition, global climate changes may seriously impact the long-term viability of conserved habitat. No HCPs have even considered the potential impacts of global warming.

These concerns raise a question about the level of habitat protection needed to support approval of a Section 10(a) permit.

Conservation Decisions in the Context of Limited Knowledge

It is axiomatic that conservation decisions must be made without full and complete biological knowledge. This problem is apparent with HCPs as well and is particularly troubling given the magnitude of policy decisions about endangered species and the speed with which they are made. A basic contradiction exists between the time frames of land users, such as developers, who want relatively quick answers, and the time frame of scientists and wildlife biologists who may need several years of study to adequately understand the biology of even a single species.

Examples of biological uncertainties present in HCPs are numerous; they include the extent of habitat that must be set aside to protect a species in perpetuity and the appropriate number, size, and configuration of preserves. In the Coachella Valley, scientific understanding remains uncertain, although an effort was made to poll a number of biological experts about the appropriate minimum acreage to be preserved.

As already observed, the cause of fluctuations in lizard populations remains a mystery. The Coachella Valley HCP recognizes this, and in its long-term biological program it outlines a variety of basic research and monitoring activities, including establishing a population baseline; tracking fluctuations in populations; developing reliable and cost-effective methods for monitoring; and conducting basic research to identify important factors affecting habitat quality, essential elements of lizard diet, a better understanding of reproduction and life span, identification of important predators and competitors of the lizard, among others.

While the extent of biological understanding varies from one HCP to the next, the Coachella Valley situation is not unique. Serious deficiencies in biological knowledge occur in every HCP. For example, there are considerable uncertainties about the extent to which noise, such as from automobile traffic or farm equipment, is disruptive to the life functions (e.g., mating and establishment of territory) of the least Bell's vireo in San Diego. Yet, clearly the answer has many implications for the kinds of activities and land uses that are appropriate adjacent to conserved habitat.

In the Balcones Canyonlands Conservation Plan, very little was known about the biota of the underground karst habitat (areas of porous limestone) in which a group of federally listed cave invertebrates live. Because these underground cave areas are relatively inaccessible to humans (with cave openings and fractures too small for humans to fit through) and have not received much study in the past, it is possible that numerous other rare species are living in the caves as well. Recently, a number of new species of cave-adapted invertebrates were discovered, representing five genera. These species have yet to undergo taxonomic study, let alone an analysis of their relevant biological or ecological characteristics. Moreover, understanding of the impacts of human activities on these karst habitats is crude at best (e.g., effects of water contaminants, modifications to surface vegetation, introduction of fire ants).

Unfortunately, there is probably little that can be done to adequately address these biological limitations, given the time and monetary constraints of the HCP process. Policy decisions must be made in relatively short time frames. Obviously, the best biological studies possible in the short term should be prepared as part the HCP process, and all prevailing scientific opinion and expertise should be utilized. Perhaps more fundamentally, however, these basic biological uncertainties should be clearly acknowledged in the HCP process and conservation measures should err on the side of caution and conservatism. Retaining much larger undisturbed areas may be more appropriate for species where knowledge of life cycle or habitat needs is quite limited. In the Balcones Canyonlands Conservation Plan, uncertainties about karst biota suggested a conservative strategy of protecting representative pieces of karst habitat, centered on areas of endemism in each of five biographic zones which have been identified in the HCP study area.

The Benefits of Comprehensive, Multi-species Approaches

In evaluating the merits of the HCP mechanism, one is initially struck by the failure of many HCPs to take a more comprehensive, "multi-species" approach. Several HCPs have identified other important species of concern, and have given lip service to the concept of a multi-species approach, but have remained focused essentially on one or a few key species. The single-species nature of the plans is perhaps not surprising given the structure and orientation of the federal Endangered Species Act, and given the perceived need to arrive at a "solution" to the problem at hand quickly. But it does not make much sense when considering the time and expense involved in preparing HCPs. More comprehensive approaches would generate greater bang for the buck, could serve to prevent conflicts in the future, and could save important biological resources more effectively. Moreover, such comprehensive, multispecies approaches are more likely to result in preserving ecologically viable and defensible habitat areas.

Taking a more comprehensive biodiversity approach would mean considering not just federally listed endangered or threatened species but also candidate species, state-listed species, and other species of concern, and indeed overall patterns of biodiversity in a locality or region. Such a strategy would allow the consideration of habitat needs of species that while not yet legally covered by ESA are likely to be listed in the future. Such an approach would allow the identification and protection of critical areas of overlapping habitat. Several recent HCPs, the Balcones Canyonlands Conservation Plan and the Kern County HCPs in particular, have taken such an approach. Despite the possibility of locking up large land areas in preserves, developers often support such a strategy as a way of addressing the species conservation needs in the region through a single plan and process, rather than through a myriad of sequential HCPs.

To take a comprehensive species approach, however, would not only mean examining how species habitats overlap but also examining how to preserve other species of concern within one's jurisdiction. It would have made sense for jurisdictions such as Riverside County (California) to consider protecting the Stephens' kangaroo rat at the same time it considered the Coachella Valley fringe-toed lizard, and for Monroe County, Florida, to consider simultaneously the habitat needs of the endangered key deer, Key Largo woodrat, and the Key Largo cottonmouse.

On the other hand, the monetary and time requirements of comprehensive multi-species HCPs are much greater than single-species HCPs. Comprehensive strategies may be inconsistent with the views of many participants in the HCP process, particularly landowners and developers, that the problem needs to be "solved" quickly. These difficulties suggest that state and federal agencies could play a larger role in laying the biological groundwork for comprehensive multi-species plans. Methodologies such as "gap analysis" hold particular promise in their ability to identify areas rich in biological diversity that are not currently protected through acquisition.

Gap analysis, developed by USFWS scientists, identifies areas of high species diversity through a process of overlaying information on types of vegetation and ranges and densities of species (for endangered and nonendangered species) and comparing the location of highly diverse habitat with existing protected lands to identify "gaps" in habitat protection—that is, important areas of species diversity not currently protected by parks or preserves.[8] The USFWS is successfully applying the analysis at a state level in Idaho and Oregon, and such studies could be extremely useful in facilitating local and regional multi-species HCPs.

Secretary of Interior Bruce Babbitt's proposed national biological survey also could assist in habitat conservation efforts. Federal and state resource agencies may need to expend considerably greater funds on basic biological research, at least for those species of concern whose habitat is now or is likely to be in the near future in jeopardy by urban development and other human activities. Early strategic planning might reduce the need to undertake eleventh-hour biological assessments for individual HCPs.

HCPs should fit within, and serve to implement, broader ecosystem protection strategies. The Nature Conservancy's efforts in recent years to prepare bioreserve plans, and to coordinate their acquisition and management decisions within such plans, make considerable sense. Some have called for the establishment of a system of national ecological reserves and the designation of larger bioregions that would serve as the focus for protective and management activities of federal agencies (and others). The HCP experience suggests the need to assume broader ecosystem-wide conservation strategies—strategies that might ultimately reduce the need to list species in the first place.

Integrating Species Conservation with Land Use Planning

Unfortunately, HCPs and species conservation efforts have not been closely tied to local land use planning. Ideally, local land use and general plans would incorporate the kind of comprehensive biodiversity analysis and planning discussed above, and these efforts could prevent the species/development conflicts that typically give rise to HCPs in the first place. Local plans could direct growth away from areas that are rich in biodiversity and could serve as the basis for comprehensive, long-term land protection and acquisition programs.

It seems obvious that as much emphasis ought to be given to prevention of species decline, through effective land use planning and growth management, as cures through HCPs. Kern County's current efforts to prepare an endangered species element of its general plan are encouraging in this respect. The wildlife conservation planning efforts of the three Southern California counties described in the next chapter demonstrate approaches to integrating conservation planning into general community planning programs. In the long term, these approaches may be among the most cost-effective ways of dealing with species conservation issues. The USFWS or state governments would assist wildlife conservation a great deal by spending small amounts of seed money up front to facilitate this kind of local planning (e.g., perhaps in the form of small planning grants).

Many states mandate the preparation of local land use or general plans, often stipulating in considerable detail the types of issues and policy areas that must be addressed. The importance of such a tool in preventing or minimizing species/development conflicts suggests the need for states to require specifically endangered species components such as that being prepared for Kern County.

Many jurisdictions have recognized the need to address species conservation issues, at least in part, by examining current development and growth patterns. Most HCPs assume that current patterns and types of growth are appropriate and that the HCP is primarily intended to find a way to overcome the legal obstacles presented by the ESA, and thus to facilitate existing growth patterns. Yet further examination might show that by modifying growth patterns or characteristics—for instance, by encouraging denser, more compact and contiguous growth patterns, and by encouraging infill—development pressure on open space and natural areas can be substantially reduced. In many localities and regions with substantial amounts of endangered wildlife and important biological resources, it may no longer be justifiable to accept existing inefficient and wasteful patterns of development. Habitat conservation increasingly must be placed in the context of promoting *sustainable communities* and sustainable patterns of local and regional growth.

The Immense Problem of Funding HCPs

Perhaps the most striking aspect of many of the more recent HCPs is the amount of money necessary to undertake the habitat acquisition and other activities for protection of species of concern. For example, land acquisition in the preservation areas identified in the Balcones Canyonlands Conservation Plan may have ultimately cost more than $200 million (including management costs). Funding may be the single most pressing implementation obstacle influencing the effectiveness of HCPs. Where will the funds come from to finance HCPs and habitat conservation in the future and who will bear the burden?

Habitat acquisition costs represent the largest component of HCPs. It is paradoxical, but typical, that species are not usually endangered until the occurrence of significant human development. However, by the time such species are in jeopardy and society recognizes the need to protect remaining habitat, the market value of habitat lands is extremely high. A recent survey of land prices for Stephens' kangaroo rat habitat in eastern Riverside County, for example, found some land selling for as much as $400,000 per acre.[9]

Many of those involved in preparing HCPs hope that the federal government will fund most habitat acquisition costs. The federal government funded approximately 60 percent of land acquisition in the Coachella Valley HCP, through a combination of appropriations from the federal Land and Water Conservation Fund and BLM land swaps. To many this is an equitable solution, since it is a federal law—the Endangered Species Act—that creates the need for HCPs in the first place. Species conservation, the argument continues, is a public good, and thus its costs ought to be borne by the broader public. Recent indications from Washington, however, suggest that Uncle Sam cannot be counted on to bail out HCPs. This heightens the need to explore other long-term funding sources. This is perhaps the greatest single challenge facing the HCP process in the future.

One component of a potential solution is to expand contributions made by the development community, specifically in the form of mitigation fees. It can be argued that the extent of development contributions often is low, particularly in light of the fact that it is these very activities (e.g., development in habitat areas) that are threatening loss of species. The Coachella Valley HCP is perhaps a case in point. Under this funding scheme, the $600 per acre mitigation fees will ultimately generate approximately $7 million toward the total $25 million cost of the preserve system, or about 28 percent. Given the tremendous profits to be made in opening up development in the Valley, such a per-acre assessment seems modest.

Furthermore, early in the fringe-toed lizard controversy some participants, such as the Riverside County Planning Department, were arguing that development fees should be assessed at least on the basis of an acre-for-acre replacement—that is, a per-acre fee should be assessed which would be sufficient to purchase and protect an acre of lizard habitat somewhere else. Given that habitat land in Coachella Valley was selling for between $3,500 and $8,000 per acre in the early 1980s, a $600 per acre mitigation fee falls very short of a one-for-one replacement ratio. Indeed, landowners and developers are being asked to protect habitat at only about a one/fifth-to-one ratio at best.

The simple per-acre mitigation fee used in most HCPs, however, may not be the most equitable way in which to assess new development. In Clark County, Nevada, a developer of a four-acre parcel would pay the same mitigation fee per acre regardless of whether the land was to be used for new detached single-family homes or a multi-million dollar hotel and casino. Equity would suggest the need to explore other ways of imposing such fees to take such differences into account.

There is some validity to the arguments of developers that the costs of HCPs should be shared by the general public. Often, previous growth and development in a community, which may benefit the entire community, may be responsible for bringing a species to the brink of extinction. Is it not equitable, therefore, for the broader public to contribute to these conservation costs? This is an especially compelling argument when the resulting habitat set-asides serve important open space, aesthetic, or recreational functions for the community or region. Local governments faced with HCP costs in the future should consider utilizing other sources of revenue in addition to exactions and development fees on new development.

Local funding for land acquisition is not a novel idea; there are numerous examples of successful locally funded acquisition programs: Boulder, Colorado, uses a sales tax; the Mid-Peninsula Open Space District in the San Francisco Bay Area uses an annual property assessment; Nantucket, Massachusetts, uses a land transfer tax. The size of the funds needed for habitat acquisition also suggests the need to continue to move toward greater state funding, such as the bond referenda considered in several states: Question 5 in Nevada, providing funds for the desert tortoise, and California's Proposition 117 (the California Wildlife Protection Initiative).

A number of mechanisms exist to reduce the cost of habitat preservation, such as utilizing alternatives to fee-simple acquisition (e.g., some combination of regulation/transfer of development rights; easements and other forms of less-than-fee-simple acquisition); adopting a much longer time horizon and acquiring land well in advance of when it is needed (this ties in closely with the advantages of a comprehensive/multi-species approach); and perhaps utilizing mitigation funds generated in one jurisdiction to buy habitat areas in other jurisdictions, particularly where land is less expensive and larger so that more ecologically viable lands can be obtained. Again, comprehensive regional HCPs, which simultaneously consider the habitat needs of many species, will serve to facilitate these types of cost efficiencies.

There also is merit in local and regional proposals that seek to contain development and growth. By doing so, and by satisfying housing and growth demands through infill, redevelopment, and higher density development, pressures on habitat areas can be reduced and resulting speculative land values kept in check.

Federal and state governments must devise ways to assist local governments in funding and accomplishing habitat acquisition. Congress could create a revolving fund for habitat acquisition, from which approved HCPs could borrow monies. Under the 1987 reauthorization of the Clean Water Act, for example, Congress phased out federal grants for construction of wastewater treatment plants in favor of encouraging the creation of state revolving funds (and the provision of seed monies for such funds). A number of states now have such revolving funds from which local governments can borrow monies at little or no interest. Similar state revolving funds could be established explicitly for acquisition of habitat and open space.

Concerns about the HCP Process

One of the main issues about the HCP process is the composition and bias of the decision-making groups, such as steering committees. Should they be informal working groups, allowing anyone and any group interested to participate, or should they be more formal groups, with the membership carefully selected to reflect a genuine balance of community interests and perspectives? Concomitantly, should decision-making procedures reflect this objective of more formal representation, as perhaps through voting, rules of order, etc.?

While the HCP committees included representatives from a variety of interest groups and perspectives, not all interests were well represented in the planning processes. For instance, environmental interests appear to be underrepresented on the Clark County desert tortoise steering committee. While each meeting is typically attended by a host of representatives of resource users and developers, often only one environmental group is represented consistently. There is little doubt that the tenor of discussion and the substance of the policy decisions of such a committee will be influenced by this membership composition. In addition, the North Key Largo HCP process was probably overrepresented by large landholders, while smaller landowners were underrepresented. Representation and public accountability of HCP groups will remain sticky issues in the HCP process and may determine the success or failure of HCPs.

Perhaps the most troubling issue to participants involved in HCPs is the shear length of time typically required to complete the process. While the Coachella Valley HCP started in the early summer of 1983, for example, a Section 10(a) permit was not officially issued by USFWS until April of 1986. Moreover, some plans, like the North Key Largo HCP, initiated in 1984, were derailed for a variety of political and technical reasons. These lengthy plan preparation and adoption periods are particularly troubling to developers, to whom even modest delays can be costly. Such delays also are of concern from a species conservation standpoint in that failure to complete the HCP in a timely fashion may place species of concern in greater jeopardy (e.g., the gradual replacement of natural grasslands on San Bruno Mountain). While earlier recommendations concerning the need for comprehensive multi-species approaches may seem to work against such concerns, in the long run such efforts may prevent the constant and continual preparation of more limited species HCPs. The temporal demands of any carefully prepared HCP, however, do suggest the need to explore possible interim conservation measures (described more fully in the following section).

The Problem of Interim Conservation

A final issue deals with the question of timing. While an HCP is being prepared, how should a species be protected? In some cases, such as the Coachella Valley, the USFWS has allowed a taking of listed species while an HCP is being prepared. In other cases, it has adamantly refused to allow any interim habitat loss.

The basic political and economic difficulties here are obvious. It often would be economically disastrous and politically infeasible to expect to completely shut down development in a community, particularly in high growth areas, while an HCP is being prepared. On the other hand, to permit a "take" to occur prior to any protective actions is certainly risky.

The preparation and approval by USFWS of several recent "short-term" or interim HCPs is one solution that appears to be working fairly well. For example, a two-year HCP was approved for the Stephens' kangaroo rat. Large areas of Riverside County have been identified in which few rats are likely to be found and where development will be allowed to proceed while the full HCP is being prepared (i.e., a Section 10(a) permit will be issued for these areas). Development generally is not permitted to occur (unless developers obtain individual Section 10(a) permits on their own) in nine designated study areas encompassing some 20,000 acres of habitat where the vast majority (some 95 percent) of kangaroo rats are found (see Figure 3.3). During this two-year period, the long-term, full-blown HCP will be prepared. Separating major habitat study areas from minor, mostly nonhabitat areas may prevent the county from coming to a development standstill. While a small amount of habitat may be lost outside of the study areas (perhaps on the order

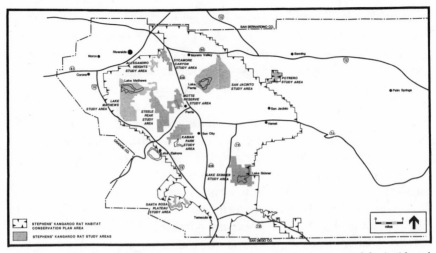

Figure 3.3 Stephens' kangaroo rat conservation plan area (area proposed for incidental take of Stephens' kangaroo rat) [courtesy of Regional Environmental Consultants (RECON), San Diego, California].

of 5 percent), this approach seems a reasonable compromise. The short-term Riverside plan has worked fairly well—some 2,100 acres of habitat has been secured during the interim period, exceeding the amount of habitat loss through development.

A similar interim approach has been taken for the desert tortoise in Clark County. Under this short-term HCP, a take is allowed within Las Vegas Valley, which includes Las Vegas, for a three-year period, in exchange for certain short-term habitat conservation measures, primarily in the form of changing allowable land uses on BLM land and taking certain BLM habitat areas out of livestock, mining, off-road vehicles, and other environmentally damaging uses.

Under the desert tortoise short-term HCP, habitat destruction is tied explicitly to protection and conservation of habitat areas. During the HCP process, 14 potential tortoise management areas (PTMAs) were identified, based mainly on earlier BLM analyses. Specifically, these are areas identified by the BLM as containing from 20 to more than 250 tortoises per square mile. Two priority management areas were also identified. The short-term HCP established conservation thresholds that must be achieved over time in order for allowable take to continue. These thresholds specified not only the amount of habitat to be conserved but the location and type of these areas. Specifically, the four thresholds established that:

1. At least 100,000 acres will be conserved within either of the two priority areas before any take is allowed in the permit area

2. At least 200,000 acres will be conserved by the end of the fourth quarter after take is allowed

3. At least 300,000 acres will be conserved before take exceeds 2,000 tortoises or habitat loss exceeds 13,000 acres

4. At least 400,000 acres will be conserved, with at least 200,000 acres in either of the two priority areas, before take exceeds 3,500 tortoises or habitat loss exceeds 18,000 acres

Overall, no more than 3,700 tortoises may be killed during the three-year period. The 10(a) permit covers approximately 300,000 acres in the Las Vegas Valley. Habitat is to be conserved through several different types of land use controls, including the acquisition of grazing rights, additional restrictions on off-road vehicle use in habitat areas, and review of mining claims on BLM lands.

The Clark County short-term HCP has thus far been quite successful, already resulting in the protection of some 400,000 areas of BLM habitat (through acquisition of grazing rights). Tortoise losses also have been considerably less than the permissible levels, and considerable progress has been made toward completing the long-term HCP.

While the short-term HCP option seems to represent a viable and reasonable approach to dealing with interim conservation, USFWS must be cautious in approving such plans. Short of a clear and logical plan for protecting the bulk of species habitat and regional biodiversity during the preparation of the long-term HCP, prohibitions against interim takes should be strongly enforced by USFWS.

Conclusions

This chapter has attempted to summarize the main experiences to date with the use of regional habitat conservation plans. Because the HCP provisions are a relatively recent addition to the Endangered Species Act, and because there have been relatively few completed and approved HCPs, a definitive critique or accurate assessment of the success of these plans is perhaps premature. Without a doubt, however, the next decade will witness even greater conflicts between urban development and protection of endangered species, and HCPs undoubtedly will be even more extensively utilized. Thus, this is an excellent time to reflect on its limitations and to suggest possibilities for improving this conservation tool.

Generally, HCPs have many pluses. HCPs appear to provide a pressure relief valve under the ESA and have resulted in the protection and preservation of substantial amounts of species habitat. Furthermore, the HCP process has generated substantial monies for conservation and management activities which would otherwise not have been available.

Despite these positive outcomes, however, a number of concerns remain, including (1) the amount of habitat loss permitted through HCPs, (2) the defensibility and long-term viability of conserved habitat areas, (3) the failure to take more comprehensive and multi-species approaches, (4) the necessity of making habitat and management decisions in the face of limited biological understanding, (5) the common failure to integrate species conservation with local land use planning and growth management, and (6) the failure to adequately address the long-term funding needs of HCPs.

While it is easy to berate USFWS for failing to provide leadership on these issues, responsibility lies at a number of levels, including with local and state governments. State governments, for instance, tend to have the financial and other resources to facilitate the preparation of efficient comprehensive habitat protection plans, as well as considerable revenue-raising capabilities.

One role which USFWS must continue to play, perhaps more aggressively than it has in the past, is in the area of enforcement. Clearly, if developers and land users do not perceive the liabilities of undertaking activities in habitat areas to be significant, they will be less inclined to participate in HCPs. Expanding enforcement activities, of course, may be difficult in this period of fiscal austerity. But USFWS must make it clear that the alternative to a strong HCP that protects a large proportion of species habitat is a local development moratorium, as politically unpopular as this may be.

It is also clear that there are many situations where private development has deleterious effects on listed species but where no HCP was required by USFWS under a narrow interpretation of a take. For example, on Big Pine Key, Florida, development in the northern end of the island is substantially increasing traffic along the major north-south road (Big Pine Boulevard), in turn leading to increased road kills of the endangered key deer. USFWS should make development in these circumstances conditional upon the submittal and implementation of an acceptable HCP.

The increasingly frequent use of HCPs also suggests an important research role in documenting and disseminating information about successful strategies and approaches. Until recently, participants involved in preparing HCPs have had relatively little information about the experiences and issues confronted by HCPs prepared or in preparation in other areas. While each HCP will have its own unique circumstances, much can be learned from other HCPs.

NOTES

1. This chapter draws extensively from Timothy Beatley, *Habitat Conservation Planning: Endangered Species and Urban Growth*, Austin, Texas: University of Texas Press,1994, with updates and revisions by the author.

2. Todd Kent Hemingson, *A Nationwide Survey of Habitat Conservation Plans*, University of Texas, Austin, Texas, unpublished master's thesis, December 1992.

3. Habitat conservation plans consulted for this analysis are identified in Table 3.1 and published as follows:

Austin Regional Habitat Conservation Plan, *Comprehensive Report of the Biological Advisory Team*, January 1990.

Clark County, *Short-term Habitat Conservation Plan for the Desert Tortoise in Las Vegas Valley, Clark County, Nevada*, prepared by Regional Environmental Consultants, August 1990.

Coachella Valley Habitat Conservation Steering Committee, 1986. See also, *Coachella Valley Fringe-Toed Lizard Recovery Plan*, prepared by the U.S. Fish and Wildlife Service, Portland, Oregon, 1985.

Kern County Department of Planning and Development Services, 1989.

North Key Largo Study Committee, *Habitat Conservation Plan and Final Report*, September 15, 1986.

Riverside County Planning Department, *Interim Habitat Conservation Plan for the Stephens' Kangaroo Rat*, prepared by Regional Environmental Consultants, March 1989. See also, U.S. Fish and Wildlife Service, *Final Joint Environmental Impact Statement/Environmental Impact Report for Proposed Issuance of a Permit to Allow Incidental Take of Stephens' Kangaroo Rats in Riverside County, California*, prepared by Regional Environmental Consultants, March 1990.

San Bruno Mountain HCP Steering Committee, *San Bruno Mountain Area Habitat Conservation Plan*, November 1982.

San Diego Association of Governments, *Comprehensive Species Managment Plan for the Least Bell's Vireo*, prepared by Regional Environmental Consultants, 1989.

The author also conducted interviews with many participants in the Coachella Valley, North Key Largo, San Diego, Metro-Bakersfield, Clark County, and Marina HCPs.

4. See Stephen Kellert, *Public Attitudes Toward Critical Wildlife and Natural Habitat Issues*, Washington, D.C.: U.S. Fish and Wildlife Service, 1979. Kellert has undertaken extensive surveys of public attitudes toward wildlife issues. In one survey he asked respondents to identify, from a list of animal and plant species, those species that they would favor protecting

if protection resulted in higher energy costs. While 89 percent favored protecting the bald eagle, 43 percent selected the eastern indigo snake, and only 34 percent identified the kanai wolf spider.

5. "Rancho Mirage Favors Desert Preserve," *The Press-Enterprise,* October 3, 1983.

6. For further discussion of this issue, see David Ehrenfeld, *The Arrogance of Humanism,* Oxford: Oxford University Press, 1978; Bryan G. Norton, *The Preservation of Species: The Value of Biological Diversity,* Princeton, NJ: Princeton University Press, 1986; Paul Taylor, *Respect for Nature: A Theory of Environmental Ethics,* Princeton, NJ: Princeton University Press, 1986; Timothy Beatley, "Environmental Ethics and Planning Theory," *Journal of Planning Literature,* Vol. 4, No. 1, Winter, 1989, pp. 1–32.

7. Richard E. Webster, "Habitat Conservation Plans Under the Endangered Species Act," *San Diego Law Review,* Vol. 24, p. 255 (1987).

8. See J. Michael Scott, et al., "Beyond Endangered Species: An Integrated Conservation Strategy for the Preservation of Biological Diversity," *Endangered Species Update,* Vol. 35, No. 10, 1987, pp. 43–48; and Timothy Beatley, David J. Brower, and Lou Ann Brower, *Managing Growth: Small Communities and Rural Areas,* prepared for the State of Maine Division of State Planning, 1988.

9. Riverside County Planning Department, op. cit. note 3.

The Balcones Canyonlands Conservation Plan: A Regional, Multi-species Approach

Timothy Beatley, T. James Fries, and David Braun

E D I T O R S '   S U M M A R Y

An ambitious plan is under way in the Hill Country near Austin, Texas, to preserve approximately 75,000 acres of habitat for over two dozen species, nine of which have been listed as endangered. The picturesque hills are coveted by developers, but the presence of endangered species halted or delayed several development projects. The plan seeks to protect critical habitat areas while identifying other areas where development could more readily occur. According to Beatley, Fries, and Braun, funding for acquiring habitat remains the greatest obstacle. Land for the proposed habitat preserve will cost an estimated $134 million to acquire. The U.S. Fish and Wildlife Service plans on acquiring roughly half of the land as part of a newly established wildlife refuge. And Austin alone has raised $40 million for land acquisition. The rest will come primarily from developer contributions. The collaborative planning effort illustrates the potential pitfalls and rewards of establishing a multi-species habitat protection preserve in an area under strong development pressure.

Background

The Austin, Texas, region is biologically rich and is home to a number of rare and endangered flora and fauna. The Balcones Canyonlands in the hill country and Edwards Plateau west of the city, with its steep canyons, ridge tops, and plateaus, contains habitat for two species of endangered migratory songbirds. Under the surface lies an extensive limestone cave system that harbors specially adapted invertebrates found nowhere else on Earth. Several species of rare plants are also found in the region. In recent years, however, this unique flora and fauna has been increasingly threatened by development pressures, including housing developments, road construction, and shopping malls.

The presence of endangered species became a significant issue in Austin in 1988 when a number of public and private projects threatening the habitat of the endangered black-capped vireo, including several road improvements and a 4,500-acre residential development, were halted. The Austin chapter of Earth First!, a national environmental organization, was instrumental in raising public awareness locally by staging protests and threatening to sue the local governments and private developers under the federal Endangered Species Act (ESA). In an effort to protect the cave invertebrates, members of Earth First! occupied several caves in one proposed development area for a few days. These and other actions of Earth First! brought national, as well as local, attention to the presence of endangered species in Austin.

In the past, many endangered species versus development conflicts of this type resulted in expensive, drawn-out litigation, with questionable results for either the species or developers. The habitat conservation plan (HCP) mechanism was seen as a way to positively resolve the impasse in Austin. What follows is a description of the innovative HCP currently in preparation in the Austin area, its principal components, and a number of planning and implementation issues being addressed by the plan. In many ways this HCP is unique and ground breaking, and it represents a model that could be emulated elsewhere.

Initiating the HCP

In 1988 The Nature Conservancy of Texas and the city of Austin's Department of Environmental Protection (now called the Environmental and Conservation Services Department) jointly proposed the initiation of an Austin Regional Habitat Conservation Plan, later called the Balcones Canyonlands Conservation Plan (or "BCCP"). The idea was accepted by leaders in the community, and an executive committee was formed to guide the preparation of the plan. David Braun, director of The Nature Conservancy of Texas, was asked to chair the committee. Efforts were made to ensure representation on the committee of all major stakeholders, including environmental groups, developers, and local and state government agencies. The U.S. Fish and Wildlife Service (USFWS) participated on the committee as an observer. The environmental community was represented by the Audubon Society and the Sierra

Club. Attorneys and consultants for several local developers represented the development community. Initially, four local governments were represented on the committee, including Travis County, Williamson County, the city of Austin, and the city of Georgetown, but Williamson County and Georgetown later withdrew after deciding not to participate in the regional conservation planning process. Four state agencies were represented: the Texas Parks and Wildlife Department, the General Land Office, the Texas Department of Transportation, and the Lower Colorado River Authority. Finally, two private landowners were added to the committee during its last three months of operation.

A biological advisory team (BAT) was appointed by the executive committee. This group was charged with overseeing the preparation of all necessary biological studies and advising the executive committee on preserve requirements (e.g., size, shape, and management of the preserves). The BAT included scientists and biologists, with expertise on endangered species issues, from the University of Texas, Texas A&M, University of North Texas, University of Oklahoma, the city of Austin, the Texas Parks and Wildlife Department, and The Nature Conservancy of Texas, among others. A number of the basic biological studies were prepared by consultants, under the supervision of the BAT.[1]

A local planning consulting firm was hired to coordinate the planning process and to prepare the final plan. In December 1990, after two years of extensive work, the plan was nearing completion; an initial draft was presented to the executive committee on December 5, 1990. The committee spent several weeks scrutinizing the plan, making numerous recommendations for changes. The most significant revision was the decision to protect habitat by land acquisition alone rather than through a combination of acquisition and land use controls. Relying on acquisition alone would substantially increase the cost of implementing the plan. Land use controls are anathema in Texas. In fact, Travis County, like many other counties in Texas, has no enabling legislation to adopt land use controls. Obtaining such authority from the state is unlikely.

A final plan was submitted to the committee in February 1992 and was submitted for public review and to the local jurisdictions and state agencies shortly thereafter. Following a review period, the plan was to be submitted to the USFWS for approval. Uncertainty over financing the acquisition of land, however, kept the plan in limbo for over a year. Then in November 1993 the plan suffered a severe setback when voters in Travis County, rejected a $49 million bond issue that would have financed the purchase of approximately 12,000 acres of habitat in the county. Poor voter turnout and lack of strong support from the environmental community was blamed for the bond issue's defeat. Less than 20 percent of the county's registered voters bothered to vote.[2]

Species of Concern

The city of Austin lies on the Balcones fault, separating the Blackland Prairie region to the east and the Edwards Plateau to the west. The majority of endangered species habitat in the Austin area occurs in the Balcones Canyonlands to the west and northwest of the city. The canyonlands are home to nine federally listed species, which are the centerpiece of the BCCP: the black-capped vireo, the golden-cheeked warbler, and seven cave-adapted invertebrates (including a spider, two types of beetles, a pseudoscorpion, and a daddy long legs). In addition, three species of rare plants and three salamanders are being considered in the plan (see Table 4.1). By simultaneously considering the needs of multiple species, the Balcones Canyonlands Conservation Plan is more biologically comprehensive than many of the other HCPs.

The black-capped vireo, federally listed in November 1987, is a small migratory songbird that nests in Texas during the summer months (as well as parts of Oklahoma and northern Mexico). It relies on a mid-successional habitat of clumps of shrubs and trees, including shin oak, hawthorne, and sumacs, in otherwise open and grassy locations. Vireos prefer this type of "edge" environment and will not inhabit densely wooded areas. Vireo population nesting in Austin has declined substantially in recent years. In the summer of 1989, for instance, only 59 breeding pairs were found in the study area.

Among the threats to the vireo are overbrowsing of vegetation by sheep and goats, which makes vireo nests more visible and therefore vulnerable to predators; direct loss of habitat or potential habitat to development; the introduction of domestic cats, and the proliferation of brownheaded cowbirds, which parasitize vireos by laying their eggs in vireo nests and displacing vireo chicks. The vireo spends its winters in the foothills of the Sierra Madre Mountains in southwestern Mexico.

The golden-cheeked warbler is also a migratory songbird, but its habitat requirements are quite different, consisting of fairly dense, mature, closed-canopy juniper and mixed oak woodlands on steep canyons. The warbler's entire nesting range lies within Texas, with most of it located in a crescent-shaped area extending from west of San Antonio to north of Austin. The warbler spends its winters in the tropical highlands of Mexico, Guatemala, Honduras, and Nicaragua.

TABLE 4.1   Species Addressed by the Balcones
Canyonlands Conservation Plan

Birds	Salamanders	Cave invertebrates	Plants
Black capped vireo	Barton Springs salamander	Bee Creek Cave harvestman	Canyon mock-orange
Golden-cheeked warbler	Jollyville Plateau salamander	Bone Cave harvestman	Bracted twistflower
	Buttercup Creek salamander	Coffin Cave mold beetle	Texas Amorpha
		Kretschmarr Cave mold beetle	
		Tooth Cave ground beetle	
		Tooth Cave pseudoscorpion	
		Tooth Cave spider	

The tiny black-capped vireo is one of the Canyonlands endangered species. (Photo courtesy of Jim O'Donnell.)

The golden-cheeked warbler inhabits extensive forest areas around Austin.

The number of existing warblers is much higher than that of vireos, with an estimated 1,100 to 2,300 breeding pairs in the area. The existing remaining habitat of the warbler in the Austin area is also much greater, representing an estimated 40 percent of the best remaining habitat in the bird's breeding range. Nevertheless, the Austin area has experienced about a 6 percent annual loss in warbler habitat over the last few years. The threats to the warbler are similar to those facing the vireo. The warbler was emergency-listed in March 1990 and permanently listed in December 1990, largely in response to the belief by USFWS that significant amounts of warbler habitat were being cleared by developers in the Four Points area. Members of Earth First! again played an instrumental role in monitoring habitat alteration and in bringing this habitat alteration to the attention of USFWS.

The limestone geology of the Edwards Plateau has permitted the development of an intricate system of caves, sinkholes, and fissures, home to specially adapted cave invertebrates found nowhere else in the world. Gradual erosion of the plateau by streams and rivers has carved the limestone layers into discrete blocks that isolate different cave systems in the area. This has permitted the biota of these karst islands to evolve separately. Some have described the karst habitat as a kind of subterranean archipelago. While seven of these invertebrates have been federally listed (in September 1988), others have been

Residential subdivisions are spreading into the habitat of the golden-cheeked warbler.

discovered recently and have yet to even undergo taxonomic study. (Some 30 cave-adapted invertebrates have been discovered so far, many of which have not been scientifically named.) While these invertebrates live in subterranean caves, they are very dependent on nutrients and moisture from the surface. There are a variety of potential threats to these cave ecosystems, including urban development, water pollution, and fire ants. Generally, however, these cave ecosystems are not well understood and the potential long-term impacts on the caves are uncertain. While the larger caves have been more thoroughly explored and most of the species inhabiting them identified, the smaller, interconnected limestone openings between the caves may also harbor similar invertebrates.

In addition to the cave invertebrates, three rare subterranean salamanders live in the aquifer of the Canyonlands and emerge in springs that originate along the Balcones Fault Zone. To survive in this aquatic environment, the two- to three-inch salamanders retain their larval gills throughout their life. The greatest threats to the salamanders are degradation of water quality and disruption of groundwater flow patterns associated with construction.

Two plants addressed by the plan, the canyon mock-orange and bracted twistflower, are currently being considered for listing as threatened species under the ESA. The Texas Amorpha, originally thought to be quite rare, is

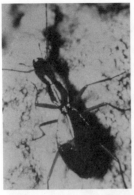  

Not all endangered species are warm and cuddly: herewith (left to right) the Tooth Cave ground beetle (courtesy of Robert W. Mitchell), the Tooth Cave pseudoscorpion (courtesy of William R. Elliott), and the Bee Creek Cave harvestman.

apparently more abundant than originally believed and is not likely to be listed. The Amorpha has, therefore, been dropped from the plan. The third rare plant species that will be considered by the plan is a recent discovery and may also be considered for federal listing. The plant is either a species not currently known to science or a specimen of Alabama Crotan, already being considered for listing as a threatened species. The primary threats to the twist-flower and mock-orange are urban development and browsing by animals. Besides saving the plants themselves, it will be important to protect the natural pollinators of these plants (bees primarily), as well as the natural microclimates within which these plants thrive (natural temperature, moisture, and light).

Elements of the HCP

Development of the BCCP involved a number of key steps, including establishing goals, conducting basic biological studies necessary to understand the needs of species of concern, developing a preserve design, identifying habitat lands to acquire, and developing long-term funding and management strategies. The major planning process and the elements of the plan are discussed below.

Biological Assessment

The first year of the planning process, from January 1989 to January 1990, was spent preparing the background biological assessment. The BAT began by reviewing a list of endangered and threatened wildlife and determining which should be targeted in the plan. Nearly 160 species were screened for inclusion, based on recommendations of the USFWS, the Texas Parks and Wildlife Department, the Texas Natural Heritage Program, and the Texas Organization for Endangered Species. Recommendations on which species to include were made based on "whether there was a significant population in the study area, the degree of threat, and the capability of a regional habitat conservation plan to materially affect its conservation."[3] A number of specific studies were then conducted as part of the comprehensive biological assessment, including vireo population studies, botanical studies, and studies of the karst ecosystems.

The comprehensive biological assessment report, summarizing the recommendations of the BAT, was issued in January 1990. It contained specific habitat conservation recommendations for each species of concern. For the black-capped vireo, the BAT report concludes that minimum populations of between 500 and 1,000 breeding pairs are necessary, and because of the transitional nature of its habitat, a preserve should protect a minimum of 123,500 contiguous acres of habitat. For the warbler, the BAT report recommends a minimum population of between 500 and 1,000 breeding pairs and at least two separate preserves, each of which should be at least 12,000 contiguous acres in size. For the cave invertebrates, the report recommends protection of the known caves where listed species live, and it also concludes that the smaller interconnected cavities in the limestone may be inhabited by endangered invertebrates and that actions should be taken to protect them. Finally, to protect the remaining habitat of the salamanders, the BAT recommended establishing water quality standards, ensuring adequate recharge of the aquifer, and establishing a spill prevention and response program.

The overall recommendation of the BAT report was that large contiguous tracts of habitat should be secured to ensure the long-term survival of the species. While the BATs comprehensive report was not officially adopted by the executive committee until February 1992, it served as a guiding document for the work of the consultants in identifying preserve areas and preserve design. Some of the recommendations, particularly the proposal for a 123,500-acre contiguous vireo preserve, refer to the effort necessary to ensure preservation of the whole species and thus were not considered applicable to the Austin area, where only one small population of vireos exists.

The overall thrust of the document, which had been widely accepted, was that the preservation effort should be directed at the ecosystems of the area rather than habitat needs of individual species. Consideration of the needs of 43 species with such different but interrelated habitats inevitably results in an ecosystem approach.

In combination with the BAT studies, a series of habitat maps were prepared by the planning consultants. These maps identify potential habitat areas for the black-capped vireo and golden-cheeked warbler, potential locations of the bracted twistflower and canyon mock-orange, potential habitat areas for karst invertebrates, and a composite habitat map showing areas of overlapping habitat. These maps have been used by the consultants in identifying preserve sites and priority acquisition areas. The maps were based on a combination of vegetation, geologic, and topographic data, and, in the case of the golden-cheeked warbler, on satellite imagery.

Habitat Acquisition and Protection

Acquisition and preservation of habitat comprised the main conservation strategy for the BCCP, as with most other HCPs. The BCCP was somewhat unique, however, in the size of the preserve system and the amount of habitat acreage protected. In developing the preserve design and plan acquisition priorities, the consultant identified those lands already owned by the public (e.g., the Emma Long City Park, which contains a sizeable block of golden-cheeked warbler habitat) and those lands which are essentially undevelopable under Austin's comprehensive watershed protection ordinance, with the intent of securing lands that are contiguous to these already protected areas. In addition, the consultants also identified FDIC and Resolution Trust Corporation (RTC) lands, acquired as a result of bank and savings and loan failures, and a number of these lands have been secured through below-market sales. For example, in January 1993, The Nature Conservancy purchased 5,280 acres from the RTC for $8 million, and immediately sold it at cost to the city of Austin. Much of this land contains significant habitat. In February 1994, the Conservancy purchased another 4,269 acres from the RTC for about $7.5 million. The Conservancy then sold the land to a developer, who kept 204 acres and donated the remaining 4,065 acres back to the Conservancy.

From this habitat and land use analysis, six macrosites were identified: the 46,000-acre Post Oak Ridge site and five smaller sites totalling about 29,000 acres in western Travis County (see Figure 4.1). The six areas together contained the largest blocks of remaining habitat in the area. The consultants recommended that these six areas, totalling about 75,000 acres, be set aside as a preserve. All 75,000 acres were to be acquired: 46,000 to be purchased by the USFWS, 9,600 from the RTC, and 11,600 by local governments. Approximately 7,800 acres are already owned and protected by government agencies, private businesses, and nonprofit organizations. About 1,500 acres of the 11,600 will be protected through conservation easements and gifts of land. Land acquisition by the FWS would not occur all at once but rather would likely take place over a ten-year period.

As of February 1994, the FWS had purchased 10,938 acres.[4] The nonfederal acquisitions are scheduled to be completed in three years. Theoretically, the Section 10(a) permit could have been issued and would have allowed a taking

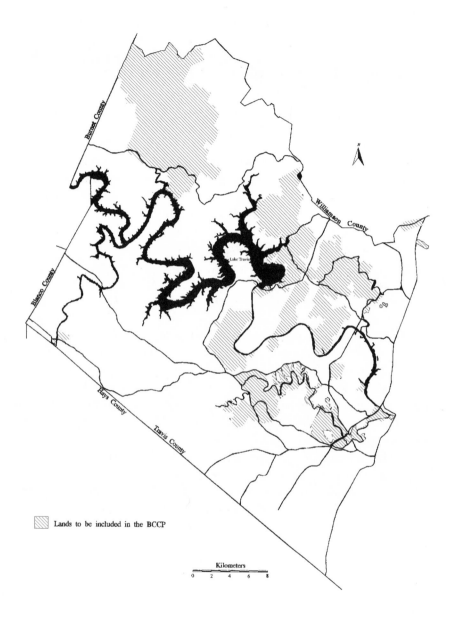

Lands to be included in the BCCP

Figure 4.1   Balcones Canyonlands Conservation Plan.

of listed species habitat as long as the plan's acquisition and protection milestones were met.

Funding and Long-Term Management

Funding for the BCCP was comprised of two parts: funding for the preparation of the plan and funding for its implementation. Preparation of the plan was not inexpensive. Nearly $900,000 was spent, including the cost of preparing the background biological studies, conservation plan, and environmental impact statement. Over $70,000 was spent to trap cowbirds. The plan-preparation costs were covered through a variety of grants and contributions. The Nature Conservancy of Texas initiated the funding with a pledge of $20,000, followed by a number of other contributions, including:

City of Austin	$430,000
Travis County	$150,000
Private sector	$150,000
U.S Fish and Wildlife Service	$50,000
Lower Colorado River Authority	$ 20,000

The larger question was how the implementation of the BCCP was to be funded, particularly the very expensive acquisition of habitat lands. The 76,000 acres recommended for acquisition would have cost an estimated $134 million, and an additional $25–75 million would have been required for operation and management, depending on the degree of public access allowed. Over $200 million would have been needed to implement the provisions of the BCCP.

A number of different sources of funding were under consideration.[5] The federal government will likely contribute a major part of the funding. The USFWS may be asked to spend as much as $46 million over the next ten years for acquisitions in the Post Oak Ridge site, where it is establishing the Canyonlands National Wildlife Refuge. Over $8 million has already been appropriated from the federal Land and Water Conservation Fund for this purpose. State funding sources were also being considered, including appropriations through the Texas Parks and Wildlife Department and donation of land by the Lower Colorado River Authority.

Much of the funding was to have come from local sources. The city of Austin approved over $40 million for habitat acquisition through two bond issues: Proposition 10 ($22 million) and Proposition 11 ($20 million). Unfortunately, a similar bond issue (for $49 million) in Travis County failed to win voter approval on November 2, 1993, which killed the original plan to purchase 75,000 acres. As a result, Austin presented a revised conservation plan known as the pay-as-you-go plan. The areas targeted for preservation in the new plan are the same as in the BCCP, but the funding mechanism for acquiring the land differs. Rather than purchase and preserve large blocks of land with bond money as proposed under the BCCP, land within the preserve system would be purchased piecemeal as development occurs in and around the preserve areas. The purchase of land would be linked directly to development in endangered species habitat. As envisioned by Austin's pay-as-you-go scheme, developers seeking to mitigate for the taking of endangered species habitat in Travis County would contribute money or land to a mitigation bank run by the USFWS, which is considering a proposal to establish such a bank for the preserve areas identified in the BCCP.[6]

Legislation to create a special habitat taxing district, to capitalize on the increased land values which will accrue to private lands around the habitat preserves, failed in 1991.[7] For these remaining developable parcels, the adjacent or surrounding preserve lands will represent undevelopable open space and a positive selling feature. Given that increased land values will likely result from the establishment of preserves, it seems only fair that these landowners be asked to contribute to the funding of the habitat preserve.

For the BCCP to have worked, execution of an interagency agreement to manage the land would have been necessary. Legally and institutionally, the BCCP was very complicated, with numerous agencies and landowners involved, including The Nature Conservancy, Travis County, Austin, Lower Colorado River Authority, USFWS, as well as private landowners. In 1993, a coordinating committee was established to develop an interagency agreement. To pay for operation and maintenance, a habitat management fee of $2,000 per acre of land developed was established. While this fee initially seemed high to developers, individual permits have been estimated to cost about $9,000 per acre.[8]

Prospects for Success

The preparation of the BCCP was a tenuous balancing of development and environmental interests. The development community appeared to recognize the need to solve the endangered species problem and clearly saw the regional BCCP as a cost-effective approach. Most environmental groups in the community were also optimistic about what could have been accomplished through the process, but members of Earth First! informally expressed an intention to sue over the plan if it did not protect enough habitat. The sharp downturn in the Texas economy during the late 1980s and early 1990s lessened pressures from the development community and provided a window of opportunity to implement the plan. Recently, however, land prices have begun to climb again, increasing the estimated cost of land acquisition for the preserve from about $55 million a few years ago to about $70 million in 1994.

Development interests, however, were not without their concerns about the BCCP. While actively supporting the BCCP process, some developers expressed serious reservations about the plan. Perhaps most significantly, many developers saw the plan as overly ambitious and financially unrealistic. Furthermore, some expressed the view that Austin was being unfairly forced to assume the entire burden of protecting the species of concern, when, in the case of the migratory birds, the habitat loss is a range-wide problem.

Similar to this view is the feeling that land development was unfairly singled out as the primary cause of habitat loss when, historically, agricultural and other activities have been responsible for much of the habitat loss. There was also the feeling that USFWS unfairly focused on the development activities and habitat threats in the Austin area, in large part, it was believed, because of the presence and aggressive actions of local Earth First!. To be sure, some of these concerns were understandable, since efforts to protect warbler and vireo habitat in other areas were only beginning.

While the sluggish real estate economy reduced development pressures in the area, some developers sought to move ahead on their own prior to completion of the BCCP, primarily by going through Section 7 consultation, but also through Section 10(a). USFWS discouraged this, however, and attempted to coordinate private Section 7 and Section 10(a) actions with the BCCP, as occurred with the expansion of the 3M complex on RR 2222.

Because the 3M Company planned to clear approximately 11 acres of golden-cheeked warbler habitat, the provisions of the Endangered Species Act applied. The Section 7 consultation was available to 3M because the expansion required an amendment to its air pollution permit required under the federal Clean Air Act (it operates a cogeneration plant on site). The mitigation offered by 3M is impressive and includes the acquisition of 215 acres of warbler habitat (located in a desirable preserve area) and establishment of a $50,000 trust fund to manage the site; a cash donation of $15,000 to the BCCP; a three-year golden-cheeked warbler census; and a three-year cowbird trapping program, among other things. The company also agreed to minimize adverse impacts to warblers on the 3M development site by controlling the timing of land alteration and revegetating altered areas. The 3M mitigation package is so extensive that it may in fact serve to discourage others wishing to circumvent the regional conservation plan in the future.

Other Section 7 consultations, however, are generally not as impressive and serve to effectively illustrate the benefits of a regional HCP. For example, at the 4,500-acre Steiner Ranch, developers went through a Section 7 consultation because they needed a federal Section 404 wetlands permit from the U.S. Army Corps of Engineers. The resulting level of mitigation, however, was disappointing. In the end, the project was required to set aside only 115 acres of vireo habitat (the warbler had not yet been listed).

Individual Section 7 consultations or individual parcel-by-parcel Section 10(a) HCPs will likely serve to protect only small, disconnected slivers of habitat, with little coordination or overall sense of how they will fit together to ensure the long-term survival of the species of concern. Project-by-project mitigation is also likely to be much more expensive. While the BCCP ultimately may have cost $200 million, individual Section 7 consultations or 10(a) plans could easily reach a combined cost of $400 million.

Undoubtedly, the greatest uncertainty about the BCCP was funding. While federal funding has already been appropriated for a portion of the total cost, future appropriations under the federal Land and Water Conservation Fund to create a national wildlife refuge are not assured. And Travis County's November 1993 rejection of a $49 million bond issue to purchase lands for the preserve virtually ensures that both the size of the preserve and the number of species addressed by the BCCP, as well as the new plan, will be rolled back. It is too early to tell whether the new (pay as you go) plan will in fact ensure the survival of the species of concern. From a biological standpoint, the BCCP was on strong footing, and the careful work and scientific credentials of the BAT may prove useful later in prioritizing the acquisition of habitat. Most agree that the BCCP was a much-preferred alternative to the more fragmented approach resulting from parcel-by-parcel Section 10(a) or Section 7 permits and that it represented the best chance of protecting the species of concern. The plan generally responded to the recommendations of the BAT, and when completed the preserve system would have protected large contiguous blocks of habitat. And, though the new plan will protect far less than the 123,500 acres of contiguous vireo habitat recommended by the BAT, it will protect as much as feasible in the Austin area, given existing development patterns and limited financial resources.

Moreover, even if major blocks of vireo and warbler habitat in the Austin area are protected, serious habitat destruction may occur elsewhere in their breeding range and in their wintering areas: highland habitats in southwestern Mexico for the vireo and tropical highland in Guatemala, Honduras, and Nicaragua for the warbler. Though not yet a serious threat to the species, significant deforestation in Central America is cause for great concern. This represents a fundamental biological limitation for any HCP involving migratory species, and comprehensive long-term protection may ultimately require international agreements and cooperation.

The reaction of the USFWS to the plan was also somewhat uncertain. Staff from the USFWS offices in Arlington and Austin, Texas, attended most BCCP meetings and strongly supported development of the plan. But USFWS staff, while supportive of the process, were unable to indicate exactly what type of plan would or would not have been acceptable under Section 10(a). There were several issues which may have been of serious concern to USFWS in reviewing the plan. One issue was, again, the question of funding. USFWS would have been given the plan and asked to review and approve it prior to having all of the funding mechanisms necessary for the plan in place. Another major issue was the plan's time frame. While a "take" would have been allowed following the approval of the plan, the actual habitat acquisition would have occurred over a ten-year period. Would USFWS have been comfortable allowing a take in the short term when it would have been a number of years before full habitat protection was achieved?

While the BCCP proved to be politically and economically unfeasible, the Austin approach represents a major improvement over many of the other habitat conservation programs prepared or in preparation in other parts of the country. The Balcones Canyonlands Conservation Plan would have represented an important model of how HCPs should be prepared and implemented, for several reasons. Its geographical focus was regional and multi-jurisdictional, covering a very large portion of the ranges of the species of concern. Moreover, the magnitude of the habitat to be set aside was impressive, potentially encompassing as much as 76,000 acres. The Balcones Canyonlands plan was also admirable in its attempt to take a multi-species approach, considering the habitat needs of not one but nine federally listed species and several other species of concern. Such a multi-species approach makes sense from both a biological and an economic viewpoint. Development of individual species HCPs would likely be less effective in protecting each one and would likely be much more expensive as well. The plan also took an ecosystem approach and would have accomplished other important regional environmental objectives, such as the protection of critical watersheds.

The Austin experience is not without limitations, however. While it does take a multi-species, multi-purpose approach, it is still largely driven by the requirements of the federal Endangered Species Act and the need to protect listed species. Many nonlisted species of flora and fauna will be protected by the new plan, yet no attempt has been made to consider regional patterns of biodiversity. And, it was decided early on that the BCCP could not, as a practical matter, focus on all species that could be listed. In addition, while the BCCP took more of an ecosystems view than most HCPs, a species orientation still resulted from targeting specific species of endangered flora and fauna. In these cases, less emphasis is frequently given to protecting biological communities. In the Balcones Canyonlands it could be argued that the BCCP, while regional in nature, would not have protected certain endangered communities, notably native Blackland Prairie to the east of the city. As yet, no endangered species have been listed there, but natural prairie communities in Texas are becoming quite rare. This suggests that while the BCCP was ambitious, it could not have been expected to protect and preserve all biological resources of importance.

The Balcones Canyonlands plan illustrated the failings of local land use planning and growth management. Years earlier, Austin adopted a growth plan known as Austin Tomorrow which would have directed much of the city's growth into a corridor running from the southwest to the northeast, away from the region's most environmentally sensitive areas to the west (City of Austin, 1980). For a variety of reasons this plan was never fully implemented, and much of the city's growth in recent years has occurred in precisely the most biologically sensitive areas where development should not occur. The reasons for the plan's failure are numerous and include the ability of developers to obtain services through the creation of municipal utility districts (MUDs) and the failure of Austinites to pass the bond referenda necessary to extend public facilities into the proposed growth corridor (e.g., see Butler and Myers 1984). Much of the development pressure that has jeopardized habitat areas might have been deflected had an effective growth management program been in place. Such efforts would also have the effect of reducing habitat acquisition costs, making the protection of large habitat preserves much easier.

Nevertheless, the accomplishments of the Balcones Canyonlands plan were impressive. A potentially conflict-ridden planning process occurred relatively smoothly, and normally warring factions joined together to resolve a common problem. A biologically sound plan was prepared and, if implemented, would have represented one of the largest habitat acquisition programs in a metropolitan environment. Although Travis County's rejection of the $49 million bond issue posed a financial setback, this was offset somewhat by the existence of 7,800 acres of habitat already protected, by Austin's obligation of over $40 million for acquisition, by land purchased by or donated to The Nature Conservancy, and by the possibility of creating a developer-financed habitat mitigation bank. In the end, protected areas will serve the needs of a number of species of concern, as well as protecting other important components of the regional environment. And, developers and landowners in the region will benefit from greater predictability and a more expeditious, less-costly development review process.

NOTES

1. See Biological Advisory Team, *Comprehensive Report of the Biological Advisory Team of the Austin Regional Habitat Conservation Plan,* January 1990.
2. Personal communication with Deborah Holle, Refuge Manager, Balcones Canyonlands National Wildlife Refuge, Austin, Texas, August 31, 1994.
3. Biological Advisory Team, op. cit. note 1, p. 4.
4. Personal communication with Tom Tollefson, Realty Officer, USFWS, Canyonlands National Wildlife Refuge, August 31, 1994.
5. See Seth Searcy and Kent Butler, "Memo to Executive Committee, Balcones Canyonlands Habitat Conservation Plan, Synopsis of Local Bill Authorizing Enforcement and Financing of the BCCP," October 12, 1990.
6. Personal communication with Deborah Holle, op. cit. note 2.
7. See Seth Searcy, "Memo to Executive Committee, Balcones Canyonlands Habitat Conservation Plan, Draft Interlocal Contract Creating the Balcones Canyonlands Habitat Conservation Authority," August 24, 1990.
8. George W. Gau and James E. Jarrett, "Economic Impact Study: Balcones Canyonlands Conservation Plan," Bureau of Business Research, Graduate School of Business, University of Texas–Austin, September 1992.

Southern California's Multi-species Planning

Douglas R. Porter

E D I T O R S '   S U M M A R Y

Three counties in Southern California, a region harboring an immense diversity of wildlife amidst a rapidly growing conurbation, are embarking on innovative and imaginative programs to plan in advance for protecting endangered species in urbanizing areas. Porter describes how their approaches promise to establish a new standard of integrated planning for reconciling conservation and development objectives. The county planning efforts are providing a framework for multi-species habitat conservation plans, coordinated through a new state program.

Until recently, developers have encountered the habitat conservation requirements of the Endangered Species Act mostly by accident. They purchase a development site, draw up plans, even obtain construction permits, and then someone finds evidence of the presence of a rare species of wildlife. Construction halts while plans are redrawn or, equally likely, a ferocious controversy erupts over just how endangered the species might be and whether it actually inhabits the site. Developers and entire communities are drawn into conflicts with conservation groups and federal and state agencies over whether, how, and where endangered species should be protected.

Habitat conservation planning has proven to be a useful approach for bringing together multiple interests to reconcile such conflicts. But habitat conservation planning has tended to focus on protection of a single species within an individual development project. Increasingly, however, as previous chapters have emphasized, it is recognized that the case-by-case approach fails to meet conservation needs and needlessly disrupts the development process. Among other problems, current procedures fail to account for cumulative impacts of incremental development, ignore broader concerns for maintaining biodiverse ecosystems, generate high costs for habitat preservation, and set up an adversarial process to resolve issues. In addition, federal and state requirements and procedures for habitat conservation traditionally have not dovetailed well with local or regional planning for urban development and environmental protection.

Proactive Planning for Wildlife Conservation

In an admirable attempt to provide a more rational response to wildlife conservation needs, the Southern California counties of Orange, Riverside, and San Diego, assisted by the new state Natural Communities Conservation Program, are undertaking ambitious planning efforts to delineate multi-species conservation areas in advance of project proposals. They are also attempting to work out long-range programs to conserve and manage wildlife habitats to avoid reduction of species to the point that they are endangered or threatened.

The planning efforts were stimulated in part by the recent settlement of three lawsuits in which the U.S. Fish and Wildlife Service (USFWS) agreed to speed up listing of 401 species of animals and plants identified by the USFWS as biologically imperiled. In addition, the recent listing of such species as the Stephens' kangaroo rat and the California gnatcatcher potentially affects the use of major proportions of the three counties: the coastal sage scrub habitat of the gnatcatcher, for example, extends over 400,000 acres from Los Angeles to the Mexican border.

The listing of the gnatcatcher as a threatened species virtually shut down most new construction in Southern California. Although private activity is minimal in this moribund 1994 economy, public facility construction is also affected. And major private development companies, such as the Irvine Company and Santa Margarita Company, discovered that they cannot solve this problem alone. New coalitions have formed to pursue coordinated habitat planning and, says James Whalen, vice president of Newland California in La Jolla, both developers and conservationists agree that "habitat-based, comprehensive land use planning is an idea whose time had come."

The California Natural Communities Conservation Program

A bold new approach proposed by state and federal agencies promises a better answer. In 1991, the California legislature enacted the Natural Communities Conservation Program to promote multi-species habitat protection. The program's pilot effort brings together the USFWS, the California Resources Agency, local governments, and the private sector to develop a strategy for preserving the coastal sage scrub habitat of the threatened California gnatcatcher in the face of continuing urbanization. Secretary of Interior Bruce Babbitt proposed a special rule that authorizes the incidental taking of the California gnatcatcher under plans approved by the Natural Communities Conservation Program.

The first permit was issued under the terms of the new rule in late 1993, when the Unocal Land and Development Company announced that it was initiating development on a 380-acre site in Fullerton, California, pursuant to a Section 10(a) permit granted by the USFWS. The habitat conservation plan on which the permit was based calls for Unocal Land to set aside 125 acres of coastal sage scrub, habitat to the rare California gnatcatcher and cactus wren.

The hope is that the union of private, local, state, and federal interests in wildlife conservation will also protect as many as 90 other species before they become endangered. Commenting in the *The New York Times* (March 26, 1993), John C. Sawhill, president of The Nature Conservancy, said "This is a bold new step for protecting endangered species. It looks at a whole ecosystem . . . and gives significant involvement to state and local governments. It's going to be a model for other states." Secretary Babbitt said the approach will avoid "the environmental and economic train wrecks we've seen in the last decade."

The current planning efforts of Southern California counties are building on this concept of multi-species, multi-interest planning for wildlife conservation.

San Diego County Conservation Planning

The USFWS has identified over 90 wildlife species in San Diego County as candidates for listing as endangered species. At the same time, the county has experienced phenomenal growth rates that continue to expand the population by 70,000 new inhabitants a year.

As described in Chapter 3, planning was initiated in 1985 for a "comprehensive species management plan" for the least Bell's vireo, a small migratory songbird. State legislation designated the San Diego Association of Governments (SANDAG) as the lead agency to coordinate preparation of the plan and a number of concurrent habitat conservation plans for watersheds in the county.

More recently, three major multi-species conservation programs have been initiated to protect large, ecologically viable habitat areas and open space interconnections before species become endangered. Preparation of a multi-species conservation plan for the southwestern part of the county is being led by the Clean Water Program of the city of San Diego in connection with planned expansion of sewage treatment facilities for the metropolitan area. Another planning effort for the northern part of the county is led by SANDAG with participation by eight cities, the county, and the county water authority. The third, in the southern and eastern parts of the county, is a multi-species habitat and open space plan undertaken by San Diego County for all unincorporated sections of the county. SANDAG is assisting in coordinating all three efforts.

The plans will be further detailed and implemented for sub-areas in the form of habitat conservation plans. For example, the city of Carlsbad is preparing a habitat management plan for the entire city as part of the larger SANDAG plan. Plans are also being prepared for large-scale development projects such as La Costa Villages, being developed by The Fieldstone Company (see accompanying feature box), and Rancho San Diego, being developed by Home Capital Corporation. The plans will allow developers to define in advance the amount and location of land that must be protected for one or more species.

Riverside County Conservation Planning

Riverside County is enormous, stretching from the eastern edge of the Los Angeles metropolitan area to the Arizona border. Almost all of its residents live in the westernmost one-third of the county, where most of the valuable wildlife habitat also occurs.

Riverside County and the seven municipalities within the county formed the Riverside County Habitat Conservation Agency to coordinate planning and financing programs for wildlife protection. The agency developed a short-term habitat conservation plan for the endangered Stephens' kangaroo rat, under which Section 10(a) permits have been granted. Now it is formulating a long-term conservation plan that may be incorporated within a multi-species plan.

A key component of the short-term plan was the establishment of an environmental mitigation fee of about $2,000 an acre of new development. The fees are intended to pay for acquisition and management of habitat lands. County officials expect to raise some $50 million over ten years. Most of the funds will be spent for acquisition; already, over 5,000 acres have been purchased. In addition, Riverside County has been working with the Metropolitan Water District (the wholesaler of water to Southern California) to acquire lands valued at more than $40 million in connection with development of a major reservoir.

New development in Riverside County is threatening the habitat of the Stephens' kangaroo rat. (Photo courtesy of Timothy Beatley.)

Habitat Conservation Planning for the Fieldstone La Costa Projects in Carlsbad, California[1]

The Fieldstone Company is developing land in Carlsbad, California, just north of San Diego. Over a two-year period, the firm cooperated with city, regional, state, and federal officials in reaching an agreement for habitat conservation on the properties. The plan is coordinated with other planning by the city and the regional agency for habitat conservation in San Diego County.

The Site and Habitat

Fieldstone owns three tracts of land within the city of Carlsbad, totaling 2,300 acres, on which it planned to develop 3,700 homes over a 12–15 year period. The land was purchased in 1988 for $180 million. About 950 acres was covered by coastal sage scrub that is inhabited by at least 48 pairs of California gnatcatchers, a bird that is proposed for listing as an endangered species but is not yet listed. There are also 33 other sensitive species inhabiting the property, of which as many as 16 may be listed as endangered in the next few years.

The city, developer, local environmentalists, and state and federal resource agencies were all concerned with prospects for development on these sites. The Fieldstone Company anticipated moving ahead with plans for development, but listing of the gnatcatcher in particular, and other species as well, loomed as potential obstacles to development. A long-planned road improvement, the city's top priority public facility project, would cut through the Fieldstone sites across prime coastal sage scrub lands and could not be financed except through development of bordering lands. To enable development and the road improvement, the city considered approval of a previous environmental impact report, although local environmentalists were entirely opposed to its proposed mitigation plan. Environmentalists also knew that acquisition of the habitat was infeasible, given the price tag of $150,000 or more per acre.

Conditions were ripe for a meeting of minds. That was initiated in 1989 when Fieldstone and local environmental leaders began laying the groundwork for habitat conservation planning on a large scale.

The Planning Process

In early 1990, Fieldstone arranged a tour and briefing for staff of the secretary's office at the U.S. Department of the Interior. The city sponsored public discussions on environmental issues. A group of development firms that collectively control 80 percent of the developable coastal sage scrub habitat in San Diego County formed the Alliance for Habitat Conservation. These efforts were only part of a series of actions pointed toward reaching a consensus on ways to reconcile wildlife concerns with development opportunities.

A year later, after many discussions, the USFWS agreed to use the habitat conservation plan process even though the gnatcatcher was not yet listed. In July 1991 state and federal agencies signed a Memorandum of Agreement to that effect. In September 1991 the USFWS announced that it would propose the gnatcatcher for endangered status, beginning a year-long study of that possibility. All during the fall of 1991, intensive planning was undertaken regarding options and opportunities for reconciling development objectives with conservation of the coastal sage scrub habitat.

In January 1992 the city of Carlsbad formed a habitat conservation plan committee comprised of representatives of the city, the USFWS, the state Department of Fish and Game, the Fieldstone Company, and various local and regional conservation groups. By May the committee had reached an agreement in principle on the habitat conservation plan, including appropriate mitigation for the road construction and residential development. In December 1992 the habitat conservation plan was formally submitted to state and federal agencies.

The Plan

The plan sets aside about 500 acres of the total of 950 acres of coastal sage scrub habitat on the sites, plus 100 acres of other sensitive habitat land. Most of this reserved land is located in a broad (1,000 to 2,000 feet) wildlife corridor bisecting the sites. In addition, Fieldstone will acquire 200 to 300 acres of habitat on a nearby tract as mitigation for on-site development. A reserved riparian corridor will permit movement for large animals such as coyotes.

The new development plan was formulated in tandem with habitat conservation planning, requiring a complete redesign of the project. In the process, the developer converted many proposed sites for low-density estate homes to clustered housing and gave up about 200 home sites. The developer also agreed to stringent, unprecedented revegetation requirements. The city, for its part, revised its planned road alignments, instituted density transfers for planned development areas, and granted variances for grading of sensitive slopes.

Efforts are now under way to define a long-term management program for the reserved habitat areas. It is expected that the HCP will require at least six months of agency consideration before approval.

Financing

The developer expects that the HCP will require outlays of $12.5 million. Of this, about $2.8 million will be spent for extra engineering, planning, environmental studies, management, and legal expenses in connection with planning and approval processes. Another $9.7 will be required for city fees, landscape revegetation, and off-site land acquisition. This amount represents $418,000 per gnatcatcher pair, or $13,933 per acre of habitat. The developer also will be responsible for $376.1 million in public facility construction, exclusive of land.

Issues/Lessons Learned

Developer John Barone observed that commitments to these major costs were made when financing was much more available than it will be in the next few years. He pointed out that future developers might not be able to bear HCP planning costs, indicating a need for state and federal assistance. The fact that at least 20 other major developments and scores of smaller developments in the region are now pursuing HCP agreements suggests that a great deal of planning money is being spent in ways that might be better coordinated at the local and regional levels.

Jeff Opdycke noted that funding for collaborative planning comes from a variety of sources, none of them adequate for present needs.

Some funding is obtained by local and regional agencies from congressionally sponsored line items in federal legislation. Other funding is available through the Section 6 grant program of the USFWS, which makes grants through regional offices. Recent proposed, but not enacted, federal legislation would have established a revolving planning fund of $20 million to be repaid by charges on subsequent development. Otherwise, local and regional agencies provide staff support as available, and developers contribute major funding for special studies and participation in collaborative efforts.

Barone identified several lessons learned in the HCP planning process:

- HCP plans are expensive to prepare and negotiate agreement on, without dependable funding sources available for either public or private planning expenditures

- The issue of multi-species planning is becoming a major concern in Southern California and is having major impacts on the development process

- Planning obstacles include the lack of any clear set of procedural or other rules, inadequate agency staffing levels, and a short supply of data

- To reach agreement, a collaborative effort is essential and focused regional planning would help

Barone also suggested several improvements in the HCP process:

- Add more certainty to the process by providing better agency support at early stages, including incentives to developers to take part in habitat-based planning

- Address financial needs, both in planning and in conservation, that will retain the economic viability of developers and provide for adequate coordination of resource planning and management efforts

- Encourage more interaction of habitat conservation planning with regional planning efforts

- Establish approaches for involvement of third parties such as water districts

Jeff Opdycke underscored the fact that listing of species as endangered or threatened will continue, indicating that comprehensive conservation planning will be required on a broader scale than in the past.

Yet funding levels for federal and state agency involvement in collaborative landowner/municipal planning efforts are insufficient to meet such
needs. He noted that while adequate funding of USFWS involvement in
"pre-listing" conservation plan development is costly, it is far less expensive than the traditional reactive approach, which frequently extends
over a ten- to twenty-year period.

Orange County Conservation Planning

As the smallest of the Southern California counties, Orange County encompasses only 782 square miles but is the most urbanized, with a 1990 population
of 2.4 million. Although it has relatively little remaining developable land, it
supports at least 300 species of wildlife and at least eight types of natural habitats. Most of the undeveloped land in Orange County contains coastal sage
scrub, home to the threatened gnatcatcher, which covers 61,000 acres. Shortly
after the governor signed the Natural Communities Conservation Bill in 1991,
the county began preparation of a plan to protect the coastal sage scrub habitat.

The county's Environmental Management Agency has involved state and
local governments, nonprofit organizations, and private landowners in the
program. Four sub-regional planning areas were delineated, and planning
agreements have been negotiated for three of them. The agreements establish
overall guidelines and procedures for further planning. When the plans are
completed, the USFWS proposes to permit limited takes of selected species in
accordance with the plans.

Financing

Planning for conservation has not been cheap. Riverside County has already
spent about $1 million on planning for the Stephens' kangaroo rat and an-
other $700,000 for multi-species planning. In San Diego County, SANDAG,
the county water district, and various cities have invested almost $5 million to
date. Orange County has spent $1 million for planning. In addition to public
funds, developers have spent even more for major studies and redesigned
plans to meet conservation needs, and conservation groups have invested substantial time and effort.

The larger funding question regards land acquisition. Much of the habitat
conserved so far has been contributed in the form of exactions from developers and reservations of public lands. The thousands of habitat acres that

remain to be reserved cannot all be obtained from similar public and private contributions. Mitigation fees such as those Riverside County is imposing will provide one additional source, but state and federal funds will be necessary to acquire much of the land identified in the current planning process.

Unfortunately, Congress has authorized spending only a small proportion of funds available in the Land and Water Conservation Fund, the primary source of federal funding. Over the past 15 years, authorizations have averaged $900 million per year for the entire nation, while the fund's unappropriated balance has risen to almost $9 billion. With current concerns over budget deficits, however, these funds probably will not be released for the foreseeable future. For that reason, conservation and development groups are looking to other potential funding sources, including tax credits and incentives. Just as important, they understand that collaborative funding efforts, tapping many sources of funding, will be necessary to implement the plans now being prepared.

Looking to the Future

Finding ways to reconcile wildlife conservation with economic development has emerged as an important national, state, and local policy issue, not unrelated to concerns over global sustainability. Southern California governments, conservationists, and developers are tackling the issue head on by providing a data base and proactive plans to assure conservation in urbanizing areas. Although controversies remain, the current approach that unites efforts of all levels of government with those of conservation and development interests provides a new, more clearly marked playing field in which to resolve wildlife issues constructively and effectively.

NOTE

1. This description is based on presentations by Jeffrey Opdycke of the U. S. Fish and Wildlife Service, and John Barone of the Fieldstone Company, both based in San Diego, at a March 1993 meeting of the Federal Permitting Working Group, cosponsored by the Environmental Law Institute and the Growth Management Institute.

Managing Wetlands through Advanced Planning and Permitting: The Columbia River Estuary Study Taskforce

Scott T. McCreary and Mark B. Adams

E D I T O R S '   S U M M A R Y

The Columbia River Estuary Study Taskforce (CREST) is a local consortium of individuals appointed by municipal governments in the states of Washington and Oregon. The task force's mission has been to prepare and implement a regional management plan for the waters and shorelands of the Columbia River estuary, one of the richest and most productive estuaries of the Pacific Northwest. Although CREST's mandate extends to economic development and land use planning for uplands, many of its activities have a direct bearing on the maintenance, use, and restoration of wetland ecosystems in the Columbia River estuary on the boundary between the states of Oregon and Washington. Federal funding channeled through a strong state planning infrastructure allowed local efforts to reach fruition. CREST's collaborative efforts with local governments to guide wetland conservation and development throughout the estuary have continued. Although the planning process is considered successful, support by some federal agencies is perceived as equivocal and some important issues remain unresolved.

Background: The Planning Context[1]

The Columbia River estuary, one of the largest estuarine systems on the West Coast, encompasses an estimated 120,000 acres.[2] As shown in Figure 6.1, the planning region of CREST includes aquatic areas and shorelands from the three-mile limit offshore, upstream to the end of Clatsop County in Oregon and Wahkiakum County in Washington, plus all tributary streams to the head of the tide and adjacent shorelands.[3]

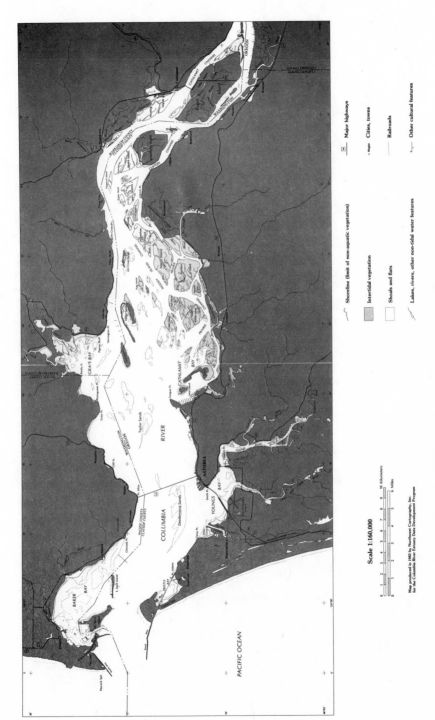

Scale 1:160,000

0 1 2 3 4 5 6 7 8 9 10 Kilometers
0 1 2 3 4 5 6 Miles

Map produced in 1983 by Northwest Cartography, Inc.
for the Columbia River Estuary Data Development Program

⌐⌐ Shoreline (limit of non-aquatic vegetation)

Interidal vegetation

Shoals and flats

Lakes, rivers, other non-tidal water features

⊞ Major highways

· Major Cities, towns

Railroads

Other cultural features

Figure 6.1   Columbia River estuary.

Wetlands along the Columbia River provide habitat for a variety of shorebirds. (Photo courtesy of the Columbia River Estuary Study Taskforce.)

The watershed of the area in the planning region is enormous. Indeed, many of the activities that affect the estuary, such as forest practices within tributary watersheds and upstream dams that alter flows, occur well outside CREST's jurisdiction and are beyond the reach of local planning. The politics of the state's salmon fisheries influence decision making in many state agencies and are played out at the highest levels of state and regional governance.

Subject to diverse uses, the estuary has been identified as one of three Oregon estuaries suitable for deep-draft port development. Major resource-based industries include forestry, fishing, and agriculture. Industrial processing sites also dot the estuary. More sites have been proposed to increase the employment base of the area, but environmental concerns have stalled their development. Economically, the tax base is inadequate to support needed public facilities in local communities. Astoria, the only major port in the estuary, is suffering from a shortage of space for expansion. On the Washington side, in particular, in towns on Baker Bay, port development is hampered by the lack of road, rail, or air access. Some observers, however, believe that port managers have overestimated demands for port development.

Due in part to these economic activities, the Columbia River has undergone significant habitat changes. Between 1870 and 1981, tidal marsh habitats declined 43 percent—from 16,190 acres to 9,200 acres. Forested tidal swamps decreased 77 percent—from 31,020 to 6,950 acres.[4] Stream flow alterations from dams and water encroachment on the Columbia River have adversely affected fish habitat.

To appreciate the CREST story, it is important to keep in mind the tradition of strong state involvement in land use planning on the West Coast, particularly in Oregon and, to a lesser extent, Washington.

Coastal Planning in Oregon

The CREST program evolved to a large extent in concert with Oregon coastal zone and statewide planning programs and with local government planning and zoning efforts during the 1970s.[5] Motivated in part by grassroots organizing to protect coastal resources, the Oregon legislature created the Oregon Coastal Conservation and Development Commission in 1971, one of the first comprehensive coastal planning initiatives in the United States. The commission was created as an autonomous blue ribbon study panel of appointed members to study resource-based economic problems such as decreasing fish harvests due to overexploitation. Additionally, the commission was to investigate both inappropriate land use in sensitive and hazardous coastal areas and encroachment upon productive estuaries and shorelands.

The commission's principal finding was that government jurisdictions managing the coast did not effectively coordinate their activities. The commission recommended a state-coordinated land use planning program to take maximum advantage of limited financial resources, provide an improved vehicle for citizen involvement, and implement sound land and water use policies.

Incorporating some of these recommendations, the legislature enacted the Oregon Land Use Act of 1973 (Chapter 197 Oregon Revised Statutes). The act established the Land Conservation and Development Commission (LCDC), a seven-member panel appointed by the governor and confirmed by the senate. The commission oversees the act's mandate for each Oregon local government to prepare and adopt a comprehensive plan that meets statewide goals. Oregon adopted statewide planning goals in 1975 (amended in 1987). In the late 1970s, four coastal goals were added to the statewide planning goals to address estuarine resources, shorelands, beaches and dunes, and ocean resources. Table 6.1 lists all 19 issues addressed by the statewide goals and summarizes eight of these goals, along with their implementing regulations and guidelines.

The goals are implemented by the commission and its professional staff, which are housed in the Oregon Department of Land Conservation and Development (DLCD). The LCDC has adopted guidelines to interpret each statewide planning goal but does not prescribe a specific method for satisfying each goal. Once a municipality adopts a comprehensive plan, it is referred to

TABLE 6.1   Issues Addressed by Oregon's Statewide Planning Goals

1. Citizen involvement	9. Economic development
2. Land use planning	10. Housing
3. Agricultural lands	11. Public facilities and services
4. Forest lands	12. Transportation
5. Open spaces; scenic, historic; and natural resources	13. Energy conservation
	14. Urbanization
6. Air, water, and land resources quality	15. Willamette River Greenway
	16. Estuarine resources
7. Areas subject to natural disasters and hazards	17. Coastal resources
	18. Beaches and dunes
8. Recreational needs	19. Ocean resources

Summary of Eight Key Planning Goals Relevant to Wetland and Coastal Resources

1. *Citizen involvement:* Requires cities and counties to establish citizen involvement programs and citizens' committees. Requires participation in all phases of planning. Requires that state and federal agencies use the involvement programs. Requires annual evaluation of the effectiveness of citizen involvement.

2. *Land use planning:* Sets requirements for inventories and plan policies. Requires implementing measures consistent with a comprehensive plan. Requires that government land use decisions conform to acknowledged plans. Requires periodic updates, including amendments to urban growth boundaries and management plans for urbanizable lands.

5. *Natural resources:* Requires appropriate planning for the protection of natural ecological, historical, and scenic sites based on an analysis of economic, social, environmental, and energy consequences of alternative uses.

7. *Natural disasters and hazards:* Prohibits building in natural hazard areas unless adequate safeguards are provided.

16. *Estuarine resources:* Requires recognition and protection of economic and social values of each estuary to maintain natural diversity. Requires designation of estuarine areas for water-dependent uses. Requires a clear presentation of the impacts of proposed estuarine alterations; requires maintenance of water quality and minimization of human-induced sedimentation. Requires management of important estuarine habitat for long-term protection through preservation of certain areas and careful management of others.

17. *Coastal shorelands:* Requires designation of shorelands for water-dependent uses. Requires designation of mitigation sites and dredged material disposal sites to offset impacts of development. Requires mitigation for dredge and fill activities in tidal or intertidal marshes. Requires management of floodplain areas consistent with hazards to life and property; requires that riparian vegetation be maintained and that nonstructural solutions to erosion be given priority over structural solution. Requires protection of shorelands with significant resource value including headlands, major marshes, and significant wildlife habitat.

18. *Beaches and dunes:* Requires protection of active foredunes and other dunes subject to erosion. Prohibits new development on dunes subject to erosion. Requires local government and state and federal agencies to regulate land use on beaches and dunes, including actions and permits to protect against groundwater drawdown. Prohibits breaching of foredunes in situations other than emergencies. Allows limited grading of foredunes to maintain views of existing homes in developed areas where a detailed plan has been approved and where dunes are more than four feet above the 100-year flood.

19. *Ocean resources:* Requires conservation of the long-term values, benefits, and natural resources of the nearshore ocean and the continental shelf.

LCDC for an acknowledgment review. After the DLCD staff prepares a plan analysis and obtains agency reviews from other state departments, it may acknowledge a part or all of the plan or indicate nonacknowledgment (approval or nonapproval). In practice, the LCDC suggests specific changes that would make it possible for acknowledgment to be conferred.

The LCDC developed a draft coastal program with the principal objectives of establishing working partnerships among all levels of government, encouraging research, strengthening local planning through financial and technical assistance, ensuring citizen participation, and setting milestones for comprehensive planning at all levels of government. The coastal program was formally certified in 1977 by the Office of Coastal Zone Management in the National Oceanic and Atmospheric Administration (NOAA), the second program (after Washington's) to reach certification.

The coastal program is based on three coordinated sets of regulatory authority: the statewide planning goals, comprehensive plans developed by local governments and approved by the LCDC, and specific statutory authorities that guide the actions of various state agencies. For example, the Department of Transportation regulates navigation and transportation in compliance with estuarine planning goals. Similarly, the Department of Fish and Wildlife manages production and utilization of wildlife and fisheries in compliance with the four statewide coastal planning goals (estuarine, coastal, ocean, and natural resources).

Comprehensive plans have been completed and approved for the entire coast. Local government expertise has been strengthened, and a substantial level of intergovernmental coordination has been achieved. Additionally, specific standards for port development, estuarine mitigation, and habitat inventory have been adopted, and a number of standing advisory groups are being maintained.

Coastal Planning in Washington

Washington has 2,337 miles of marine shoreline, 34 miles of which front the Columbia River. Compared with the Puget Sound coastal area, the Columbia River is relatively free of development, population is sparse, and water quality is pristine.

Within Washington, the Columbia River estuary was not subject to the same development pressures as the Puget Sound area, and thus it had not, until recently, received as much planning attention as other parts of the state. When Oregon municipalities were beginning to develop local zoning ordinances in the mid-1970s, municipalities in the state of Washington had not yet begun to address local planning. However, a state supreme court decision in 1969 cast doubt on private rights to fill within navigable waters and prompted

Cape Disappointment lighthouse overlooks the rugged waters at the Columbia's entry into the Pacific. The remains of a shipwreck lie in the foreground. (Photo courtesy of the Columbia River Estuary Study Taskforce.)

new legislation providing comprehensive coastal planning rather than case-by-case judicial review of wetland filling. By 1971 the legislature had enacted the State Environmental Policy Act (SEPA) and created the Department of Ecology. In 1972 citizens' petitions put a coastal management initiative on the ballot, and the legislature responded by enacting the Shoreline Management Act of 1971 and making it retroactive by almost 18 months to 1971.[6]

The act mandates that local governments prepare shoreline master plans for areas within 200 feet of the shoreline and associated wetlands. The coastal boundary is designated in two tiers. The first tier includes all of the state's marine waters, lakes over 20 acres, streams with a mean annual flow exceeding 20 cubic feet per second, and associated wetlands. The second tier includes the coastal county lands outside the first tier. The 51 local jurisdictions have authority under the act to issue or deny permits for activities within the first-tier management area, guided by locally developed, state-approved shoreline master plans.

Local governments also may designate environmentally sensitive areas to promote sound coastal management. Such areas include those with unstable soils, unique plants or animals, wetlands, or floodplains. Attention is focused on parts of these areas that would normally be exempt from environmental review. County and city governments are free to administer designated areas in any manner as long as the areas are clearly mapped, adopted, and filed with the Department of Ecology.[7]

The Department of Ecology adopted rules and regulations for development of shoreline master programs in 1972 to provide a uniform, statewide system for classifying shoreline environments and determining priority uses.[8] The classification categories are natural, conservancy, rural, and urban, and they are based on existing development patterns, the land's biophysical capabilities, and the land use goals of the community. These categories do not impose strict zoning controls on each type of land but instead rely on performance standards to ensure that any permitted uses are carried out with the minimum environmental impact.

In practice, the "natural" designation has been applied sparingly, mostly to publicly owned lands, since its restrictions allow little resource degradation. The "conservancy" designation is applied to managed lands where the demand for recreational and other resource uses is high. "Rural" lands recognize priority for agriculture; and "urban" lands are targeted for a variety of more intense uses. Many municipalities also have added a "rural-residential" category for low-density or suburban development.

Local shoreline master programs are forwarded to the Department of Ecology for state and federal agency review. Approved plans are incorporated into the Washington Administrative Code. Once the plans are in place, "substantial" developments require permits from local governments. Each local government permit decision is reviewed by the Department of Ecology and the attorney general, either of which may appeal the decision to the Shorelines Hearings Board. Decisions of the board may be further appealed to the state superior court. About 7 percent of all permit decisions are heard in court.[9]

Washington's Coastal Management Program, approved under the Federal Coastal Zone Management Program in 1976, consists of the local shoreline master programs, state permitting functions for development activities within the coastal zone, and a multiplicity of state agencies that review and comment on activities affecting coastal water quality and land use. The program provides state administrative review of local master programs and final authority over most permits within the coastal zone.

In general, Washington municipalities in the Columbia estuary are more rural than their Oregon counterparts, and they have less funding and expertise to bring to environmental planning and management, particularly for estuarine management. This explains why the shoreline management program retains substantial permitting control at the state level. Consequently, local programs in Washington are much less specific than Oregon local plans.[10]

A 1983 survey and analysis of Washington's shoreline master program (SMP) found that most local programs were used almost exclusively as regulatory tools. Program policies were seldom used unless a controversial permit decision was at stake. Land use regulations were applied inconsistently among comparable programs, and local zoning ordinances often were not in conformity with the shoreline master program. Generally, the process was reactive and not well integrated into local comprehensive planning.[11]

State guidance of conservation and land use was strengthened with the enactment of the Washington State Growth Management Act. Adopted in 1990 and broadened in 1991, the act requires urban counties and cities to adopt plans consistent with 13 state goals. The plans are required to delineate urban growth areas and to recognize natural resource areas and critical areas. Local plans are to be reviewed and approved by a state board. Although this process is barely under way, Washington's local governments are now addressing planning concerns more thoroughly than in earlier years.

Developing the CREST Plan

The Columbia River estuary, most of which lies within Oregon's boundaries, is the subject of a fully coordinated plan that blends the Oregon and Washington coastal management programs and integrates federal and local permitting authorities.

The plan was prepared over a four-year period by CREST, a voluntary consortium of two states, multiple federal agencies, and 10 local governments. The lead agencies were Oregon's LCDC and Washington's Department of Ecology.

CREST was created in 1975 and produced the Columbia River Estuary Regional Management Plan in 1979.[12] The plan has no separate legal authority but its policies and recommendations are incorporated into municipal plans and ordinances. The 261-page plan includes regional policies, development standards, and local land use plans. The plan designates all shorelands as either "natural," "conservation," "rural," or "development." These four broad classifications are further divided into 19 land use categories for which specific development standards are provided. Eight other land and water use activities, such as dredging and filling, are the subject of specific standards and guidelines. In addition, the plan incorporates plans for dredged-material management, restoration and mitigation, and implementation.

Full state approval in 1983 of the local plans contained in the CREST plan culminated a nine-year planning effort. A final structured mediation process was necessary to bring the process to closure and solve some key remaining conflicts. Although some minor land use conflicts remained, they were not significant enough to prevent acknowledgment of the plan.

The period of active planning in the 1970s generated a high level of expertise and involvement. CREST now operates with fewer staff than in the early days, due to both the early resolution of most conflicts and a smaller constituency (i.e., funding and political will) for planning. The remaining conflicts are unlikely to receive much focused attention.

Impetus for the Plan and Key Participants

While some people believe that CREST owes its agenda to federal and state coastal management initiatives, former director James Good saw CREST as a grassroots initiative that provided a model for the state as a whole. In his view, the initial CREST goals inspired coastal and estuarine planning at the state level. He also believed that the Yakima Bay planning effort (the first major estuarine planning process on the West Coast) helped provide the ground rules for addressing the Columbia River's needs. But local planning would never have been initiated without federal funds disbursed to the state through Section 306 of the Coastal Zone Management Act.[13]

Participants in developing the CREST plan included the CREST council, a representative body of local officials; 11 major committees convened to advise on discrete subjects; and three technical advisory committees. (Table 6.2 summarizes the CREST organization.) The CREST council included, from Oregon, representatives of Clatsop County (3), the city of Astoria (1), the port

TABLE 6.2   The CREST Organization in Its Planning Context

UMBRELLA OF FEDERAL AGENCY REVIEW AND PERMITTING
[NATIONAL MARINE FISHERIES SERVICE, ENVIRONMENTAL PROTECTION AGENCY, U.S. FISH
AND WILDLIFE SERVICE, AND ARMY CORPS OF ENGINEERS SECTIONS 10 AND 404]

FEDERAL COASTAL ZONE MANAGEMENT ACT

OREGON

- Statewide Planning Goals
- Land Conservation and Development
  Commission (LCDC)
- Department of Land Conservation
  and Development (DLCD)
- DLCD Quarterly Reporting
- Periodic Review
- Additional Review by Oregon State
  Lands Commission, Department of
  Fish and Wildlife

WASHINGTON

- SEPA
- Shoreline Management Act
- ECPA
- Shoreline Hearings Board
- Additional Review by Multiple
  State Agencies

CREST GENERAL POLICIES AND DEVELOPMENT STANDARDS

CREST LAND USE PLAN: SPECIFIC SUBREGIONAL PLANS AND LOCAL LAND DESIGNATIONS

MUNICIPAL PLANS AND ORDINANCES
- Port of Astoria
- Astoria
- Clatsop County
- Warrenton
- Ilwaco
- Port of Ilwaco
- Cathlamet
- Wahkiakum County

LOCAL PERMIT DECISIONS AND APPEALS

of Astoria (2), the city of Warrenton (3), and the town of Hammond (2). In Washington, representatives came from Pacific County (1), the port and town of Ilwaco (2 each), Wahkiakum County (2), and the city of Cathlamet (2). (By 1994 Cathlamet had dropped membership, Wahkiakum Port District Number 2 had joined the task force, and the town of Hammond had merged with Warrenton.) All representatives were appointees of local governments or sitting local officials. In some instances, staff such as city managers and planning directors represented their local governments. The emphasis was on appointing actual decisionmakers for the area they represented.

Below the CREST council, 11 major committees were established, including a regional policy committee, land and water use planning committees for each subregion, a dredging and mitigation committee, and an implementation committee. Additionally, there were subcommittees on fisheries, restoration, refuge management, public access, and recreation. Each committee included local citizen representatives and the press was also represented, by invitation, at all early workshops and meetings. These committees helped to maximize opportunities for community participation and local control of planning.

Moreover, three technical advisory committees were convened—one for Oregon agencies, another for Washington agencies, and a third for federal interests. Representatives included officials of various departments and offices in state government (e.g., Department of Natural Resources, Planning and Community Affairs Agency, and Department of Transportation).

Federal and State Participation in Developing the CREST Plan

CREST became a pilot planning program for the Oregon Department of Land Conservation and Development, as state policies were being refined in the late 1970s while local governments were actually completing their plans. DLCD field representatives worked directly with cities and counties to provide planning assistance and interpretation of state planning standards. DLCD participated in conflict resolution efforts, both informally at the local level and in formal state-board mediation. DLCD also provided implementation grants to cover the administrative costs of developing the plans and to provide additional assistance in preparing amendments and the periodic plan update.

Federal agency participation was achieved through the Pacific Northwest River Basins Commission, a cooperative council of agencies established to protect fisheries from water quality degradation and to help mesh water resources with local land use planning actions. The commission organized representation from the U.S. Army Corps of Engineers, the U.S. Fish and Wildlife Service, the National Marine Fisheries Service of NOAA, and the U.S. Environmental Protection Agency. Other federal participants included representatives of the Geological Survey, the Soil Conservation Service, and the Forest Service.

The commission provided essential funding to CREST for Phase I data development and administrative costs. An estimated $5 to $6 million was committed through the commission over a five-year period to fund the Columbia River Data Development Program, in which researchers at the University of Washington and Oregon State University provided baseline planning data. However, only about $4.5 million was actually granted and the commission was completely dismantled in the early years of the Reagan administration. Paul Benson, the director of the commission during CREST planning describes the CREST plan as a "pioneering effort," although he characterized the actual participation of federal agency representatives on policy issues as peripheral.[14]

CREST used an extensive outreach program that included hearings in each affected community. CREST followed procedures for public participation outlined in goal 1 of the Oregon planning goals; they emphasize direct citizen involvement in information gathering and policy making, set procedures for advisory committees, and require two-way communication including an official response to all citizen inquiries. The planning effort is intended to "ensure effective two way communication, involve citizens in all phases of the planning process, make technical information understandable, ensure that citizens receive response from policy makers, and secure funding for citizen involvement programs." The public was included in all policy development sessions in both workshops and hearings, and draft plans were made available for public review at each stage.

The Plan: Overview of CREST General Policies

The CREST plan was prepared in response to planning issues identified through interviews and a series of workshops. The four major issues were economic (land and water use); fish and wildlife (biological/chemical problems); physical alterations and hydraulics; and political and resource management fragmentation. The CREST plan includes 158 policy statements: 27 general policies and 131 specific policies. To illustrate this range of concerns addressed by the plan, the major policies relevant to wetlands issues are summarized in Table 6.3.

Several policies address fisheries, for example, by recognizing that fish resources have played a major role in the cultural development of the estuary

Table 6.3   Major Issues Addressed by the CREST Plan

Economy—Land and water use problems

• The economic base has shown little growth since 1950 and is not well balanced.
• The area has not identified or designated suitable and adequate sites for industrial and economic base expansion.
• Determination of compatibility of a variety of land uses and coordination of land use developments does not occur.
• The area's nonwater transportation network is inadequate for economic expansion.
• Some public facilities are inadequate to support development.

Fish and wildlife—Biological/chemical problems

• For some species, such as the dungeness crab, production and harvest does not equal previous years; for others, production potential is not achieved.

Physical effects—Alterations

• The biology and chemistry of the Columbia River estuarine system are not understood fully enough to inform management programs.
• Industrial and other effluents discharged into the river cause adverse effects.
• Wildlife management and enhancement programs are incomplete.
• The effects of channel dredging are cited repeatedly as major problems.
• Sand movement and shoaling problems are numerous.
• Best methods to respond to flood and other flow conditions are not agreed upon.
• Sedimentation problems and effects are diverse.
• Log storage has adverse effects.
• Wave action of oceangoing vessels adversely affects beaches, wildlife, and recreation.

Political and resource management fragmentation

• No system exists to assign management responsibility for program implementation to appropriate levels of government agencies.
• No system exists for recording and tabulating local citizen attitudes toward estuarine resource management.
• Current planning and study methods are fragmented.

area and that the dramatic decrease of fish is due partly to habitat destruction and degradation resulting from human interaction in the environment. The plan calls for traditional fishing areas to be protected from dredging, filling, and other disruptive in-stream activities and for the establishment of minimal tributary stream flows necessary to maintain aquatic life. In addition, tributary streams should be evaluated for their potential for future fish populations. The plan also encourages enhancement programs.

Other policies recognize the importance of deep-water navigation, shallow draft ports and marinas, and industrial development along the Columbia

A cargo ship passes beneath the span of the Astoria-Megler Bridge. (Photo courtesy of the Columbia River Estuary Study Taskforce.)

River, but they stress that new facilities should be constructed only where existing facilities cannot be improved or expanded to meet demands. Biological productivity and habitat values are to be considered in siting new ports or marinas. In addition, public or community marina facilities are favored over single-purpose mooring facilities, and navigational access is to be maintained.

Recognizing that the Columbia River estuary has been substantially altered, the plan establishes the overall policy that all habitat restoration projects should serve to return, replace, or otherwise improve the estuarine ecosystem. Priority should be given to projects that restore habitat types or resources that are in shortest supply, with particular emphasis on aquatic and riparian restoration. Creating shallow water or other habitat areas through disposal of dredged material in water and wetland areas is strongly discouraged. Breaching dikes to restore wetlands in diked tidelands is acceptable if no loss of either productive farmland or significant habitat occurs.

Land and water use policies for residential, commercial, and industrial development focus on the shoreline. Priority is given to water-dependent or water-related projects. All approved uses should minimize environmental impacts, promote visual attractiveness, and provide appropriate visitor access. Conversion of existing agricultural land is discouraged. New developments must maintain natural vegetated buffers along wetlands and rivers.

The shoreland capacity for dredged material is likely to be exhausted within

20 years. Selection of new disposal sites should consider areas where material may be stockpiled for future use, where material will restore degraded habitat, and where toxic or polluted material will present minimal hazards.

Given that the Columbia River estuary has lost more than 15 percent of its volume in the last century, the plan cautions against future loss of estuarine surface area and volume. Fill and dredged material shall not be placed in productive subtidal, intertidal, or tidal marsh areas or in areas that support important benthic communities unless such placement is part of an approved development project. Although maintaining and improving dikes to provide flood protection is permissible, construction of new dikes in wetlands and tideland areas must be carefully evaluated to avoid destructive effects on the estuarine ecosystem.

Intergovernmental coordination is to be provided by CREST, which will provide planning and technical assistance to member agencies and act as a liaison to the Pacific Northwest River Basins Commission. Additionally, CREST will evaluate state and federal activities as they affect local governments and will operate a Columbia River Estuary Information Center.

Another key element of the CREST plan is the designation of important land and water uses, summarized in Table 6.4.

Within each aquatic and shoreland area, the plan defines specific land and water uses that are permitted with standards, allowed conditionally on an individual basis, or not permitted. The plan sets forth detailed standards for each use. The net effect is to guide development away from the natural aquatic areas and natural shorelands. The designated development aquatic areas or aquatic shorelands allow most uses that meet permit standards, although water-dependent development is preferred over non-water-dependent development.

The most controversial areas, from the perspective of state and federal permitting agencies, were shorelands and wetlands designated for development. Development areas include 3,455 acres of shorelands, of which 1,950 are considered water-dependent development. In wetland areas, 680 acres were designated for development, of which Youngs Bay–Astoria had the greatest acreage, 361 acres or 8.3 percent of the total wetlands in the subarea. Baker Bay had 221 acres designated for development, and Eastern Clatsop had 76 acres; Wahkiakum had 22 acres. All wetlands in the lower river and islands were designated as natural, with no development proposed. None of the development proposed in wetlands was water-dependent. As discussed in later sections, this issue sharpened during the state review process.

Former CREST director Mark Barnes said that the key issues in local planning were demands for deep-draft port development and marina expansion, as well as the constant need for channel-maintenance dredging and dredge-spoil disposal.[15] On the Washington side, the ports of Ilwaco and Chinook

TABLE 6.4 CREST Land and Water Use Classification System

	Acres	Percentage	Percentage of category
Total planning area	175,676	100	
Water	78,054	45	
Wetlands	42,564	24	
Natural			85
Conservation			12
Rural			1
Development			2
Shorelands	54,058	31	
Natural		4	
Conservation			40
Rural			46
Development			6
Water-dependent development			4

Explanation of key categories:
- Natural aquatic: Areas managed for resource protection
- Conservation aquatic: Areas managed for low to moderate use intensity; may include open-water portions of the estuary and valuable tidal marshes
- Rural aquatic: Areas managed for resource conservation and uses associated with agriculture
- Development aquatic: Areas managed for navigation and other water-dependent uses
- Natural shorelands: Areas managed for resource protection or preservation
- Conservation shorelands: Areas managed for timber production, wildlife, or recreation
- Rural shorelands: Areas managed for agriculture, timber production, and recreation
- Development shorelands: Areas managed for a wide range of uses; may include areas presently developed or suitable for residential, industrial, or commercial use
- Water-dependent development shorelands: Water-dependent uses are emphasized, with water-related or other uses allowed if associated with water-dependent uses

needed opportunities to maintain and expand their shallow-water fishing facilities and marinas.

Five subareas were defined for planning purposes, including Lower River and Islands, Youngs Bay–Astoria, Eastern Clatsop, Wahkiakum, and Baker Bay. They represent distinct geographic subregions defined by watershed divides, current use intensity, and other features.

As an example of detailed treatment by the plan, Youngs Bay–Astoria includes the most intensively developed shoreland and aquatic areas in the estuary region, with the greatest potential for additional development. This subarea includes the Tongue Point site as well as shorelands in Hammond, Warrenton, and Astoria. Historical patterns of rail, highway, and deep-water channel development have concentrated population growth in the area be-tween Youngs Bay and Astoria. Public opinion polls identified development as a major value, particularly that of flat land on which to expand the industrial base of Astoria, residential development in Hammond, and other uses such as log storage, transportation facilities, dike maintenance, and public access. In these urban areas, the plan designates most shorelands for development or water-dependent development: a total of 1,677 acres of shorelands for devel-opment and another 886 acres for water-dependent development (a total of 30 percent of the land in the subarea). Potential port development sites desig-nated by the plan include Tansy Point, east and west spits of the Skipanon River mouth, Smith Point (port of Astoria), and Tongue Point.

Existing and potential shallow-draft marina sites were designated in Ham-mond, Warrenton, Lewis and Clark River, Youngs River and Bay, and Astoria. These areas include numerous sites designated for dredged material disposal. The plan designates most biologically important marshes and subtidal areas for natural or conservation use. Shorelands outside urban growth boundaries were designated rural or conservation to give priority to agriculture and forestry.

Three important policies will guide development in the subarea. Log storage is given priority even as a nonconforming use in natural areas, except where logs would rest on the bottom at low tide. Existing transportation cor-ridors are recognized as development areas regardless of the surrounding habitats or designations. New transportation routes are given priority even through natural or conservation lands. Public access is recognized as a major value to be enhanced through small waterfront parks in urban areas, fishing piers, viewpoints, boat launches and walkways, or in conjunction with any new major water-dependent development.

Another subarea, Baker Bay, is the more developed of the two subareas on the Washington side, although the population and workforce are sparse. Reg-ulatory jurisdictions include the town and port of Ilwaco, port of Chinook, Pacific County, and Clatsop County, as well as state and federal agencies. The overriding issue in the planning area is maintaining the viability of the two ports and keeping navigation channels open. Protection of natural habitat, public access, and potential mineral extraction are other important planning issues. Fishing and tourism are important economic activities, but the area lacks rail, air, and deep-water access to accommodate heavy industrial devel-opment. Nonetheless, the ports of Chinook and Ilwaco are designated for modest expansion.

Baker Bay's several hundred acres of tidal marsh and rich benthic commu-nities are biologically important. Sand shrimp, dungeness crab, and finfish—

particularly juvenile starry flounder and salmon—use shallow areas of the bay. The area is also important for waterfowl, particularly gull and Caspian tern rookeries in the sand island area. Most of these shoreland and aquatic areas are designated for natural resource protection, but many shallow subtidal areas also are designated for conservation with some moderate-intensity uses.

The plan recognizes the need to support the economic and social stability of the ports and the tourist and fishing industries. Improved landside and waterfront facilities are envisioned to take advantage of the 200-mile limit. Because shoaling is a major problem, the plan emphasizes study of the hydraulic system and long-term measures to maintain navigability while preserving the biological functions of the bay. The plan encourages public access but considers current information inadequate to protect many natural areas from alterations caused by development. More complete biological surveys are needed. Mineral extraction is also a potential future use, particularly if technological advances reduce environmental impacts.

Plan Adoption Process

State Reviews

Local plans in both states were subject to much refinement during state reviews, but the task was much less arduous in Washington.[16] As state agencies in Washington retain a broad appeal power over all local decisions, the Department of Ecology allowed local land use plans to be much less detailed than Oregon local plans. Because Oregon's system essentially delegates its permit power to local government upon the acknowledgment of plans, the DLCD requires much more precision in local plans before relinquishing its authority.

The initial CREST plan was adopted by all of its member governments in June 1979, shortly after the arrival of Director Michael Delapa. Local approvals set in motion the Washington and Oregon state review, which necessitated lengthy negotiations and mediation procedures to reach full agreement. Final approval by the state agencies came in 1983. According to Delapa, the plan presented another dilemma to the Oregon DLCD. It was widely recognized, according to Delapa, that a piecemeal review of local plans would be contrary to the intended regional perspective of the plan. Departmental regulations, however, did not provide for the review of a regional document, and there were no established procedures for such a process. To this day, it is unclear whether DLCD had the jurisdiction to review a regional plan.[17]

Once the DLCD opted to review the plan, some previously unresolved conflicts began to surface. These disagreements generally concerned the plan's lack of specificity regarding the type and intensity of proposed land uses and the amount of discretion open to local planning officials for deciding the fate of wetlands areas and establishment of new port facilities. As originally submitted to the DLCD, the CREST plan appeared to some state officials to be pro-development. State goal 16 requires that "all estuarine resources be protected unless there is a proven need for development." For this reason, the state required that the plan justify proposed development.[18]

The plan arrived at DLCD with many conflicts resolved (such as those between local governments and ports), but it proposed that 4 percent of estuarine lands and waters be designated for development. Of that 4 percent, very little was proposed for actual shorefront development in the intertidal zone; the remaining development lands were designated for navigational uses and other subtidal uses not requiring fill.

Another major issue involved the plan's treatment of wetlands. Less than 1 percent of the areas identified as wetlands were designated as potential development sites. Delapa viewed these wetland sites as insignificant in the context of the entire estuarine system, but federal reviewers, particularly at the National Marine Fisheries Service (NMFS), argued that any habitat loss—no matter how slight—was unacceptable. Both the NMFS and CREST staff regarded the entire estuarine area as a valuable salmon nursery habitat, and management of the salmon fishery was an overriding principle, both politically and with regard to natural resource protection. Many of the impacts on the salmon fishery, however, were caused by events occurring well outside the planning area, including dams and other streamflow alterations, forest practices, and overfishing.

In response to the five areas of disagreement, CREST prepared a regional economic analysis and the state economic development department completed a study of Oregon ports in 1978. These studies, along with a set of DLCD ground rules, became the starting point for the mediated agreement. In spite of these deficiencies, CREST was considered by DLCD to be further along in applying statewide planning goals in practice, so the CREST plan policies were influential at the state level in applying and testing statewide policy.[19]

THE DLCD also found fault with the plan's specification of uses and sites for water-dependent development. CREST had designated about 20 areas within its planning jurisdiction for water-dependent development. The DLCD agreed with CREST that the sites were suitable for some water-dependent development and that acreage allocations were appropriate. But the department did not believe that the land uses to be allowed at each site were sufficiently well described. The DLCD believed that the plan should assign specific types of uses and acreages at sites earmarked for water-dependent development.[20]

The Wetlands Debate in a Nutshell[21]

Section 404 of the Clean Water Act authorizes the U.S. Army Corps of Engineers (Corps) to issue permits for filling navigable waters, including wetlands. Wetlands are often drained and filled before being developed. The Corps issues permits, however, in accordance with guidelines developed by EPA—the so-called b-1 guidelines. Moreover, EPA may veto the Corps' decision to issue a permit, although EPA seldom does.

For over a decade, Section 404 has been the subject of pitched battles and heated debates. Here is why.

1. *What Is a Wetland?*

   There is little disagreement that places with permanent water and water-loving plants such as the Everglades or the Great Dismal Swamp qualify as wetlands. But what about shallow depressions in the landscape that become wet briefly now and then, yet may remain dry for months, like the prairie potholes in the upper midwest and vernal pools in California? Should they be considered wetlands? How long must an area remain wet to be considered a wetland: one week, one month, six months, all year? And must there be standing water or will saturated soils be sufficient?

2. *Whose Land Is It Anyway?*

   Approximately three-quarters of the remaining wetlands in the coterminous states lie on private land. The benefits of wetlands protection—clean water, habitat for wildlife, flood control, etc.—are shared by society, while the "costs" are borne by individual landowners. That's the rub. How can society's interest in protecting wetlands be balanced with the rights of property owners to develop their land? If wetland regulations restrict development of private land, should government have to pay for that land?

3. *How Should Wetlands Be Protected?*

   The Clean Water Act was not designed to protect wetlands.[22]

4. *Who Is in Charge?*

   Two fundamentally different agencies, EPA and the Corps, are responsible for administering the federal program for regulating development in wetlands. The Corps, traditionally concerned with large public works projects like dams and canals, runs the program, with guidelines established by EPA, whose main concern is environmental protection. In splitting authority from responsibility, Congress committed a cardinal management sin.[23] Should one agency only be responsible for running the program? If so, which one, the Corps, EPA, or some other agency? Should states, rather than the federal government, regulate activities in wetlands?

5. *Where Does a Wetland End and Dry Land (Upland) Begin?*
Wetlands typically occupy low-lying areas in a gradient between dry land and open water. They often occur along rivers, streams, lakes, and oceans. Unlike property lines, wetland boundaries are dynamic, often shifting from year to year or from one flood or drought to the next. What criteria or techniques should be used to delineate wetlands from uplands?

6. *Are All Wetlands Alike?*
Wetlands come in all shapes, sizes, types, and conditions. Some are more common than others. Some are pristine, others defiled, and still more lie somewhere in between.

Are some wetlands more valuable than others? If so, should wetlands be classified according to their value and then regulated accordingly? How should they be classified? By what methodology? In some parts of the country, like the Hackensack Meadowlands in New Jersey, soiled and sullied wetlands are all that's left; yet these wetlands still provide habitat for birds. Should these wetlands be classified as low-value and therefore relinquished to development?

7. *Does Wetlands Mitigation Work?*
In exchange for a permit to fill wetlands, the Corps usually requires that an applicant create a new wetland of similar size or larger, a practice known as mitigation. Can new wetlands be created from scratch? Will they replace all values and functions of the wetland that was destroyed? The track record of developers in creating wetlands is unimpressive: most created wetlands fare poorly, due to inadequate design, poor site selection, lack of maintenance, and in many cases failure to implement a mitigation plan properly, if at all.

Another problem was that CREST's plan was one of the first reviewed by DLCD pursuant to the 19 statewide planning goals. In this start-up plan, state agencies took the opportunity to develop more detailed interpretations of goal requirements, which were then applied to the CREST plan. The first review found five major concerns:

1. Local governments provided insufficient information to justify the development exceptions they requested.

2. Many shorefront development sites appeared to be alternatives to each other—that is, they were not all needed.

3. Development envelopes surrounding each site were not sufficiently specific or restrictive.

4. A regional economic analysis was needed to provide a basis for development plans.

5. A port study was needed to assess the feasibility and types of new port development.

Overall, DLCD found that "proper planning should determine very specific envelopes for all future uses."

Mediation to Resolve Conflicts

A formal mediation process was central to settling these disagreements and completing the CREST plan. In 1979 the Environmental Mediation Institute (EMI) offered to help mediate CREST's dispute with the DLCD. At that time, CREST did not believe that neutral assistance was needed, as the parties had not reached a full impasse; but one year later, motivated by pressures to move ahead with economic development under the plan, including anticipated increased tax base benefits and employment opportunities, CREST commissioners decided to ask for EMI's help.

Verne Huser and Sam Gusman, the mediators from EMI (which had changed its name to the Mediation Institute) met with the staff of state and federal resources agencies, local members of CREST, representatives of environmental groups, and others. In designing the negotiation process, one challenge was to persuade the U.S. Army Corps of Engineers, the LCDC, and the Oregon Division of State Lands to sit at the negotiating table with local government representatives. The regulatory agencies worried that direct participation in the negotiations might compromise their subsequent decision making on permit issues, so a special category of "review advisors" was created to differentiate direct participants from active observers.

Huser and Gusman devoted two two-day sessions to resolve preliminary issues, such as determining the parties that should participate, in what capacity, on what issues, and with what expectations of resolution. The LCDC and the DLCD suggested that the discussions focus on appropriate locations and acreages for water-dependent development. The mediators and participants all agreed to a strict deadline.

The discussions took a positive turn when the parties reached agreement about Tongue Point, the first proposed development site. They drafted findings that designated appropriate land uses and drew up detailed conditions to govern site development.

Coalitions formed among the resource agencies and the development interests; most local interests lined up on the development side. Even with the advent of coalitions, however, the participants were able to agree on desirable land uses and development conditions for each of the four remaining sites.

A final negotiating session scheduled just days before the imposed deadline was devoted to working out further details regarding the type of development that would be allowed in each area. The mediators prepared a 36-page summary detailing the agreements, and the parties signed it. The document outlined appropriate development at each site, designated areas where development was prohibited, and specified limits for dredging and filling.

The CREST effort gave news reporters access to all formal negotiating sessions. The mediators believed that because recalcitrant parties were apt to be depicted in a poor light by the news media, news coverage would encourage constructive discussions. For most participants, it was important to appear reasonable rather than hardheaded. The mediation effort also provided opportunities for broader public participation in the negotiations.

Former CREST director Michael Delapa observed that "[O]ne outcome of the mediation process was to further scale back the amount of development proposed for wetlands."[24] A spinoff benefit of the mediation effort was to increase the amount of technical information available to decisionmakers at all levels. Technical resources were heavily weighted on the side of federal and state agencies. Delapa noted that local representatives, especially from the ports, had neither the credibility nor the competence to match those on the other side of the table. Throughout the process, CREST staff served as neutral advisors, taking on tasks such as preparing background information and developing briefing books. The staff did not back any particular position on development.

In Delapa's view, negotiators agreed to pare back proposed development because the development community declined to commit to develop the areas designated in the earlier drafts of the plan. He added that the lands designated for development were more than sufficient for present needs; the right balance of conservation and development was achieved.

Almost 90 percent of the wetlands were slated for preservation in the final plan, according to a subsequent CREST director, Mark Barnes.[25] A small proportion (about 5 percent of nontidal wetlands) could be developed under the plan although the actual acreage would probably be less after site-specific planning and permit review.

Position of Federal Agencies

Federal agencies participated in the mediation process but never fully supported the agreement on the plan. State and local participants in the planning process observed that federal agency members provided a cursory review of plan policies as they were being developed and identified areas where future conflicts seemed likely. But agency representatives were not empowered to make commitments to plan policies until the final stages when key conflicts became evident.

In discussions of issues, Bud Forrester commented, federal and state resource agencies were less compromising than were local representatives, often assuming what some participants believed were "impossible" or "extreme" positions against any kind of development that compromised resources.[26] Federal agency representatives only reluctantly signed off on the final plan.

According to other participants, federal agency officials acted more as observers, gave "agreements in principle," and generally drew a basic distinction between planning and permitting. Federal permit review, particularly under Section 404 of the Clean Water Act, centers on case-by-case consideration of specific proposals. The Corps of Engineers review criteria are broad and nonspecific. Federal regulations are not flexible enough to allow an advanced determination of specific development quotas.

One participant observed, "The permit process encourages a 'battle mentality' and creates an adversarial stance intended to stop any loss of important resources. Planning, on the other hand, acknowledges that some development will occur, and that proper planning should determine the scope of development while specific permit review should decide the details of design intensity and location."[27]

During and after the mediation process, local government representatives have been disappointed in federal agencies' lack of commitment to the spirit of the agreement. According to Paul Benson, who coordinated much of the federal participation, federal agencies wished to retain full authority to make future permit decisions case by case.[28]

Implementation of the Plan

CREST Role: Assisting in Local Planning and Permitting

CREST has several roles under the approved and acknowledged plan:

1. Permit applicants may preview their projects with CREST staff to determine which sections of the plan apply and to refine project details.

2. After full federal, state, and local permit applications are made, the CREST staff prepares a staff report and technical presentations for local government permit hearings.

3. CREST recommends relevant permit conditions, predicts issues that may arise in federal and state permit reviews, and makes suggestions at the local level to ensure consistency in local approvals.

CREST staff has been reduced from seven full-time professionals to two, which the current director considers adequate to operate in a maintenance mode now that the plan is substantially in place. These professionals also act as staff to the ten member municipalities, many of which have no full-time planning staff. CREST's staff typically review two or three permit applications per month and take on additional temporary staff or consultants as required for plan updates or studies.

CREST is currently assisting local jurisdictions with permitting issues, zoning ordinances, comprehensive plan and shoreline master program amendments, estuarine impact analysis, wetlands related issues and restoration, and dredging and dredge material disposal issues. Special projects include development of a geographic information system natural resource and planning database, environmental education programs, and habitat restoration.

State Role under the Approved Plan

Once local plans are acknowledged by the state, the Oregon DLCD and the Washington Department of Community Development interact with local planning agencies in two principal ways. The DLCD reviews the land use decisions of Oregon's local governments through a quarterly reporting process. All local decisions are forwarded to enable a test of compliance with comprehensive and statewide planning goals. The field representative assigned to Oregon's North Coast region described the review as "brief but thorough."[29] She emphasized that DLCD is not involved in day-to-day decision making. Both state agencies review local plans every five years. Most of the issues under review involve policy updates and deletion of irrelevant policies. For example, one of the main items that arose in the Clatsop County review was the need to rewrite the regulations on forest uses to comply with 1987 state legislation on forest practices. Warrenton, a small town with large areas of both tidal and nontidal wetlands, had not identified all wetlands and designated them for protection in the town's comprehensive plan. A more precise mapping of wetlands was required to enable closer scrutiny of proposed development sites. To that end, the city is now (1994) identifying non-tidal wetlands and designating them for preservation, restoration, or limited development.

In the town of Astoria, the Alderbrook deep-draft development site that was identified in the initial plan has required some modification. Strong local opposition arose to development at Alderbrook because of perceived conflicts with adjacent residential land uses. Since the development designation for the Alderbrook site was part of the original mediated agreement, this conflict has created a dilemma for state planners. Although there is a clear process for amending a plan, the mediated agreement included no provisions for remediation should circumstances change, and state agencies, in particular, have viewed the mediated agreement as cast in stone. Rather than reconvening the mediation process, the DLCD recommended an addendum to the agreement.[30]

On the Washington side, the state growth management act requires local governments to designate critical wetlands as part of their planning process. Most jurisdictions in the lower estuary have completed this task.[31]

The Federal Role

For all plan amendments, the state agencies provide notice to other state and federal agencies and act as a clearinghouse for review comments. Among the federal agencies they work with are the U.S. Fish and Wildlife Service, Environmental Protection Agency, National Marine Fisheries Service, Soil Conservation Service, Forest Service, and U.S. Army Corps of Engineers.[32]

Many of the agency representatives who were involved in plan development have moved on to other posts. Newly recruited staff are only generally aware of the efforts and formal commitments that shaped the CREST plan. This lack of continuity means that federal agency staff have less stake in upholding and carrying out the plan. Unfortunately, high rates of staff turnover also have greatly complicated the task of securing adequate comments, to the frustration of the state agency staff.[33]

Mark Barnes reported that federal agencies did not consider themselves bound by the provisions or agreements worked out under the CREST plan. They continue to review permit applications case by case. Although the Corps of Engineers and the National Marine Fisheries Service participated in the agreements that delineated wetlands and designated certain lands for development, they generally conduct a new mapping and site analysis for each permit application, often finding more extensive wetlands than were originally designated in the CREST plan. Nontidal wetlands are the source of the most uncertainty and conflict.[34]

Conclusions: Measures of Success and Future Prospects

A 1984 review characterized CREST as the flagship of Oregon's coastal program:

> The Columbia River Estuary Study Task Force, a group of experts funded by LCDC, conducted an intensive study aimed at coming up with the data base and policies necessary to implement the estuarine goal. Once completed in draft the plan was reviewed by state and federal agencies and revised in light of their response. The study is regarded as the best done on coastal problems and has given LCDC more confidence in instructing other local governments in what will be required of them. At the other extreme, the Coos Bay Task Force spent about $1 million, the money is gone and due largely to a recalcitrant city and port district there are few results and no plans ready for acknowledgment.[35]

Intergovernmental Cooperation in Conserving Wetlands

The CREST plan has been valuable in guiding local, regional, and state efforts to conserve wetlands. As evidence, Paul Benson, the former director of the Pacific Northwest River Basins Commission, cited the continuing support that CREST receives from its local government members (including the development-oriented port districts).[36] Bud Forrester observed that the plan and permit procedures allow development to proceed in an orderly manner while ensuring that natural resources are protected, an arrangement that has resulted in very constructive working relationships among state and local government agencies. However, Forrester sees the increasing number of proposals for reuse of waterfront buildings as a growing issue. For example, conversions to office or retail uses have been proposed for fish-processing facilities, a change that would erode the water-dependent economic base. Additionally, because of the burgeoning demand for housing within view of the ocean, Forrester predicted an insatiable demand fueled by people with "California checkbooks."[37]

In the view of Gail McEwan, formerly the DLCD North Coast field representative, "The CREST plan protects wetlands well. But more importantly, it has established a good working relationship between the towns, the ports, and state agencies. During the comprehensive planning process, CREST was viewed negatively by the port of Astoria, but now CREST has gained credibility and has proved beneficial in identifying development sites and ensuring predictability."[38] Before the CREST plan, the local port districts had a free hand to develop their waterfront sites. Consequently, they were initially reluctant to cooperate with local planning agencies. The CREST program brought them to the table as full participants. Because the benefits of orderly, predictable development became evident during the planning process, port directors conceded their previous right to fill waterfront land without oversight.

An undisputed achievement of the CREST process has been its education of local public officials and local constituencies about the values of estuary-wide planning, wetlands conservation, and improvement of the quality of planning. Local planning officials in Oregon jurisdictions within the estuary have been committed to sound comprehensive planning across local jurisdictions and have sought mediation services to resolve their remaining conflicts. This effort was another example of local initiatives moving the planning process past a key obstacle.

Some observers of the CREST program, however, believe that local governments were given too much control in the planning process and retain a significant amount of control over the plan's implementation. They regard the regional plan as simply a collection of local plans rather than a full-fledged strategic plan for the estuary.[39] Former director Delapa takes a different view: he believes that the plan was a completely integrated regional policy document.[40]

Nevertheless, the plan has its weak points as well as strong points. According to Mark Barnes, the plan has been quite successful in preserving the tidal parts of the estuary where most of the critical shorelands are publicly owned and where there is broad agreement about wetland designations and appropriate uses. Planning for critical nontidal wetlands has been less successful. Federal and state agencies differ with CREST and local plans about how to designate nontidal wetlands.

Patricia Snow, DLCD federal liaison planner, agreed that tidal wetlands were well identified in the plan. At the time the plan was created, however, the fact that nontidal wetlands were not granted as much attention has created a considerable amount of uncertainty in the permitting process. Since the plan is for an entire estuary, the definition of estuarine lands excluded many upland, nontidal wetlands. Goal 17 (the estuarine goal) specifically mentions "major marshes" but leaves the status of smaller freshwater wetlands undefined. Snow noted that state estuarine policy does not require evidence of water dependency to enable inland wetlands to be filled.[41]

Coastal Zone Management Act Section 309 funds may be the main tool to help resolve the status of inland wetlands. State planners at Oregon's DLCD proposed the use of EPA's advanced identification procedure and a Corps of Engineers general permit. In effect, they are seeking a complete inventory and an agreement with federal agencies on the status of inland wetlands. Several commentators believe that the Corps never accepted the CREST plan's identification of nontidal wetlands as final, and as a rule, the Corps has found nontidal wetlands to be more extensive than those identified in local plans.

Only recently has the Corps undertaken an advance identification of wetland areas in the Warrenton area.

All in all, Snow said, "[T]he planning process worked well, particularly in designating appropriate conservation lands. Federal agencies, however, don't have the same commitment to a plan that state and local agencies do." She balanced these comments with the observation that "current efforts at EPA to incorporate comprehensive planning into wetlands protection seem hopeful."[42]

Effects on the Private Development Approval Process

CREST now offers a more systematic review process for developers at the local level. Permit applicants may preview their project in consultation with CREST staff to ensure full information sharing and compliance with plan policies.[43] CREST staff also provide technical assistance in presentations at local hearings such as the Shoreline Hearing Board in Washington and planning commission meetings in Oregon.

Barnes noted that the plan has created a consistent standard for project approval across the entire planning area. Permit denials are rare because projects that fail to meet CREST goals do not survive the pre-application review. Although there are no formal statistics, Barnes "could not think of any project that had been denied."[44]

Furthermore, CREST staff provide a working knowledge of federal and state standards that may not be explicitly stated in the CREST plan. Proposed development projects may appear to comply with plan policies but still raise objections from the U.S. Army Corps of Engineers or the federal Environmental Protection Agency. Since local decisions come before federal or state agencies act, CREST staff recommendations can streamline the rest of the permit process. Although Oregon state law requires that local decisions be handed down within a total of 120 days, a standard that is consistently met, federal permit decisions are frequently subject to long delays in spite of consistency with plan standards.[45]

One of the outcomes of the CREST planning process was improved access to information and locally available expertise. Additionally, CREST provides a readily accessible data base for planners, drawing together available information into a useful form and generating new information on key issues. CREST's new geographic information system, completed in 1993, has greatly expanded the usefulness of its data base.

Adapting the Plan to Changing Conditions

Several CREST communities in Oregon were obligated to begin reviewing their local plans in the late 1980s. A significant feature of the plan update process was that the DLCD expected to review local plans individually rather than as an integrated CREST plan revision. Additionally, updates were being handled administratively by the DLCD staff and referred to the LCDC only if staff objected to a proposed revision. In this way, the review process was less restrictive overall.

According to Jon Graves, the current CREST director, changes in local plans during the review process were relatively modest. He observed that since CREST staff participated in the review process in its technical assistance role to local governments, CREST was able to provide the regional overview required to keep local plans consistent with the estuary plan. Beginning in 1994, the next review process is being initiated, with a similar involvement of CREST expected.[46]

The 1984 plan left several issues incompletely resolved; these have been subject to continuing efforts to reach satisfactory consensus between CREST, local governments, and state and federal agencies.

One major development issue has been the specific types and intensity of uses appropriate for Tongue Point, for which the outcome is still uncertain. Proposed as a development site before CREST's inception, the Tongue Point area was an important element in the mediation process, and active debate over development on this site continues. Since the CREST plan was adopted, the State Lands Commission acquired the development site and acts as both a permitting authority and a leaseholder for any future development. Although a number of development projects have been proposed, none have materialized. At the moment, in 1994, only a film production studio occupies part of the site.

Federal resource agencies such as the Corps have been quite concerned over the possibility of more intensive development at Tongue Point, for several reasons: (1) Tongue Point is an important nesting site for bald eagles; (2) it lies at the center of an area considered to be an important feeding habitat for a larger population of bald eagles; and (3) because the point is the site of a former Navy base, there is a suspected reservoir of hazardous wastes in the bottom sediments. The latter problem resulted from indiscriminate dumping in the estuary of uninventoried material from hundreds of decommissioned ships after World War II. Such wastes may include barrels of chemicals and obsolete equipment. Therefore, any development that would involve dredging raises a red flag for resource agencies reviewing the project, although, in Barnes's opinion, the river contamination would be considered clean by the standards of Boston Harbor.[47] Dredging in this area, however, would subject bald eagles and salmon—politically critical types of wildlife—to unknown levels of contamination as contaminants previously adsorbed to sediments are resuspended and rendered more biologically available. Jon Graves observes that in 1994 this problem still exists, although with continued sedimentation over time the contaminated sediments are slowly being buried.[48]

Decisions about the fate of Tongue Point are critical, because it is one of a few suitable sites available for marine industrial development. According to Bob Cortright, "[N]eeds have changed and there may not be a demand for as many development sites as have been designated. Ten years ago, for example, a coal export facility was seen as highly desirable, but that demand has evaporated. Still, options for future development use of key sites should not be traded away just because there is no current demand."

Cortright predicted that the resource agencies may use an issue like bald eagle nesting habitat to stop any kind of development at Tongue Point, in spite of the mediated agreement that accounted for habitat issues at the time. Thus, it may be difficult to hold federal agencies to the commitments they made under the CREST plan. However, some recent development has been occurring in the Tongue Point area under conditions, such as height restrictions and construction phasing, that will limit impacts on bald eagle habitat.[49]

Another issue has been development in the town of Warrenton. Warrenton is the location of extensive wetlands habitats but is also the only town in the estuary planning area that is experiencing development pressure. Although local and federal agreements on wetland designations were controversial for some time, most recently a comprehensive mapping of wetlands in the Warrenton area was completed by the Corps, and state and federal agencies are proceeding with plans to issue a general 404 permit that will allow the town to control future development in wetland areas.[50]

Maintenance of water quality is another emerging issue, but one well beyond the scope of CREST's plan. Barnes estimated that 99 percent of water-quality problems originate upriver and are caused by forest practices on tributaries and dam-induced flow alterations. Michael Delapa commented that this issue was not part of the original agenda for negotiation. Because no decision-makers or experts from forestry agencies took part in the negotiations, he said, the views of federal forestry interests were not considered. Forestry is so critical to the health of Oregon's statewide economy, explained Delapa, that "forestry beats resources head to head in any conflict." As a small local agency with little influence at the state level (now that the highly publicized mediation process is past), CREST has no means of attacking water-quality problems.[51]

A long-standing issue for CREST is the conversion of disused fish-processing plants to compatible water-dependent uses. In the research conducted in 1988, one respondent identified this as the largest potential conflict yet to be resolved. Yet in 1994, Jon Graves notes, the dilapidated remains of fish canneries still are found throughout the estuary, along with active canneries. Because tourist investment has centered on the coastal area rather than upriver, little conversion of the wharves and buildings has taken place and the primary controversy has been over preservation of what some people perceive as historic structures.[52]

Comment on Future Prospects

CREST has solid support from its member governments and has become a valued channel of federal funds for local planning assistance. Yet the ports and municipalities within the estuary pay only 10 to 20 percent of CREST's operating costs. About 30 percent of CREST's budget comes from federal Coastal Zone Management Act Section 306 allocations through state agencies and the remainder through grants and contracts. If these funding sources should change, CREST would have to turn to economically unstable local government sources and user fees which, according to Mark Barnes, is essentially unrealistic, because if applicants had to pay the full permit processing costs they would find ways to avoid the process altogether. He suggested that fees should be kept low enough to induce applicants to participate.[53] Current director Jon Graves concurs with this view.

NOTES

1. This chapter is based on a similarly titled study prepared under the supervision of and copyrighted in 1989 by The Environmental Law Institute, Washington, D.C., and which was funded in part by the U.S. Environmental Protection Agency (Office of Wetlands Protection and Office of Policy, Planning and Evaluation) through EPA contract number 68-01-7378. It is reprinted in edited form with the permission of the Institute and the authors.

2. James W. Good, "Oregon Estuary Planning and Management." Proceedings of the Fifth Annual Conference of the Coastal Society, November 6–8, 1979.

3. Columbia River Estuary Study Taskforce, *A Program for Increased Understanding and Improved Use of the Columbia River Estuary,* Astoria, Oregon: Columbia Review Estuary Study Taskforce, 1975.

4. R. Bartl and M. Morgan, *An Economic Evaluation of the Columbia River Estuary,* Astoria, Oregon: Columbia River Estuary Study Taskforce, 1981.

5. Much of the information in this section is taken from the following sources: National Oceanic and Atmospheric Administration, Office of Coastal Zone Management, *State of Oregon Coastal Management Program and Final EIS* and *State of Washington Coastal Management Program and Final EIS,* Washington, D.C., 1977 and 1973, respectively; Scott T.

McCreary and Mark B. Adams, *Alternative Institutional Arrangements for State Coastal Management Programs: An Assessment of Their Strengths and Weaknesses*, prepared for the New York State Department of State, Division of Coastal Resources and Waterfront Revitalization, October 1988; and Oregon Land Conservation and Development Commission, *Oregon's Coastal Management Program: A Citizen's Guide*, Salem, Oregon, 1986.

6. Washington State Department of Ecology, *Washington State Coastal Zone Management Program*, Olympia, Washington, June 1976.

7. M. Jennings, J. Alfonso, and W. Budd, 1988. "Use of the Environmentally Sensitive Areas Rule by County Governments in Washington State," *Environmental Impact Assessment Review*, Vol. 8, No. 1, pp. 63-70 (1988).

8. Chapter 173-16, Washington Administrative Code.

9. Washington State Department of Ecology, op. cit. note 6.

10. Personal communication from Mark Barnes, former director of CREST, Astoria, Oregon.

11. Nancy Fox and Susan Heikkala, *Shoreline Master Program Handbook and Shoreline Master Program Study: Analysis Report*, Olympia, Washington: State of Washington Department of Ecology, 1983.

12. Columbia River Estuary Study Taskforce, *Columbia River Estuary Regional Management Plan*, adopted June 1979. Also see the initial program proposal: Columbia River Estuary Study Taskforce, *A Program for Increased Understanding and Improved Use of the Columbia River Estuary*, 1975.

13. Personal communication from James Good.

14. Personal communication from Paul Benson, Oregon Coastal Zone Management Association. Benson was a former coordinator of federal agencies for the Pacific Northwest River Basins Commission.

15. Personal communication from Mark Barnes.

16. Personal communication from Mark Barnes.

17. Personal communication from Michael Delapa.

18. Personal communication from Robert Cortright, coastal policy specialist with the Department of Land Conservation and Development, Salem, Oregon.

19. Personal communication from Robert Cortright.

20. Verne Huser, *Mediation in a Coastal Estuary. Proceedings of a Conference on Conflict Resolution for Coastal Zone and OCS Resources*, Cambridge: Massachusetts Institute of Technology, 1984.

21. Adapted with permission from David Salvesen, "Wetlands: Mitigating and Regulating Development Impacts," The Urban Land Institute, January 1994, p. 8.

22. The Clean Water Act is a water quality statute designed to regulate dis-

charges from industrial and municipal point sources; it never mentions the word *wetlands*. Yet, wetlands protect water quality, among other things.

23. Virginia Albrect, "The Wetlands Debate," *Urban Land*, May 1992, p. 21.
24. Personal communication from Michael Delapa.
25. Personal communication from Mark Barnes.
26. Personal communication from Bud Forrester, publisher of *The Astorian* in Astoria, Oregon, and former member of the Land Conservation and Development Commission.
27. Personal communication from Robert Cortright.
28. Personal communication from Paul Benson.
29. Personal communication from Gail McEwan, field representative for the north coast region for the Department of Land Conservation and Development, Salem, Oregon.
30. Personal communication from Gail McEwan.
31. Personal communication from Jon Graves.
32. Personal communication from Robert Cortright.
33. Personal communication from Robert Cortright.
34. Personal communication from Mark Barnes.
35. John M. DeGrove, *Land, Growth and Politics,* Chicago: American Planning Association, 1984, p. 59.
36. Personal communication with Paul Benson.
37. Personal communication from Forrester.
38. Personal communication from Gail McEwan.
39. Huser, op. cit. note 20.
40. Personal communication from Michael Delapa.
41. Personal communication from Patricia Snow, coastal planning specialist and federal agency liaison with the Department of Land Conservation and Development, Salem, Oregon.
42. Personal communication with Patricia Snow.
43. Personal communication from Mark Barnes.
44. Personal communication with Mark Barnes.
45. Personal communication from Mark Barnes.
46. Personal communication from Jon Graves to the editors, 1994.
47. Personal communication from Mark Barnes.
48. Personal communication from Jon Graves to the editors.
49. Personal communication from Jon Graves to the editors, 1994.
50. Personal communication from Jon Graves to the editors, 1994.
51. Personal communication from Michael Delapa.
52. Personal communication from Jon Graves to the editors, 1994.
53. Personal communication from Mike Barnes.

Special-Area Management Planning in New Jersey's Hackensack Meadowlands: An Emerging Model for Cooperative State-Federal Planning

Edwin W. Finder

EDITORS' SUMMARY

The Hackensack Meadowlands in northern New Jersey were used for many years as a dumping ground for garbage and chemical wastes. About one-third of the 32-square-mile region is occupied by wetlands which, although degraded, have endured. Rising development pressures threatened their existence, while environmentalists called for restoration and preservation. In 1988 the Hackensack Meadowlands Development Commission signed a Memorandum of Understanding with state and federal agencies to prepare a special-area management plan that would incorporate the Clean Water Act's Section 404 "practicable alternatives" within a regional land use master plan. Finder describes how the plan was prepared and how it incorporated and consolidated a variety of planning and regulatory concerns. If successful, the integration of planning and regulatory processes at local, state, and federal levels of government will provide many lessons for other communities seeking to balance environmental and development objectives.

Background

In northern New Jersey, just five miles west of Manhattan, lies a vast soggy area called the Hackensack Meadowlands. About one-third of the 32-square-mile region is wetlands; it is probably the largest remaining wetland acreage in the northern part of the state. Most of the wetlands, however, are degraded; they are the legacy of years of abuse by local municipalities and private property owners who used the Meadowlands as a large garbage dump, and by industries who found the area a convenient place to dispose of chemical wastes. Yet, the wetlands have endured and continue to provide valuable wildlife habitat.

Over the last decade, the fate of the wetlands in the Meadowlands has been the subject of intense debate. In the 1980s, due to the Meadowlands' proximity to New York and their easy access from major thoroughfares like the New Jersey Turnpike (see Figure 7.1), it became one of the area's real estate hot spots. Developers were anxious to convert the wetland to sites for houses, offices, and warehouses. At the same time, environmentalists were demanding that the remaining wetlands be restored and preserved.

In late 1988, after nine months of negotiations, the Hackensack Meadowlands Development Commission (HMDC)—the regional planning agency for the Meadowlands—the New Jersey Department of Environmental Protection, and federal resource agencies, such as the Environmental Protection Agency (EPA) and the U.S. Army Corps of Engineers (though not the U.S. Fish and Wildlife Service), signed a Memorandum of Understanding under which the parties agreed to prepare a special area management plan (SAMP) for the Hackensack Meadowlands.

A principal objective of the SAMP is to demonstrate that federal environmental regulations and state legislative mandates can be compatible. Specifically, the Meadowlands SAMP seeks to incorporate the Clean Water Act Section 404(b)1 practicable alternatives requirement in a regional master plan. If it is successful, the plan could be a model for integrating local and area-wide master planning into federal environmental regulations.

For over a century, the Meadowlands District, comprising about 20,000 acres, has endured repeated encroachment by ever-expanding garbage dumps, and more recently by land development. Until relatively recently, much of the Meadowlands was regarded as worthless swamps that should be reclaimed through filling or draining. These and other conditions were among the factors that allowed the Meadowlands to become the region's dumping ground— literally a vast depository for massive, largely unregulated landfilling operations. Rail and automotive transportation corridors were laid out haphazardly across the area. The ostensible criteria for the location of these transportation facilities was simply the need to connect the Port of New York and New York City with other urban locations outside of the Meadowlands.

In addition, local zoning by 14 separate jurisdictions relegated most land to low-intensity railroad, warehousing, trucking, or undesirable industrial use. Accordingly, by the mid-1960s, the Meadowlands consisted of vast stretches of vacant land whose potential for development or ecological preservation had been seriously undermined.

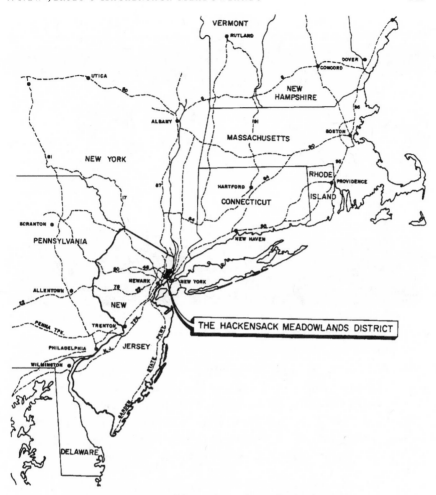

Figure 7.1 Location of the Hackensack Meadowlands District.

By the late 1960s the Meadowlands area had become the repository for one-third of New Jersey's solid waste stream destined for some 24 landfills, which occupied 13 percent of the land area within the district. More than 10.5 million tons of waste were dumped annually in the district. According to HMDC, nearly one million tons of waste arrive in the district annually. Only one operating landfill remains; it occupies 17 acres of land.

During this same time, 13 sewage treatment plants discharged effluent directly into the Hackensack River; today, there are four plants still in operation. The location of several power plants along the river affected the diverse marine life of the river. The dumping of waste by chemical manufacturers and other heavy industrial facilities since the early 1900s resulted in serious

This telescopic photograph underscores the contrasting pressures on the district: warehousing, transportation, new development, and wetlands.

contamination. Today, some 30 sites within the Meadowlands are known to be contaminated (three are Superfund sites), and mercury and chromium contamination is widespread, the result of uncontrolled industrial processes.

By the mid-1960s, the quantitative and qualitative loss of tidal wetlands was visibly evident. More than 2,500 acres of wetlands had been converted to landfill. Disastrous land use policies finally prompted state action.

The Hackensack Meadowlands Development Commission

In 1968 the New Jersey Legislature enacted the Hackensack Meadowlands Reclamation and Development Act in recognition of the significant environmental degradation that had been inflicted on the Meadowlands. The legislation also officially recognized decades of wasted opportunities as a result of a totally uncontrolled and unmanaged environmental process that had inflicted such widespread social and economic damage. The 1968 legislation created the HMDC and entrusted it with an array of important powers, including complete zoning and planning authority within the 32-square-mile district. The district is now a unified planning entity, empowered to regulate land use and construction in portions of 14 municipalities in two counties.

The state legislature charged the commission with the following three somewhat conflicting principal mandates:

- Orderly, comprehensive development . . . for industrial, commercial, residential, public recreational, and other uses

- Protection of the balance of nature

- Continued provision of facilities for the disposal of solid waste

The legislature charged HMDC with developing a plan for the district that fulfills certain state policy objectives that include creating jobs and maintaining the economic competitiveness of the region; fostering the development of housing that accommodates diverse income levels; and preserving the district's environmental resources. In addition, HMDC was made responsible for preserving a functional balance between development and other improvements (sewers, water supply, transportation, and other infrastructure) required to support residential and commercial development and recreational facilities. Finally, HMDC was responsible for maximizing aesthetic values in designing the components of the overall plan for the district as well as the interrelationships among them.

The master plan that HMDC adopted in 1972 could not address the requirements of the federal Clean Water Act, also adopted in 1972, or the subsequent Clean Water Act amendments. Nevertheless, the 1972 master plan, supported by HMDC zoning, land use, environmental, and solid waste controls, clearly succeeded in coordinating solid waste and development objectives with the preservation of substantial acres of wetlands. Also, HMDC programs and policies helped to restore wetlands, mitigate for wetland losses, and alleviate other environmental problems in an area that had long been disregarded.

HMDC authority and actions have resulted in the permanent protection and management of some 1,400 wetland acres in Saw Mill Creek basin and elsewhere in the district. In addition, HMDC's accomplishments in reducing and managing previously uncontrolled solid waste flow into the district, cited earlier, and other projects have helped substantially to reverse further degradation of the entire region's environment.

HMDC is an area-wide planning agency whose zoning and planning authority extends over parts of 14 "constituent" political jurisdictions. In addition, the commission's extensive power includes a tax sharing system, state financing powers through the issuance of revenue bonds, eminent domain authority and redevelopment powers. As a state regulatory agency, the HMDC also regulates and monitors compliance with its own specific zoning and with other land use regulations and building codes that apply in the district, as well as with detailed environmental regulations and standards.

HMDC must balance competing needs and demands within the district in a manner that maximizes its ability to meet the policy mandates and obligations imposed on it by the state legislature. It is principally through its master plan, first adopted in 1972, its zoning, and its other regulatory actions that HMDC is able to fulfill these state policy mandates.

Conflicts with Federal Regulatory Programs

Beginning in the early 1980s, it became apparent that federal environmental regulations were impeding HMDC's ability to meet its statutory obligations. Federal regulations and policies, focusing principally on the protection of wetlands, prevented projects from moving forward that were otherwise consistent with the 1972 master plan. From 1983 to 1990, a period characterized by unprecedented growth in the region and strong pressure for construction permits, only one fill permit allowing development was granted in the district by the U.S. Army Corps of Engineers.

The morass of conflicting and overlapping federal and state environmental regulations undermined HMDC's ability to continue its assigned functions. The scheduled completion, in the mid-1980s, of the major revisions to HMDC's 1972 master plan was delayed, as federal regulations were viewed as undermining HMDC's planning responsibilities.

It became evident by the mid-1980s that the project-oriented federal process for regulating wetlands was in direct conflict with HMDC's legislatively mandated, comprehensive, long-term approach to planning for the district. This complicates HMDC's dual role as both a planning and a regulatory agency. On the one hand, HMDC must view the district as a "region" in which long-term, sometimes competing development and preservation needs must be balanced. On the other hand, HMDC must be concerned with immediate or short-term impacts of its actions within each of its constituent municipalities. The foundation for HMDC's regulatory actions is the master plan, which attempts to achieve land use equity over the legislature's decision to assemble the land use regulatory authority of constituent municipalities under HMDC.

The 7,300 acres of wetland in the district (one-third of which are privately owned, with ownership of the remaining two-thirds divided among numerous governmental jurisdiction, utilities, and quasi-public entities) represent virtually the only remaining developable land in the Meadowlands.

The abuses that resulted from past actions have degraded much of the district's wetlands. Vast tracts of wetlands need restoration rather than simple protection. Actions to remove, contain, or restore contaminated sites and the ability to address other pollution problems, however, often are outside the purview of the federal case-by-case wetlands permitting process.

Determining whether a specific action involving development in wetlands should be approved by governmental authorities would begin with planning, a process in which responsible parties establish the rules and standards that will apply to a geographical area. Subsequently, only those proposals deemed to comply with rules and standards established in the planning process would be allowed to proceed. From the perspective of a regional planning agency like HMDC, the success of a long-term master plan for the district must depend on its ability to implement the development and preservation components of the overall plan.

The Planning Process

HMDC and its SAMP partner agencies sought to integrate local and regional planning into the federal environmental regulatory procedure. Although each partner was highly sensitive about infringing upon the statutory jurisdiction of the others, there existed a commonality of respective issues, goals, and procedures.

During the summer of 1990, HMDC authorized funds for the preparation of what may well come to be regarded as a landmark document—a programmatic environmental impact statement (EIS) on the SAMP. In this case, it was an area-wide environmental assessment for the Hackensack Meadowlands. It was initially anticipated that the EIS would be completed by the fall of 1991 and, assuming consensus on the SAMP, that HMDC would then proceed to adopt a revised master plan that conforms with the SAMP. Although this time schedule has been revised, the components of the SAMP are proceeding on a new schedule that calls for completion by early 1995.

In essence, the Meadowlands SAMP partner agencies have succeeded in starting a planning process that could identify the means for state and federal regulations to operate in concert and that incorporates the Section 404(b)(1) guidelines, including the practicable alternatives test, into regional planning.

Before the SAMP was initiated, HMDC's staff had produced a substantial body of technical studies and data on the district. This data should facilitate completion of the EIS in an expedited time frame. In addition to studies of air and water quality, wetlands quality and characteristics, and wildlife habitats, the EPA and the Corps initiated a study in 1986 to identify and evaluate the district's wetlands in accordance with the Wetland Evaluation Technique

(WET) developed by the Corps. The study, known as the Hackensack Meadowlands Advanced Identification or "AVID" study, will serve as one of several important planning tools for the SAMP and master plan.

In addition to the AVID, HMDC commissioned a team of experts to prepare several key master plan revision studies. Extensive land use, housing, and demographic studies were prepared by the HMDC staff and consultants. These studies provided the basis for growth projections in the district. A highly sophisticated transportation model was developed for the district that provides the capacity to test alternate land use scenarios on an ongoing basis. A cultural resource reconnaissance of the area was also undertaken. Additionally, special water quality evaluations and studies, prepared over a period of many years, were useful in establishing environmental base conditions. These master plan background studies provide a baseline of information from which the components of the SAMP are drawn.

Early in the planning process, HMDC staff developed several alternative land use/development scenarios, comparing wetland and upland development and land use configurations at varying degrees of density. Data was also collected on environmental problem sites and needs in the district, public and community facilities, as well as profiles of business establishments within the district. The studies provided the basis for the development of the Environmental Improvement Plan.

Following the signing of the Memorandum of Understanding in 1988, the SAMP partner agencies created three working groups: a SAMP Committee, consisting of top management representatives of the partner agencies with authority to make policy decisions and to resolve conflicts and issues, and two staff-level subcommittees. One subcommittee meets regularly to serve as a "one-stop" joint processing and information resource for the public and prospective applicants and to address fill violations and other regulatory actions. A second group, the EIS Subcommittee, jointly evaluated the qualifications of prospective EIS consultants and recommended the selection of one contract. This subcommittee now meets regularly to address all EIS management and technical matters.

By the time the EIS commenced in late spring of 1990, the SAMP Committee and the two working subcommittees had worked out procedures for managing the SAMP process. However, the period between the signing of the Memorandum of Understanding in late 1988 and spring 1990 was fraught with tension and misconceptions among the SAMP partners. In part, this was due to misunderstandings about the agencies' missions. In particular, HMDC, which was established to halt uncontrolled development in the Meadowlands and to provide parks and recreational opportunities to the region, was perceived by federal resource agencies as being too pro-development. The agencies cited HMDC's role in allowing developments such as warehouses and the sports complex, which resulted in the loss of approximately 1,400 acres of wetlands in the Meadowlands.

In spring 1989, tensions among the SAMP partners had peaked. At that time, the agenda of the SAMP Committee meeting held at the EPA offices in New York City included a presentation by HMDC planners that focused on HMDC's plan for the district. The planners characterized the plan as conceptual and preliminary—and as something against which other plan configurations for the SAMP might be measured. The agency representatives assembled in the room insisted vehemently that concepts like the one sketched on the map before them only evolve out of a process that evaluates an unknown number of such configurations. Some agency staff implied that the map was evidence that HMDC had breached its obligations under the terms of the Memorandum of Understanding to develop a plan pursuant to the process outlined in the document.

During this same period, a SAMP Committee member commented, after an especially tense session, that an outsider would probably assume that all the people in the room that day conducted themselves as if they had been informed in advance that one of them would be executed by firing squad at the conclusion of the session.

In retrospect, much of the difficulty can be attributed to the relative absence of common ground among professional disciplines (engineers, scientists, planners) represented on the working groups. Remarkably, close and effective working relationships have emerged as a useful and long-term by-product of the SAMP process itself. The SAMP partners did not engage a professional mediator.

Coordination with Other Groups

In addition to SAMP Committee operations discussed above, HMDC consultations continue on a regular basis with other groups: the Meadowlands Chamber of Commerce and its several active committees; the Hackensack Meadowlands Municipal Committee, an umbrella group representing the political jurisdictions that comprise the District; and the HMDC Master Plan Advisory Committee, which consists of representatives from business, environmental, and community organizations. Additionally, the EPA and the Corps as the EIS co-lead agencies have appointed a Citizens Advisory Committee. Clearly, there has been substantial effort on the part of all SAMP partner agencies to keep local officials, environmental groups, and the business community informed and involved.

The U.S. Fish and Wildlife Service (FWS) was invited to participate in the SAMP as a full partner by signing the Memorandum of Understanding at the onset of the program in 1988. All four SAMP partner agencies have encouraged FWS to participate at least as an observer, but all of these efforts have not convinced FWS to participate.

The SAMP agencies, during negotiations of the Memorandum of Understanding, agreed that full, decision-making participation in the program required signing of the agreement. FWS proposed several conditions prerequisite to its execution of the memorandum. It was the consensus of the SAMP partners that certain conditions imposed by FWS were unacceptable principally because they did not accurately reflect the advisory role of FWS pursuant to 1977 amendments to the Clean Water Act. The conditions tended to undermine a fundamental objective of the SAMP to address a spectrum of environmental impacts in the district as part of the planning process that could prove to be a basis in the EIS (a focal component of the SAMP program) to broaden the Clean Water Act Section 404(b)(1) guidelines reliance on aquatic ecosystems.

The contention of FWS that compliance with the section 404(b)(1) guidelines specifically means that the discharge of fill cannot be permitted, even if social, economic, or environmental factors suggest otherwise, could not be deemed consistent with fundamental SAMP objectives. A pivotal component of the SAMP is to incorporate the section 404(b)(1) guidelines into the planning process at the earliest possible time. The SAMP partners felt that the conditions imposed by FWS would undermine the spirit of the Memorandum of Understanding and the SAMP at the onset by precluding a plan for the district that both demonstrates area-wide environmental benefit and also permits a minimum filling of wetlands.

A process for identifying wetlands in the district as generally suitable or unsuitable for fill placement was undertaken by EPA, supported by an interagency team, beginning in mid-1986. The process involved preparation of a data base on wetlands through the assessment of wetland functions and the subsequent development of criteria relating to suitability for fill placement. Utilizing an updated version of the WET originally developed by the Corps, the study designated and mapped the degree to which each of 147 wetland assessment districts within the Meadowlands could perform certain wetland functions at low, high and moderate levels. A rating system for AVID data was developed by EPA staff to support its "suitable/unsuitable for filling" probability ratings.

Integrating the EIS and Area-Wide Plan

Integrating an area-wide plan with the EIS raises several issues. These include:

1. The development needs of HMDC

2. The out-of-district or practicable alternatives tests

3. The development of a hybrid land use plan and preferred alternative plan

As mentioned earlier, HMDC expended considerable resources in articulating its social and economic needs in the district. This included consultant studies of the real estate and housing markets, as well as social and environmental needs. The district's needs were expressed through the ability of nonresidential development to contribute to the environmental improvements. This would be done through impact fees and other contributions which in turn would provide funding for resource protection. The residential needs were expressed through their ability to provide low- and moderate-income housing consistent with the regulations of the New Jersey Council on Affordable Housing, a state agency charged with assigning housing needs to each municipality under the state's housing laws.

Agreement among the SAMP partners with regard to the needs of the district is crucial to the development of a comprehensive land use plan. Although HMDC presented cogent arguments for the commercial and nonresidential components, the residential needs became intertwined with inner city issues. Questions were raised about whether the construction of new residential units in the district would hamper the rehabilitation of housing in older cities outside the district. HMDC was able to show that the increase in employment combined with an existing jobs-to-housing imbalance in the district would stimulate an increase in housing development as well as encourage inner city housing rehabilitation. There are presently about 70,000 jobs and 3,000 housing units in the district.

The SAMP agencies recognize that they will be breaking new ground with the programmatic EIS. The current objective of the SAMP is to prepare an EIS with the EPA and the Corps serving as co-lead agencies. In effect, HMDC is an unconventional "applicant" in the federal 404 permit process, bringing forward alternative master plan scenarios for evaluation of their impacts under a federal EIS.

These plans included designations of several areas:

1. Wetlands driven—no disturbances of aquatic sites

2. No SAMP action—continuation of existing ad hoc approach without master plan revision and continuation of federal permitting policy

3. SAMP alternatives/representative land use configurations

   (a) Selected limited growth centers/higher density, mixed-use development nodes

  (b) Linear concept development limited to highway corridor

  (c) Opportunistic scattered multi-use clusters

  (d) Redevelopment of upland sites

  (e) Development limited to low-quality wetlands

4. Out-of-district alternatives

  (a) Urban locations—older established cities in proximity to the district

  (b) Locations in the six-county region (an area identified in the Memorandum of Understanding consisting of the New Jersey counties of Hudson, Essex, Passaic, Union, Bergen, and the northern portion of Middlesex)

A standard imposed by the Memorandum of Understanding on all the SAMP alternatives to be tested in the EIS is that there can be no net loss of wetland values within the district and that a net overall environmental benefit in the district must be demonstrated. Further, the memorandum provided that no wetlands be designated for development unless the Section 404(b)(1) practicable alternatives requirement is satisfied. The overriding premise is that an evaluation of these alternative planning concepts in the EIS against criteria that incorporate the Corp's Public Interest Review, the National Environmental Policy Act (NEPA), and the federal Clean Water Act requirements would produce a SAMP and master plan acceptable to all parties.

The EIS will evaluate alternative plans, including plans that combine certain critical program elements: minimization of wetland impact; strict controls to protect wetlands; a program of environmental improvement initiatives designed to address air quality, water quality, and toxic waste problems; environmentally sensitive, mixed-use development limited to a small number of areas that discourages reliance on the automobile and achieves certain economic and social goals. A combination of such program components can incorporate Section 404(b)(1) guidelines and demonstrate both no net loss of wetland values and overall environmental benefit in the district.

The central focus of the planning process highlighted by the EIS is the goal of integrating alternative analyses into master planning. The emphasis is to address this pivotal aspect of the federal permitting process during the planning stage instead of in the conventional manner—as part of ad hoc federal actions on individual project fill permit applications. In accordance with this new procedure, HMDC could be assured, along with its constituents, that future federal permitting decisions will not undermine the master plan once it is revised to conform with the SAMP.

However, the central issue, for which "the jury is still out," is how the SAMP partner agencies can maintain a comprehensive planning perspective and still satisfy Section 404(b)(1) requirements. One of the unresolved issues is how to conduct a practicable alternatives analysis that fulfills Clean Water Act requirements when the proposal under review is a comprehensive plan instead of a specific development project and where HMDC authority is limited by statute to a geographic area that may or may not coincide with the geographic scope of conventional alternative analyses.

HMDC is legislatively mandated to address a myriad of formidable solid waste, contamination, and hazardous waste problems that impact wetlands and also have serious impacts on the overall environment. Accordingly, HMDC anticipates that a key component of its Master Plan and future agency program will be an environmental improvement program designed to harness private development and public sector resources both to protect wetlands and to effectuate other important environmental improvements in the Meadowlands. A permanent wetlands preservation and management area, incorporation wetlands areas already protected, is among the components being designed.

Constraints and Patterns That Will Shape the Master Plan

The approach taken by HMDC in the master plan adopted in 1972 was to define a "balanced community" in a traditional mold—a land use pattern dominated by a principal "downtown" and surrounded by satellite neighborhoods of lesser intensity. Industrial development was heavily represented in the 1972 master plan.

The planning concepts emerging today vary from the traditional model, shaped by several constraints and patterns.

THE WETLANDS INFLUENCE

A cursory look at the land within the district reveals the presence of 7,300 acres of remaining wetlands, which comprise most of the vacant land. The wetlands are scattered and preclude a centralized community with a single "downtown." Minimization of the number of wetland acres to be filled in the district is a goal embodied in the 1988 Memorandum of Understanding and shared by all of the SAMP partner agencies. Effectively, this goal requires a higher range of zoning densities if HMDC's economic and social program goals are to be fulfilled.

TRANSPORTATION CAPACITY

The elongated shape of the district is bisected by the Hackensack River, limiting travel opportunities. Limited river crossings and the physical layout of the existing highway and mass transit system are major plan constraints.

Further, any expansion of the transportation system to meet regional needs cannot be achieved equally in all parts of the district.

EXISTING AND FUTURE URBAN DEVELOPMENT

The district encompasses several built-up areas, including established residential neighborhoods and industrial, warehousing, and commercial districts developed since the early 1960s. Together these areas constitute a large part of the district. These existing patterns limit the types of land use that can occur on nearby tracts of land.

One of HMDC's legislative mandates is to foster the creation of jobs. Pursuant to this goal, HMDC seeks to capture a "reasonable" share of the region's future demand for commercial and residential space, because of its unique locational assets. If the district is not permitted to capture this share, a substantial portion of this activity will disperse to locations outside of the New York/New Jersey metropolitan region. Such a result would be detrimental to the region's economy and societal needs. Real estate research supports the notion that this pattern will result, both from the specific demand for space at district locations and the restrictive land use regulations and other impediments in surrounding jurisdictions that preclude the higher density, transportation oriented, mixed-use development that is feasible within the district.

There are sites within the district, located principally in upland areas, that appear eligible for treatment as redevelopment areas in accordance with applicable New Jersey redevelopment statutes. These areas are potential locations that could effectively serve future regional needs for new industrial and warehousing activities. District land values and locational factors would make such uses infeasible at other locations.

New Jersey Supreme Court rulings, New Jersey Council on Affordable Housing (COAH) regulations, and other state housing policy objectives impose additional constraints on the master plan by mandating the production of low- and moderate-income housing in the district.

WASTE DISPOSAL ISSUES

Significant contamination and toxic waste problems exist in some parts of the district. Improvement and remediation of these sites, many of which are wetlands, is one objective of the SAMP. Government regulations affecting these areas constrain and shape the land use component of the master plan. Further, the locations of both known and suspected contaminated sites serve as important constraints over adjacent development.

Managing the solid waste needs of the district and surrounding municipalities is one HMDC's legislative mandates. Almost all of its 25 landfills are inactive. Thus, in addition to finding new landfill space, the commission will focus its efforts on resource recovery, recycling, and the transfer of solid waste to other locations.

In addition to these waste disposal issues, the district's four sewer districts fragment the area and thus constrain new development.

Wetlands Policies

The February 1990 Memorandum of Agreement between the EPA and the Corps articulates policy and procedures to be used to determine the type and level of mitigation necessary to demonstrate compliance with the Clean Water Act Section 404(b)(1) guidelines. These relate to the federal agency's objective to restore and maintain the chemical, physical, and biological integrity of wetlands. The wetland avoidance-minimization-mitigation hierarchy articulated in this agreement and its special treatment of SAMPs and regional plans constrains land use planning in the district.

Furthermore, the SAMP policy of no net loss of wetlands values, specified in the August 1988 Memorandum of Understanding, and the SAMP requirement for a demonstration of overall new environmental benefit in the District, also constrains future land use. These policies effectively preclude or limit areas within the District where certain activities can occur if such locations adversely impact on EIS demonstration of overall environmental benefit.

Looking to the Future: A Multi-nodal Land Use Concept

The unusually complex and interrelated constraints and determinants in the Meadowlands together point toward a future pattern of land use that features multiple nodes of intense development that can accommodate existing and future demands and conditions in the district. Such multi-development nodes can maximize the potential of each location. The pace of development within each node would be controlled by the availability of infrastructure required to assure its proper functioning and thus would be sensitive to the environment. The various components of each node can be phased in as the required infrastructure to support the components of development becomes available. Each node offers an opportunity to integrate planning and development with appropriate environmental and preservation objectives and initiatives designed to tap the economic dynamism of private development within it.

By including residential as well as commercial and office uses, development nodes with a mix of interrelated uses would reduce peak-hour dependence on major regional highway transportation systems. Relatively high densities would minimize land coverage, increase open space within nodes, and, thus, maximize wetland preservation. The potential financial contributions to environmental initiatives from each unit of land developed within the node is likely to be directly proportional with the permitted use intensity.

Based on transportation, land use densities, and other criteria evaluated in the EIS, the master plan will establish the maximum development levels for each mixed-use node. HMDC land use regulations and zoning will assure that the permitted level of development at any time remains commensurate with the infrastructure needed to support it. This type of growth management phasing is essential to the proper functioning of the uses and facilities in the district. As required in the HMDC regulations, the nodal concept assures that all uses within each node will be " . . . suitably sited and placed in order to secure safety from fire, provide adequate light and air, prevent the over-crowding of the land and undue concentration of population, prevent traffic congestion, and, in general, will relate buildings and uses to each other so that aesthetic and use values are maximized."

Integral to the multi-nodal concept is the premise that harnessing development-generated opportunities for preservation and environmental improvements can contribute significantly to the preservation of wetlands in the district. Such a multi-nodal concept will help to fulfill the environmental and preservation objectives shared by all the SAMP partner agencies. Simultaneously, it can establish a long sought overall ecological balance between developed and preserved areas in the Meadowlands. Each of the mixed-use developments will provide for concurrent mitigation of any ecological impacts. Development phases within each node can be accompanied by a corresponding on-site or off-site mitigation.

Benefits of Planning with the SAMP

HMDC anticipates several benefits from the integrated planning and SAMP process. It is anticipated that the master plan will designate specific areas within the district for mixed-use development that will maximize the area's locational potential and at the same time is sensitive to the environment by calibrating and phasing development with the availability of infrastructure. In addition, the plan will:

- Designate specific areas for permanent wetlands preservation and management

- Identify areas in the district that may be eligible for designation as redevelopment areas under state statutes

- Develop a long-term environmental improvement program for the district, with enforceable mitigation, preservation, open space, and other needed land use regulations and procedures

- Define procedures and regulations that integrate development with preservation and mitigation requirements through the utilization of transfer of development rights, mitigation banking, zoning restrictions, infrastructure, and other tools

Based on this plan, it is expected that the SAMP agencies will endorse a district-wide federal permitting policy applicable to future district development. The new policy, which could serve as a model for planning elsewhere, will ensure that projects in conformity with HMDC's master plan are deemed to have no practicable alternative pursuant to Section 404(b)(1) guidelines. (Note: The signators to the Memorandum of Understanding provided for the possibility that in "exceptional and unforeseeable circumstances," supplemental analyses might be appropriate. However, examples of such circumstances were not specified.)

The SAMP partner agencies will obtain mutual assurances that all wetlands designated for protection will be preserved and restored and that there will be no net loss of wetland values in the district. As a result of the SAMP, HMDC will be assured by the federal agencies that future federal permitting decisions will not undermine or impede development that conforms with the adopted master plan.

Through institutionalization of streamlined joint program procedures already largely in place under the terms of the Memorandum of Understanding, a continuation of interagency permit processing and review procedures will continue to benefit both business and preservation interests.

State policy mandates in the areas of solid waste, economic development, housing, and the environment will continue to be addressed.

Conclusion

The Hackensack Meadowlands Special Area Management Plan is unique in that it will likely result in the development of a comprehensive land use plan, the implementation of a $900 million Environmental Improvement Plan, and delegation of some of the 404 regulatory process to HMDC. From a development standpoint, one of the most salient products of the SAMP will be that all development consistent with the SAMP and the resulting master plan for the Meadowlands will be relieved of the practicable alternatives test of the Clean Water Act. The SAMP would provide certainty to the development community concerning the type and location of projects that would be approved. It would also ensure that many of the remaining wetlands will be preserved and that no net loss of wetland values will occur. None of this would be possible under the existing regulatory framework.

The Meadowlands is still under strong development pressure. Each of the agencies involved in the SAMP recognizes that, under the ad hoc, case-by-case permitting system wetlands losses would continue and that no mechanism would be available to protect the most valuable wetland areas. Similarly, implementation of a master plan would be stymied by the uncertainty of the 404 permit process. All SAMP participants realized that they would have to reach a compromise in order to achieve a viable plan that would benefit everyone.

Based on the experience in the Meadowlands, some general conclusions can be drawn about the SAMP process. First, the planning process will take much longer than expected. Initially, the participants assumed the SAMP would be completed in three years. The project is now in its seventh year. Second, the level of detail required for both planning and environmental studies was much greater than anticipated. Detailed environmental and demographic baseline conditions were examined in order to understand the relationships between land use planning and the environment. Finally, the importance of establishing clear lines of communication and constructive interpersonal relationships among all the parties involved cannot be overemphasized. The Meadowlands demonstrated the importance of effective interagency coordination and of utilizing a mediator to resolve differences.

Although the integrated planning process is not complete, the Meadowlands effort has defined important issues that must be addressed in merging local, state, and federal planning and regulatory requirements, and it has indicated possible solutions that may be of use in other areas. The process has also highlighted the difficulties of marrying well-intended but narrowly oriented regulatory requirements within the basic planning functions of local and regional agencies.

CHAPTER 8

Balancing Conservation and Development in Chiwaukee Prairie, Wisconsin

Leah V. Haygood

EDITORS' SUMMARY

An 1800-acre lakefront area in the southeastern corner of Wisconsin had been partially developed when a planning effort was initiated to preserve wetlands and remnants of prairie habitat. The Southeast Wisconsin Regional Planning Commission convened a group of representatives of federal and state agencies, local governments, business and civic organizations, and property owners to prepare a plan that would balance open space preservation and urban development objectives. The planning process provided opportunities for resolving conflicting views that have forestalled probable landowner litigation. Haygood describes how the plan channels new development to upland areas and preserves important prairie uplands as well as more than 90 percent of the wetlands. Through acquisition and donations, about 60 percent of the area designated for protection has been purchased.

Background

Between late 1981 and 1985 in a quiet corner of Wisconsin, an often-intense struggle was carried on over the preservation of important wetlands and prairie and the use of properties that had been subdivided and sold as developable. During those four years, the regional planning commission prepared a land use management plan, the state environmental agency prepared an environmental impact statement (EIS); citizen groups on both sides of the issue formed and then lobbied local, state, and federal agencies; several public hearings were held; the Wisconsin Public Intervenor became involved; and the legislature passed new statutes directly relevant to the issue.

Geographic Features

The Chiwaukee Prairie/Carol Beach area, an 1,825-acre strip of land along Lake Michigan, lies in the extreme southeastern corner of Wisconsin, about midway between Chicago and Milwaukee, hence the name "Chiwaukee." Within the town of Pleasant Prairie in Kenosha County, the area is defined in part by natural boundaries and in part by political boundaries and manmade features. Lake Michigan borders it on the east, the state of Illinois on the south, a state highway and railroad right-of-way on the west, and the city limits of Kenosha on the north (see Figure 8.1). The following description of the area (referred to as the "planning area") is drawn from an EIS issued in 1985 by the Wisconsin Department of Natural Resources (DNR).

The planning area is about 72 percent open space and 28 percent urban uses. An extensive street network was laid out when parts of the area were platted. Some streets are currently in use, while others have been abandoned or lost to erosion along the shore of Lake Michigan; some streets were never constructed.

Most of the development in the area consists of scattered single-family residences. Other development includes the Trident Marina, the Kenosha Towne Club, a motel, several small farms, and a water pumping station for the Pleasant Prairie electric generating plant. Other portions of the planning area contain residential development ranging from sparsely scattered houses to well-developed residential neighborhoods. All of the residences in the area rely on on-site waste disposal systems, primarily septic tank systems, even though most of the soils in the area are unsuitable for on-site septic tank systems.

A total of 747 acres of wetlands have been identified in the planning area (see Figure 8.2). Most of the wetlands are located between the Chicago and Northwestern railroad right-of-way on the west and 1st Avenue on the east. These wetlands are part of a beach dune–ridge and swale complex in which the swales (low areas between ridges) are wetlands and the ridges, or uplands, are dry. Because the difference in elevation between ridges and swales is too small to delineate them individually, the majority of the ridge and swale areas are identified as wetlands even though there are upland areas included in them.

Among the more common wetland vegetation, a number of endangered, threatened, and watch-list prairie-wetland plant species have been identified in this area. Some of these species have been found in significant concentrations.

The Southeast Wisconsin Regional Planning Commission (SEWRPC)

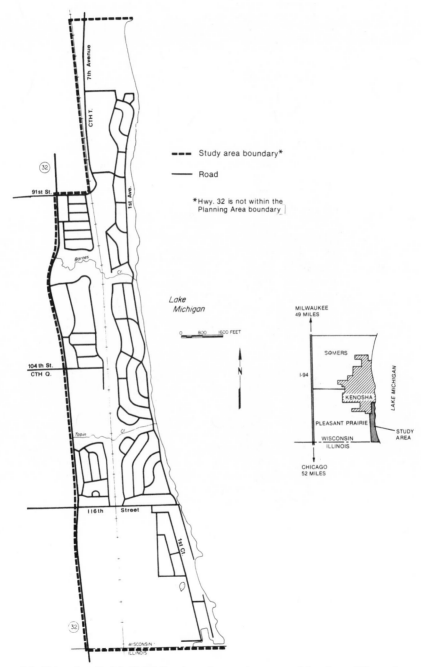

Figure 8.1 Chiwaukee Prairie/Carol Beach study area (courtesy of Southeast Wisconsin Regional Planning Commission).

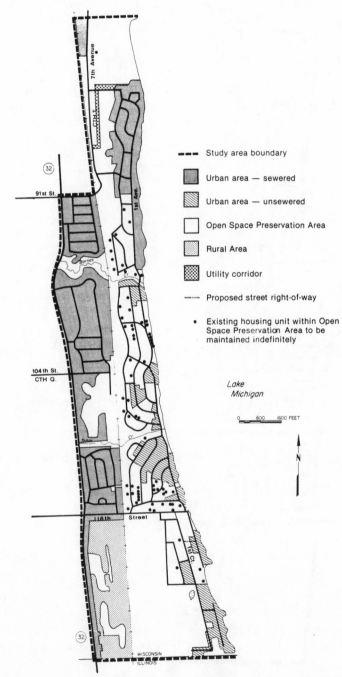

Study area boundary

Urban area — sewered

Urban area — unsewered

Open Space Preservation Area

Rural Area

Utility corridor

Proposed street right-of-way

• Existing housing unit within Open Space Preservation Area to be maintained indefinitely

Lake Michigan

0   800   1600 FEET

N

Figure 8.2 Final recommended land use management plan (courtesy of Southeast Wisconsin Regional Planning Commission).

identified 828 acres of prairies in the Chiwaukee Prairie/Carol Beach area. The significance of these prairies lies in their diversity of prairie vegetation and scarcity in Wisconsin. The vegetation cover today is much like the vegetation cover of 1833, when the original land survey took place, except for some areas of tree stand invasion.

The combination of wetlands and native prairies found in the Chiwaukee Prairie/Carol Beach area provides excellent habitat for a diversity of plant and animal species. The value of the natural resources in the planning area is supported by the designation of seven scientific and natural areas by the Wisconsin Scientific Areas Preservation Council. Together, the scientific and natural areas represent a total of 484 acres.

Over time, there have been attempts to develop the Chiwaukee Prairie/Carol Beach area for residential and private recreational purposes. About 1,246 acres, or 68 percent of the total planning area, have been platted for residential development. Residential lands occupy 237 acres, or 13 percent of the planning area, although 1,659 private interests owned 1,161 acres of real property in the area in 1980.[1]

Development Pressure

The Chiwaukee Prairie/Carol Beach area has long been the focus of development interest because of its attractive lakefront location. In all likelihood, only its poor soils (from a development standpoint), its erosion problems on the lakefront, and its location beyond reasonable commuting distance from Milwaukee and Chicago have allowed it to remain relatively undeveloped.

The first major effort to develop the area occurred in the 1920s, when Edith Rockefeller McCormick purchased about 1,800 acres for the development of a "model city." Several roads were built during the 1920s and the outlet of one of the creeks traversing the area was altered, but the model city project failed following the stock market crash of 1929.[2] Miscellaneous projects were pursued in the 1930s and early 1940s, including construction of a golf course and several summer homes.

The next major effort to develop the area came after World War II. In 1946 a Chicago real estate group purchased 1,200 acres in the area that they planned to develop as Carol Beach Estates. More than 2,700 lots were subdivided and sold. By the early 1960s, 285 homes and several roads had been built in a few densely developed neighborhoods scattered throughout the planning area. By the mid-1980s, 643 lots had been developed. Most of the undeveloped lots were held by absentee owners for speculation or eventual second or retirement home construction.[3]

The pattern of development was determined in part by the unsuitability of many soils in the area to support septic systems. The more densely settled areas occur where soils are more able to support septic systems. The soil limitations, and a growing awareness of the unique natural resources of the area, prompted the state of Wisconsin to consider designating undeveloped portions of the area as a state park. The state park plan was not pursued because of the diffuse land ownership and relatively high prices for the subdivided land. However, since 1965, The Nature Conservancy had been purchasing land at the southern end of the area, and by 1983 it owned 91 acres and the University of Wisconsin owned 55 acres as part of a contiguous preserve.

A 120-acre site at the northern end of the area has also been the focus of development proposals. In the mid-1940s the Wisconsin Electric Power Company (WEPCO) purchased 120 acres of dune property in the northernmost portion of the planning area for use as a power plant site. An additional 25 acres were acquired in 1980. Strong local opposition arose, and WEPCO eventually located the power plant five miles inland. As of mid-1979, WEPCO had stated its intention to retain ownership of the land, maintaining that it considered it suitable for utility purposes.[4]

Land Use Issues and Conflicts

By the early 1980s, the expectations created by the subdivision and sale of lots in the Chiwaukee Prairie/Carol Beach area were in conflict with the limited suitability of many of the lots for development and a growing appreciation of the area as the site of important wetlands and remnant prairie habitat. An improving economy in the city of Kenosha, north of the planning area, suggested that new housing construction might accelerate from its relatively lethargic pace. As noted in SEWRPC's Land Use Management Plan for the area, "the future of the Chiwaukee Prairie/Carol Beach area has been uncertain for some time because of the divergent natural resource preservation and urban development objectives attendant to the area, and because of the relatively large number of public agencies and private interests which are concerned with, or which may have a bearing on, future land use in the area."

At least six public agencies—the U.S. Army Corps of Engineers, the U.S. Environmental Protection Agency, the Wisconsin Department of Natural Resources, the Southeast Wisconsin Regional Planning Commission, Kenosha County, and the town of Pleasant Prairie—had some interest or responsibility in the area.

At the federal level, the U.S. Army Corps of Engineers has authority for issuing Section 404 permits for discharge of dredged or fill material into wetlands. In addition, under Section 10 of the Rivers and Harbors Act of 1899, the

Corps regulates structures that affect navigable U.S. waters, including the Lake Michigan frontage of the study area. The Corps was particularly interested in the Chiwaukee Prairie/Carol Beach area because, over the years, it had received numerous applications from landowners to fill lots for development. Because of the abundance of wetlands in the area, it anticipated receiving many more applications if development were to continue or accelerate.

The EPA Region V was also familiar with the area because of its joint responsibility with the Corps in administering the 404 program, and because of the distinctive natural features of the area.

At the state level, the DNR was responsible for implementing several policies and programs that affected the area and helped to precipitate the planning process. Chapter NR 1.95 of the Wisconsin Administrative Code sets general policies on wetlands preservation, protection, and management, including the protection of wetlands affected by state-sponsored or permitted activities, acquisition of high value wetlands, and enforcement of illegal activities.

In addition, Section 59.971 of the Wisconsin statutes requires counties to adopt shoreland zoning ordinances for all shoreland areas in unincorporated areas. The zoning is to protect public interests in these areas by preventing and controlling water pollution, by protecting spawning grounds and fish and aquatic life, by controlling land uses, and by preserving shore cover and scenic qualities. The Wisconsin statutes define shorelands as lands within 1,000 feet of the ordinary high-water mark of a navigable lake, pond, or flowage; and within 300 feet of the ordinary high-water mark or the landward side of the floodplain, whichever distance is greater, of a navigable river or stream.

The rules for establishing shoreland zoning ordinances in unincorporated areas of the state are found in Chapter NR 115, Wisconsin Administrative Code. In 1980 NR 115 was amended to require counties to establish shoreland/wetland zoning districts within their shoreland areas. The zoning districts are required to include all wetlands of five acres or more that are identified on the Wisconsin Wetlands inventory maps and located within shoreland areas. In those zoning districts, allowable activities include hunting and other recreation; harvesting of wild crops; planting, thinning, and harvesting of timber; various agricultural activities; construction and maintenance of duck blinds, piers, docks, and walkways; and maintenance of highways and bridges. These uses are permitted provided no draining, dredging, ditching, excavating, tiling, filling, or flooding of wetlands or other navigable waters occurs. Lands included in the shoreland district, but not the shoreland/wetland district, are subject to the general shoreland zoning restrictions including limits on lot sizes, required setbacks, and other regulations.

In establishing shoreland and shoreland/wetland zoning districts, counties are required to keep their regulations current and effective to remain in compliance with the statutes and minimum standards established by the DNR. If the county fails to meet the standards, the DNR is authorized to adopt a shoreland ordinance to be administered by that county. Thus, although the state shoreland law clearly contemplates the local government as the locus of zoning activity affecting wetlands, the state bears the ultimate responsibility for ensuring the effectiveness of the zoning programs.

The DNR also regulates public sanitary sewer service to protect water quality in the state. Under Chapters 144 and 147 of the Wisconsin Statutes and the Federal Clean Water Act, the DNR is required to review and take action to approve or reject plans for sewage treatment plants and sewer systems, including extensions of sanitary sewers. All sewer system plans must conform to an approved area-wide water quality management plan (known as "208" plans from Section 208 of the Clean Water Act authorizing their preparation).

All existing homes within the Chiwaukee Prairie/Carol Beach area at the time of the initiation of the planning process used septic systems or holding tanks. In the early 1980s, Kenosha County identified 11 failing residential septic systems within the area. Thus, the area was of interest to the state, which is responsible for protecting wetlands and water quality.

The Planning Process

No single event precipitated the initiation of a wetlands planning process in Chiwaukee Prairie. The DNR's requirements in 1980 that Kenosha County establish shoreland/wetland zoning, the state requirement for regulation of septic systems, the failure of septic systems within the area, and the identification of environmental corridors and farmland preservation areas (described below) all combined to suggest that the area needed a coordinated approach to planning.

In 1981 the town of Pleasant Prairie and the Kenosha County Office of Planning and Zoning Administration asked SEWRPC to bring together the concerned public agencies and private interests to address a wide range of issues relating to conservation and development of the area.

For a variety of reasons, SEWRPC was the logical planning agency for the study area: it is the region's Section 208 planning agency; it has traditionally provided technical assistance to local governments within its region in preparing plans and mapping natural and human features; it had taken the lead in identifying and developing plans to conserve farmlands; and it had pioneered the concept of "environmental corridors."

The process developed by the SEWRPC for this purpose involves a mapping overlay technique to identify areas containing concentrations of natural resource elements and natural resource–related elements, including a wide variety of lakes, streams, associated shorelands and floodlands, wetlands, prairies, wildlife habitat areas, and other sensitive lands. It also includes identification of existing and potential park and open space sites, historic sites, significant scenic areas and vistas, and natural and scientific areas.

When delineated, these mapped elements produce an essentially linear pattern of relatively narrow, elongated areas within the region which have been termed *environmental corridors* by the commission. In most jurisdictions, the environmental corridors constitute a relatively small percentage (perhaps 10 percent) of the area. In Chiwaukee Prairie/Carol Beach, however, 69 percent of the study area was considered primary environmental corridor.

The state regulations for 208 water quality plans prohibit sewer service in environmental corridors. Given development pressures on the Chiwaukee Prairie, SEWRPC had a strong interest in addressing land use issues in the area in a comprehensive framework.

Shoreland-wetland zoning caused considerable alarm among landowners because they feared that property values would decline, rezoned property might be condemned, and little or no compensation would be available. Many landowners from the area began forming associations to pressure local officials, investigate possible legal challenges, and, as wetland maps became available, challenge the accuracy of the wetland delineation.

Planning Objectives

As stated in materials distributed to attendees at a public hearing in October 1984, the primary purpose of the Chiwaukee Prairie/Carol Beach planning program was to develop a plan which would identify wetlands and uplands that should be protected and preserved in the public interest as well as other lands upon which urban growth could be accommodated. The planning process attempted to achieve a sound balance between open space preservation and urban development objectives within the area. Furthermore, it sought a way to fairly compensate those residential lot owners whose land would be placed in an open space preservation area. (The compensation issue had not been foreseen in initial statements of planning objectives. As the planning program proceeded, however, compensation to property owners emerged as an important concern.)

The resulting planning program recognized that both past platting and development activities and the past acquisition of open space areas meant that various individuals and groups had significant investments in the Chiwaukee

Prairie/Carol Beach area. Therefore, without a "compromise" plan, each group had something to lose, while with such a plan each group had something to gain.[5]

Participants in Planning

SEWRPC organized a technical advisory committee (TAC) to participate in the planning process. The lead governmental agencies on the committee included representatives of SEWRPC, the DNR, Kenosha County, and the town of Pleasant Prairie. Also involved were several federal agencies—the Corps (the voting member), EPA, and the U.S. Fish and Wildlife Service (FWS), which retained advisory status. In addition to the governmental agencies, voting members of the TAC included representatives of the Wisconsin Electric Power Company, the Kenosha Water Utility, the Wisconsin chapter of The Nature Conservancy, the Wisconsin League of Women Voters, the Carol Beach Estates Property Owners Association, and the University of Wisconsin at Milwaukee Department of Botany. At the first meeting of the TAC, held in August 1982, the committee agreed to add two representatives of property owners in the area so that residents from the northern, middle, and southern thirds of the study area would be represented.

As is customary, SEWRPC played several roles. With assistance from the other agencies, it performed technical studies, research, and mapping and drafted the Land Use Management Plan. It also convened the TAC to oversee development of the plan and, albeit informally, facilitated consensus on the plan. SEWRPC's own status on the advisory committee was as a "nonvoting member."

The commission itself consists of three members from each of the seven counties in the southeast Wisconsin region. SEWRPC also has a professional staff of planners and administrators who carry out the technical studies and plan preparation. The commissioners generally act on recommendations from the staff and also participate in activities such as recommending advisory committee members. In carrying out its planning activities, the commission must appoint advisory committees representing the various public and private interests affected by the plan. As is the case with the products of most comprehensive planning processes, the plans themselves are not usually binding—it is up to other governmental entities to implement them through zoning ordinances, acquisition of land, and other measures.[6]

The Wisconsin DNR is the lead environmental agency in the state, overseeing both environmental quality and natural resource issues. The DNR played several key roles in deciding the fate of the Chiwaukee Prairie. The department's authority to approve or disapprove the 208 plan for the area and to impose zoning on local governments that failed to zone for shoreland and shoreland–wetland areas gave them considerable regulatory power. As described below, as the planning process proceeded, the Wisconsin legislature appropriated funds with which DNR could acquire areas such as Chiwaukee Prairie. Thus, the DNR had nonregulatory tools at its disposal as well.

At the second meeting of TAC, the Department of Natural Resources' representative described its major concerns as the preservation of wetlands and other natural resources and the cost-effective correction of failing septic system problems. The DNR staff arranged to meet with SEWRPC and town and county staffs to identify "developable wetlands" within the study area. The DNR also helped with some of the technical aspects of the plan by supplying data and performing field work within the study area. In addition, the DNR applied for federal coastal zone management funds on behalf of SEWRPC to partially fund the study.

The Kenosha County Office of Planning and Zoning Administration, which is responsible for implementing shoreland zoning, was represented on TAC by its director. At the outset of the planning process, however, the county was less than convinced that shoreland and shoreland–wetland zoning would ultimately take precedence over existing zoning that essentially encouraged development. Thus, the county's aim was to achieve a balance between urban development and open space preservation in the study area. From the county's perspective, any land use management plan would need to attempt to protect areas essential to the maintenance of environmental values and at the same time, accommodate development consistent with the past commitment of the area to urban use. The county was also represented on TAC by an elected official on the Kenosha County Board.

Somewhat less central to the process, the Corps was granted status as a full voting member of the committee because of its key role in implementing any plan that called for filling wetlands. EPA was not a voting member but was invited to attend meetings and comment on technical and jurisdictional matters. Both EPA and FWS seemed to adopt an advisory rather than an advocacy role. The agencies, however, recognized the value of the planning process in resolving the wetlands issues of the Chiwaukee Prairie and, as the process neared completion, used the plan as the basis for one of the nation's first 404 advance identification actions.

The town of Pleasant Prairie was represented on TAC by the town clerk, who also served as committee chair, and by the chair of the Town Plan Commission. In addition, the town engineer and the town planner were nonvoting members of the committee. The town of Pleasant Prairie received some of the funding obtained by SEWRPC to assist in the technical plan preparation and contributed in-kind services, as well.

The town's concerns, as stated by the chair of the Town Plan Commission, were to protect the interests of both existing residents and owners of buildable property in the study area and, at the same time, to preserve the most significant environmental areas.

Technical Aspects of Plan Preparation

SEWRPC's planning process involved overlay mapping of dozens of natural and anthropogenic features, largely using available information. Natural features mapped included areas within 1,000 feet of a body of water, critical plant habitat, critical wildlife habitat, wetlands, and uplands. The plan also considered projected population levels, land use and land ownership patterns, and the legal land use management framework.

To delineate wetlands, SEWRPC biologists, in cooperation with DNR and as part of the Wisconsin wetlands inventory, mapped the wetlands and identified their type based on aerial photographs. Following initial publication of the maps, several hundred landowners requested on-site inspections to verify the wetlands identifications. SEWRPC and DNR staff conducted field inspections using the U.S. Army Corps of Engineers' definition and delineation method.

Following mapping, they evaluated the wetlands according to several parameters important to implementing the shoreland–wetland zoning ordinance:

- Stormwater and floodwater storage capacity

- Maintenance of dry season streamflow, or the discharge of groundwater to a wetland, the recharge of groundwater from a wetland to another area, or the flow of groundwater through a wetland

- Filtering or storage of sediments, nutrients, heavy metals, or organic compounds that would otherwise drain into navigable waters

- Shoreline protection against soil erosion

- Fish spawning, breeding, nursery, or feeding grounds

- Wildlife habitat

- Areas of special recreational, scenic, or scientific interest, including scarce wetland types

The method of analysis varied for the different parameters and included modeling, use of published information, and field studies.

Development of the Plan

SEWRPC initiated the planning process in March 1982. The general process involved SEWRPC's preparation, with assistance from the other lead agencies, of draft chapters of the plan for TAC review and approval by majority vote. The intention was to move fairly quickly toward outlining a plan that designated areas for conservation and development. By the third meeting, the committee reviewed a preliminary plan.

The process, however, very quickly hit some obstacles. While reviewing the legal framework for the plan, committee members raised a number of questions, particularly concerning the need to compensate owners of rezoned land. Although initial meetings were not well attended by the general public, public interest expanded rapidly, and by the third committee meeting 32 people attended, including three members of environmental groups, a reporter from the *Kenosha News,* and individuals who described themselves as property owners.

The preliminary plan provided for preservation of the Kenosha Sand Dunes at the north end of the study area (owned by the power company) and the Chiwaukee Prairie at the south end (largely owned by The Nature Conservancy and the University of Wisconsin). The two areas would be linked by a continuous environmental corridor consisting mostly of platted residential lots to be acquired and placed in conservancy zoning. The plan called for moving several existing houses out of the environmental corridor, installing sewer systems in several areas earmarked for development, and allowing extensive development of apartments or condominiums along the lakefront. The rationale for extensive lakefront development (which might have seemed inappropriate given the high rate of shoreline erosion) was that such developments might be able to support the costs of erosion control, while single-family homes probably would not. The plan also provided for a new railroad crossing and a new road along the state line.

Virtually all aspects of the plan were controversial, particularly the lack of assured compensation to owners of rezoned properties. Some members objected to the apartment and condominium plan and said that single-family homeowners could provide adequate shore protection, or that the Corps might provide it. The representative of the Corps, however, held out little hope that individual efforts at erosion control would be effective or that the Corps would step in at any point in the next several decades. The Nature Conservancy representatives were cautiously positive about the proposed plan but expressed concern about a new road adjacent to their preserve. They also were careful to state that they would not have the funds to acquire all of the rezoned land and that their interest was only in acquiring biologically significant land from willing sellers.

Local officials expressed concern about the loss of tax revenues from rezoned lands, and the power company expressed concern over the designation of the Kenosha Sand Dunes for preservation. Some members felt too much land was proposed for the environmental corridor, while others felt too much development would be encouraged. At the third meeting, the committee still was unable to reach agreement. SEWRPC agreed to present the plan to a joint meeting of the Pleasant Prairie Town Board, the Town Plan Commission, and the County Planning and Zoning Committee and to draft a chapter describing the proposed plan.

In late October 1982, SEWRPC met with local officials. A story about the meeting, printed in the *Kenosha News* on October 27, 1982, began: "Kenosha County officials will demand some answers from the Wisconsin Department of Natural Resources before a study of Chiwaukee Prairie/Carol Beach continues. The question most often asked is: Does DNR have the power to place already platted land under the confines of shoreland–wetland zoning?" The article reported that County Board Supervisor Wayne Koessl stated he would not vote to rezone the area to conservancy. On a slightly more conciliatory note, Supervisor James Fonk, a TAC member, said "Instead of trying to second guess the DNR, let's find out firsthand what they intend to do and what kind of jurisdiction they have." At that point, the law on shoreland–wetland zoning was untested. County officials decided that the zoning study should not proceed until the DNR's authority was confirmed.

A few weeks later, the DNR distributed the wetlands maps produced by SEWRPC that were to serve as the basis for shoreland–wetland zoning. Under the zoning regulations, the county government and planning-area residents had 180 days to review the accuracy of the maps and request an on-site inspection. The deadline for requesting an inspection was later extended to May, 1984, due to intense lobbying by property owners' associations and the number of requests for on-site verification of the delineations.

Along with property owners' associations, the Racine-Kenosha Sierra Club and other environmental groups joined the debate over development and preservation of the Chiwaukee Prairie. The Wisconsin Environmental Network (a coalition of environmental groups), the Hoy Nature Club, and the Sierra Club sent over 200 letters to the secretary of the DNR urging preservation of the area.

In October 1983 the DNR decided to prepare an EIS for the Chiwaukee Prairie/Carol Beach area. The EIS specifically addressed the impacts of proposed sewering alternatives, an issue over which the DNR had clear responsibility. The EIS was linked to the SEWRPC process, however, in that sewer locations depended upon the SEWRPC plan. By setting in motion a decision-making process that could proceed separately from the SEWRPC process, preparation of the EIS served to reinforce the DNR's authority in establishing shoreland zoning.[7] The EIS took about a year to draft.

The question of providing compensation to landowners affected by rezoning was beginning to be played out in the larger political arena. In February 1984 State Senator John Maurer introduced legislation to exempt lots platted before 1980 from shoreland–wetland zoning. In addition, the bill provided for compensation to owners of any rezoned wetlands. The intent of the bill was clearly to place some limits on the DNR's authority. The *Kenosha News* (February 17, 1984) reported that Senator Maurer remarked, "We knew it would get the attention of the DNR. A lot of people have been upset by the DNR's rather forceful habit of getting what they want." Although the legislation did not pass, it may have helped to pave the way for legislation introduced in January 1985 that provided the DNR with additional funds to acquire significant natural resources.

The Wisconsin Public Intervenor also became involved in the controversy. Fairly unique in state governments, the Wisconsin Public Intervenor is an individual within the Department of Justice who intervenes in various procedures as a representative of the public interest. In this case, the Public Intervenor seemed to be aligned mostly with environmental interests that were not directly involved in the planning process.

By the time the committee reconvened in February 1984, SEWRPC had prepared four alternative plans—a "maximum development" plan, a "maximum preservation" plan, a "development–preservation" plan, and a "no action" plan. The TAC reviewed the alternative plans at the meeting but requested additional time to consider the plans before voting to recommend an alternative.

In a meeting attended by over 100 people in early May 1984, the TAC reviewed the compromise development–preservation plan. SEWRPC, in what was perhaps an effort to encourage the committee to act, had announced several days earlier that it was prepared to recommend adoption of the development–preservation plan. Representatives of property owners and local government officials proposed a variety of amendments to the plan, including:

- Revision of the wetland inventory map based on lot-by-lot survey

- Acquisition of lots in the open space preservation area at fair market value

- Reservation of land for expansion of the Kenosha sewage treatment plant

- Provisions made for the expansion of the Trident Marina

- Provision of a corridor for the extension of utilities along 7th Avenue, and for sanitary service along both sides of the roads within the proposed urban areas

- Provision of a 400-foot-wide utility corridor to WEPCO's pumping station

All of these amendments and the plan were approved by the committee.

Several members, including the Corps representative, abstained. The DNR representative voted against the plan, citing concerns over the wetland mapping and extension of sanitary sewer service to all proposed urban areas. Committee members agreed to review the plan with their constituencies and meet again.

The sixth TAC meeting in September 1984 had a similar outcome, with committee members agreeing to table the plan for further review. However, they also agreed that the plan should be the subject of a public hearing. Shortly after the TAC meeting, the Wisconsin Public Intervenor recommended to SEWRPC that the plan be rejected because of its accommodation of several proposed developments, including the Trident Marina, expansion of the Kenosha sewage treatment plant, a utility corridor, and sewering of subdivisions.

On October 23, 1984, SEWRPC held a public hearing on the "preliminary recommended plan" that was attended by about 200 people. More than 70 individuals and organizations submitted written comments. The executive director of SEWRPC presented the plan at the hearing, stressing its benefits and the alternatives to its adoption—specifically, that owners of wetlands would be subject to case-by-case permit review and the possible, if not likely, denial of permits; that wetland–shoreland zoning would also preclude filling; that acquisition by the state would not be an assured alternative; and that protection of the natural resources would be incomplete.

SEWRPC's summary of comments at the public meeting grouped comments into three general categories—those who supported the plan (five, including town officials), those generally opposed to any large-scale preservation effort encompassing both uplands and wetlands and concerned about property values (21, including landowners and WEPCO), and those concerned that the plan fell short of adequately protecting the natural environment (145 individuals and organizations, including environmental groups, the Public Intervenor, and DNR).

Given its role as approver of the final plan, DNR's comments were perhaps the most significant. DNR indicated that it would not be able to approve the plan unless several changes were made, including: that all "special value" wetlands (as defined in Chapter NR 115 of the Wisconsin Administrative Code) be placed in a preservation area; that the north-south utility corridor be eliminated and the east-west corridor minimized; that the marina expansion area be redefined to exclude any significant wetlands or any plant habitat areas that contain endangered or threatened species; that the expansion area for the Kenosha sewage treatment plant be eliminated; and that proposed sewer service to homes in the open space preservation area be deleted.

SEWRPC published its response to the comments in the plan document itself. Several comments pertained to the need for more data on wetland boundaries, rare and endangered plants, groundwater hydrology, etc. In most cases, SEWRPC declined to seek more data, noting that "these requests for additional information reflect a lack of understanding of, and appreciation for, the planning process and its iterative nature. Good planning practice, as well as budgetary constraints, dictate that . . . a plan should be prepared using the information adequate for that purpose, although not necessarily adequate for later facilities, or project, planning purposes."

The final recommended plan prepared by SEWRPC incorporated the following changes from the preliminary plan:

- For consistency with Chapter NR 115 of the Wisconsin Administrative Code, all "special value" wetlands not already included in the preservation area were added. Some of the areas affected were within the expansion area for the Trident Marina and, thus, the expansion area was deleted.

- The land reservation area for the Kenosha treatment plant expansion was eliminated because of the many comments against it and lack of proponents.

- Utility corridors were reduced.

- Drainage improvements were eliminated and floodplain areas added to the preservation area.

- The recommended sanitary sewer service area was reduced to eliminate sewer extensions through the preservation area.

Thus, the changes to the plan accommodated most of the DNR's comments and eliminated several pro-development amendments adopted at the May 1984 TAC meeting. The net effect of the changes was to reduce the area proposed for development and increase the area set aside for preservation by about 18 percent. The final recommended plan would preserve 404 of the 408 acres of "special value" wetlands within the shoreland zoning area. In total, 92 percent of the 747 acres of wetlands in the area would be preserved.

The plan also would preserve 84 percent of valuable uplands and 81 percent of the 828 acres of prairie found in the study area, including 95 percent of the "high-quality" prairie area.

Seventy-two homes remained in the area designated for preservation. The plan recommended that these homes be maintained indefinitely and not rendered nonconforming uses under the Kenosha County zoning ordinance.

The final plan recommended the acquisition, from willing sellers, of 989 undeveloped platted lots totaling 310 acres within the preservation area. The price paid for lots was to be based on the cost of comparable lots in areas designated for development. An additional 171 acres of unplatted lands were recommended for acquisition.

The Technical and Citizen Advisory Committee met in January 1985 to review the recommended plan as modified in response to public comments. Legislation had been introduced to establish a natural heritage fund for DNR to use to acquire ecologically significant lands. The Chiwaukee Prairie area would receive priority as an acquisition, and DNR announced that it would accept the SEWRPC land use plan as an acquisition plan, thereby expediting the acquisition process.

The committee discussed the plan and agreed to several changes, including that the plan be modified to adapt to the timing and availability of DNR funds for acquisition. The committee approved the plan with only the Wisconsin Electric Power Company and the representative of the League of Women Voters voting against it and the Corps of Engineers abstaining.

Implementation

The SEWRPC Final Recommended Plan set out a variety of mechanisms for implementing its recommendations, most of which have been completed or undertaken.

In August 1984, before final agreement on the recommended plan, EPA Region V and the Corps jointly issued an Advance Identification (ADID) designating wetlands in the environmental corridor of Chiwaukee Prairie/Carol Beach area as unsuitable for development. The ADID covered several environmental corridors in southeast Wisconsin.

The Corps suspended its general permits in the planning area and issued a permit to the town to fill the few wetland areas designated for development. Kenosha County implemented the shoreland rezoning in stages. First, it rezoned areas in the county outside of Chiwaukee Prairie/Carol Beach; it then adopted the text of the plan and finally the maps.[8]

After DNR completed its EIS process in 1985, it accepted the SEWRPC plan as a modification to the 208 Water Quality Plan. DNR also set out to implement the acquisition process by sending a letter to the approximately 600 landowners within the acquisition area. Two-thirds responded that they were willing to sell their land, and DNR began acquiring options to purchase the highest priority lands.

DNR targeted approximately 615 acres of land for acquisition. As of June 1994, the Department had purchased 314 acres, most of it single quarter-acre lots at a time, for a total cost of $1,110,000. Lot prices range from about $8,000 to over $20,000.[9] DNR purchases land only from willing sellers and purchases only unimproved property. The Wisconsin chapter of The Nature Conservancy and the University of Wisconsin at Parkside combined own 227 acres, and a local group called the Chiwaukee Prairie Preservation Fund purchased about five acres of land in an area known as Barnes Prairie.

In addition, in September 1993 the Wisconsin Electric Power Company donated approximately 63 acres of the Kenosha Sand Dunes to The Nature Conservancy, which has announced plans to give the land to DNR. According to The Nature Conservancy, the property contains about 15 to 20 acres of wet prairie that, with considerable work, could be restored. The entire shoreline is buttressed with rip-rap, and the dunes continue to be a playground for dune buggies.[10]

Both DNR and The Nature Conservancy are still buying lots as they become available. Acquisition is complicated by the number of small landowners and by the subdividing that occurred years ago, including utility easements along virtually every road, even those never built. The Nature Conservancy is attempting to determine a means for extinguishing those easements. A chronology of events of the Chiwaukee Prairie land use plan is given in the accompanying box.

A Chronology of Chiwaukee Prairie Events

7/14/81	Preliminary field work for mapping of wetlands in Chiwaukee Prairie (DNR 1985, pp. 2–65)
8/18/82	First meeting of Technical and Citizen Advisory Committee—review of background chapters of plan; agreement to add representatives of homeowners
9/1/82	Second meeting of TAC—review of "Legal Land Use Management Framework" leads to questions of compensating owners of rezoned land
10/7/89	Third meeting of TAC—review of preliminary land use management plan; many questions and objections raised; agreement to present plan to relevant Pleasant Prairie and Kenosha County committees and boards
10/27/82	Kenosha County officials demand answers on DNR's authority to enforce shoreland–wetland zoning before study continues
11/10/82	Kenosha County Planning and Zoning Committee receives wetlands maps from DNR (DNR 1985, pp. 2–65)

2/83	Kenosha County Planning and Zoning Committee meets with chief of DNR
10/83	DNR decides to prepare EIS on Chiwaukee plan
11/83	DNR holds public hearing on proposal to prepare EIS
1/84	State legislator seeks to exempt platted lots from rezoning
2/28/84	Fourth meeting of TAC—review of four "alternative land use management plans"; approval of any plan delayed 30 days to allow additional review
5/3/84	Fifth meeting of TAC—review of compromise plan; SEWRPC recommends its adoption; majority vote to amend the plan generally in the direction of more development
5/15/84	Deadline for filing request for on-site inspection to verify presence of wetlands on property
7/84	Wisconsin Public Intervenor asks National Park Service to place Chiwaukee Prairie on "list of damaged and threatened natural landmarks"
8/13/84	Corps and EPA issue joint notice of "Advance Identification of Sites Unsuitable for Discharge of Dredged and Fill Material" covering most of the wetlands in the area (DNR 1985, A5-2)
9/6/84	Sixth meeting of TAC—review of changes to compromise plan; further suggested changes and agreement to table the plan for further review
9/14/84	Public intervenor recommended to SEWRPC that plan be rejected because it is biased toward development
10/23/84	Public hearing on plan as revised in response to TAC comments
11/7/84	DNR Draft EIS released for public comment (DNR 1985, pp. 1–3)
12/17/84	Public hearing on DNR Draft EIS (DNR 1985, pp. 1–3)
1/15/85	Seventh meeting of TAC—DNR announces availability of funds for acquisition; plan approved 12 to 2
2/85	Publication of "A Land Use Management Plan for the Chiwaukee Prairie-Carol Beach Area of Pleasant Prairie Kenosha County, Wisconsin," including "Final Recommended Plan," approved by TAC

6/85	Publication of DNR Final EIS—assesses three SEWRPC alternatives plus "phased sewer service alternative" and "no action" alternative

1985–1994 Acquisition of land by DNR and others

Sources: TAC meeting minutes and *Kenosha News,* unless otherwise indicated

Conclusions

The development of the Chiwaukee Prairie land use plan furnishes a good example of a planning process that provides the vehicle for coordinating multiple governmental authorities; for gathering, generating, and interpreting a variety of data; and for resolving conflicting views on resource use within the context of applicable laws and information.

Technically, the plan is outstanding. SEWRPC published, along with 249 pages of text, 38 full-color maps presenting a wide range of information crucial to informed decision making. The scrutiny received by this 1,825 acre stretch along Lake Michigan is truly impressive.

Substantively, the plan helped achieve a reasonable balance between development and conservation. New development is channeled toward upland areas with relatively suitable soils where other development already exists. Most of the important prairie uplands and more than 90 percent of the wetlands were preserved. Though threatened, no litigation was pursued over the wetland determinations, the plan itself, or the rezoning.

The Chiwaukee Prairie plan falls short of achieving no net loss of wetlands, however. The planning process was consistently characterized as a means of balancing development and conservation, yet the pace of development in Chiwaukee Prairie/Carol Beach was decidedly slow—averaging 13 housing units per year between 1940 and 1980, although the pace picked up somewhat in the early 1990s. Given the federal and state protections for the extensive wetlands in the area, DNR's "no action" alternative could actually have resulted in the preservation of more wetlands than the SEWRPC Final Recommended Plan—95 percent versus 91.6 percent. Previous versions of the recommended plan and the "maximum development alternative" would have preserved fewer wetlands. Thus, there is reason to believe that the planning process facilitated the development of wetlands that might otherwise have remained undeveloped in the absence of a plan.

The Corps, EPA, and DNR might have been able simply to exercise existing authorities to protect the wetlands in the planning area, but the costs of such a strategy could have been high. Landowners probably would have sued the agencies over the wetlands determinations and permit decisions, and an aggressive stance by DNR could have backfired: the legislature might have repealed DNR's authority for shoreline zoning—an outcome much more likely if controversy had persisted and litigation flourished.

The plan provides for the preservation of important prairie upland areas that otherwise would not receive the same protection as wetlands, a trade-off specifically recognized by DNR at the time. It also provides the basis for equitable compensation to landowners affected by the preservation of their land in a natural state as a matter of public interest. In addition, the plan incorporates comprehensive mechanisms for implementation through local zoning, private and state acquisition, and exercise of federal authorities. As such, the plan provides greater certainty for all interests.

The success of the plan in providing a vehicle for orderly resolution of conflicts over the use of the resources of Chiwaukee Prairie was mixed. The process was protracted, extending from the request to SEWRPC for shoreland zoning in 1981 to final rezoning in 1988. Furthermore, the planning process did not diminish the level of controversy—veteran planner and SEWRPC Director Kurt Bauer observed that preparation of the Chiwaukee Prairie/Carol Beach land use management plan was the most controversial he had encountered. There are probably several reasons for this. First, the Wisconsin shoreland–wetland zoning ordinance is an ambitious and technically complex means of regulating local land use. In the early 1980s, when the planning process began, the law was relatively untested and had never been applied to an area in which it would affect a large number of landowners. At the outset of the planning process, there was no commitment to compensating affected landowners, whose confusion and anxiety were understandable. During the development of the plan, a commitment was agreed upon in principle, but the funds needed to carry out a comprehensive acquisition program only became available in the final stages of the process. Had a mechanism for defusing the controversy over landowner's rights become available sooner, considerable conflict might have been avoided.

Second, the issue of what constituted a wetland was particularly controversial in the case of Chiwaukee Prairie. Prairie wetlands and uplands are distinguished by nearly imperceptible differences in elevation, leading to map delineations of wetlands that included uplands. Landowners were prone to question wetland determinations both because the prairie wetlands are not readily recognizable as wetlands, and because the regulatory agencies' wetland delineations included some upland areas. The significance of this issue diminished as the plan for compensating landowners took shape because acquisition was to be based on the lot's inclusion in the acquisition area, not its delineation as a wetland.

Third, some procedural issues hampered an orderly resolution of the issues. Clearly the process of preparing the land use management plan did not internalize all of the controversy. SEWRPC committees are normally established to represent the local interests in a particular planning area. However, Chiwaukee Prairie is a natural resource of statewide and national significance, and state-level environmental groups were interested in the planning process. Since they were not directly represented on the TAC, they used other channels, such as pressuring the DNR and the Public Intervenor and participating in public meetings, to air their views. At the same time, landowners were probably overrepresented on the TAC relative to their authority. After the addition of two representatives at the first meeting, landowners and local government representatives had a nearly automatic majority. DNR, which had several salient authorities, found its influence understated.

Perhaps in response to this situation, the DNR initiated an EIS process encompassing many of the same issues as the SEWRPC process. The use of two competing processes clearly led to confusion and duplication. While the SEWRPC process was more suitable for airing issues and resolving them creatively, the EIS process afforded DNR an opportunity to advance alternatives that would not have achieved consensus in the SEWRPC process.

In the end, the variety of opportunities for input, through the TAC and through public hearings and written comments on the SEWRPC and DNR alternatives, allowed the citizens of southeast Wisconsin to develop a creative plan that preserves significant natural features in both upland and wetlands, while allowing for new development at suitable sites and compensation to landowners precluded from developing their property. Though at times fitful and inefficient, available democratic mechanisms allowed the public and private interests to navigate through a complex layering of land use controls to a resolution that largely preserves a unique little stretch of prairie on Lake Michigan.

ACKNOWLEDGMENT

In addition to the persons specifically cited, the author wishes to acknowledge information obtained through interviews with Louis Dixon, Wisconsin Electric Power Company, member of Technical and Citizen Advisory Committee; Tom Gladzel, EPA Region V Aquatic Resources Unit; Phil Sander, member of Technical and Citizen Advisory Committee; and Steven Ugoretz, environmental specialist, State of Wisconsin, Department of Natural Resources.

NOTES

1. State of Wisconsin, Department of Natural Resources, *Final Environmental Impact Statement for the Land Use Management Plan for The Chiwaukee Prairie-Carol Beach Area, town of Pleasant Prairie—Kenosha County, Wisconsin,* June 1985.
2. *Milwaukee Journal,* January 7, 1962.
3. Southeastern Wisconsin Regional Planning Commission, *A Land Use Management Plan for the Chiwaukee Prairie-Carol Beach Area of the Town of Pleasant Prairie,* Community Assistance Planning Report No. 88, February 1985.
4. DNR, *Final Environmental Impact Statement,* op. cit. note 1, pp. 1–9.
5. Southeastern Wisconsin Regional Planning Commission, "Minutes of Public Hearing, Appendix A, October 23, 1984."
6. Personal communication with Kurt Bauer, Executive Director, Southeastern Wisconsin Regional Planning Commission, August 10, 1988.
7. Personal communication with James P. Morrissey, District Environmental Impact Coordinator, State of Wisconsin, Department of Natural Resources, August 10, 1988.
8. Personal communication with George Melcher, Director, Kenosha County Office of Planning and Zoning Administration, August 10, 1988.
9. Personal communication with Rick Deyarman, DNR Realty Officer, January 4, 1994.
10. Personal communication with Kim Wright, The Nature Conservancy, Wisconsin Chapter, January 4, 1994.

CHAPTER 9

Maryland Chesapeake Bay Critical Areas Program: Wetlands Protection and Future Growth

Erik Meyers, Robert Fischman, and Anne Marsh

EDITORS' SUMMARY

The Maryland Chesapeake Bay Critical Areas Law, enacted and signed into law in 1984, created an innovative program to improve water quality, preserve sensitive habitat including wetlands, and limit the extent and nature of growth in and around the Chesapeake Bay and its tidal tributaries, with a special zone extending 1,000 feet inland from the shoreline. The stated goals of the act were to minimize adverse water quality impacts, conserve valuable habitat, and accommodate future growth in the least polluting manner.

The Chesapeake Bay Critical Areas Commission, a statutorily created body whose members are appointed by the governor and confirmed by the state legislature, developed protective criteria to deal with development activities, resource utilization, and resource protection in the critical area. The commission carried out its work amid high public interest and scrutiny of affected interests and within a tight, statutorily mandated time frame.

From 1984 to 1988 the commission developed and obtained approval of the criteria and supervised and guided the development of local plans. All local governments within the critical area developed plans for commission review and approval, some with modifications required. More recently, the commission's role switched to oversight of local plan and program implementation and review of projects proposed by state and local governments in the critical area.

Although debate continues around a few unresolved issues that could obstruct achievement of environmental protection goals specified in the critical areas act, anecdotal and empirical evidence demonstrates that implementation by local governments is largely in accord with the commission's criteria. The critical area program appears to provide significant protection to wetlands by diverting development and potentially harmful activities to nonwetland areas and by buffering wetlands with transition zones.

Background [1]

The Chesapeake Bay is the largest estuary in the United States. It stretches some 195 miles roughly north to south and includes 1,726 square miles of water surface in Maryland alone. The bay's drainage area of 64,000 square miles includes most of Maryland, Virginia, Pennsylvania, and the District of Columbia and smaller portions of Delaware, New York, and West Virginia. More than 150 rivers and streams supply the bay's freshwater flow; the Susquehanna River, however, is the major source, contributing up to half of the total flow. The watershed is rich in wetlands: approximately 1.2 million acres remain, of which about three-quarters are inland, nontidal wetlands and the balance is made up of tidal wetlands.

Historical accounts dating to colonial times attest to the legendary productivity of the bay, but its rich physical environment began to decline precipitously in the 1960s and 1970s. The impact of a growing population in the bay region caused dramatic declines in fisheries, waterfowl populations, and general water quality. Submerged aquatic vegetation, once plentiful, became sparse. Oyster, shad, and striped bass or rockfish populations dropped to all-time low levels. Duck and other waterfowl populations returned in decreasing numbers to the Chesapeake region. Concerned political leaders, policymakers, and citizens demanded specific answers—and solutions—to the sources of the bay's decline.

EPA Study Finds Widespread Problems

The U.S. Environmental Protection Agency (EPA) was directed by Congress to undertake research to track down root causes of the bay's recent problems and to create the basis for solutions. In 1983, after seven years and expenditures of $27 million in research funds, EPA produced one of the most exhaustive environmental analyses of an ecosystem ever prepared. This study and similar reports prepared by state agencies traced the source of the bay's decline to the growing human population on its shores and in its watershed. EPA identified both point and nonpoint sources of pollution as culprits in the increased nutrient and sediment loading of bay waters and as sources of increased toxic pollutants. The negative impacts on water quality exacted by new post-war industry, urban and suburban development, and expanding agriculture demanded an unprecedented response from policymakers and the public at large.

Following the release of the EPA bay study in 1983, the states of Maryland, Pennsylvania, and Virginia, plus the District of Columbia and EPA, signed an

Watermen tend the jib on a Maryland-based skipjack—one of the last working sailboats in North America. The oysters on which the watermen depend have been decimated by disease, pollution, and excessive harvesting. (Photo courtesy of the Chesapeake Bay Foundation.)

extraordinary pact—the Chesapeake Bay Agreement—that committed each signatory to begin taking immediate, substantial measures to restore and protect the bay. The agreement represented the first public commitment to respond to identified problems and take steps to improve the ecological health of the bay and reverse its steep decline.

One of the most dramatic commitments was made by Maryland Governor Harry Hughes, who called for the state to create and implement a new rigorous program limiting land development and further encroachment on a number of sensitive natural habitats around the bay. Hughes' call went to a state already active in protecting bay resources. For example, the 1973 Tidal Wetlands Act sought to stem further losses of the state's 440,000 acres of tidal

Sediment running off construction sites such as this new highway near Annapolis, Maryland, often finds its way into the Chesapeake Bay. (Photo courtesy of the Chesapeake Bay Foundation.)

Small, meandering streams flowing through agricultural areas, such as the one shown here in Pennsylvania, carry polluted agricultural runoff to the Bay from as far away as southern New York and northern Pennsylvania. (Photo courtesy of the Chesapeake Bay Foundation.)

Over 13 million people live in the Chesapeake Bay's watershed. Here, development occurs along the bayshore in Kent Island, Maryland. (Photo courtesy of the Chesapeake Bay Foundation.)

wetlands, which represent 38 percent of the total state wetland acreage. In the early 1980s Maryland used coastal zone management program funds to identify critical areas needing special state protection. In 1981 the Maryland Department of State Planning began an effort to designate areas of critical state concern after local nomination. Yet, these efforts had not stopped the bay's continued ecological slide.

Passage of the Chesapeake Bay Critical Area Law

Of all Governor Hughes' "Chesapeake Bay Initiatives" passed by the Maryland legislature during its 1984 session, the Chesapeake Bay Critical Area Law (Senate Bill No. 664) and the subsequent work of the critical area commission had the most profound effects on development, land use practices, and wetlands protection in the state's near-shore zone.

The outline of the critical area law was set by a working group during 1983 and 1984. The group included the secretaries of natural resources, agriculture, and state planning; directors of environmental programs in the Department of Health and Mental Hygiene, the Tidewater Administration in the Department of Natural Resources, and the University of Maryland Center for Marine and Estuarine Studies; three members of the governor's staff, and an environmental attorney.

The new legislation (Maryland Natural Resources Code Annotated, Section 1801, et seq.) defined a "critical area" consisting of the water of the bay, its tidal wetlands and tributaries, lands under these waters, and 1,000 feet of adjoining upland (or inland from the landward boundary of the water). All tidal wetlands previously mapped by the state were included. The area amounted to about 10 percent of the total area of the state.

The law established a 25-member critical area commission to be appointed by the governor and confirmed by the Maryland senate. The commission was to develop "criteria" to guide plans and actions of critical area jurisdictions (16 counties and 45 municipal governments, four of which subsequently were excluded from coverage in accordance with provisions of the law). The criteria were to address the three protective goals set out in the law:

1. Minimize adverse impacts on water quality that result from pollutants that are discharged from structures or conveyances or that have runoff from surface lands

2. Conserve fish, wildlife, and plant habitat

3. Establish land use policies for the development in the Chesapeake Bay critical area which accommodate growth and also address the fact that, even if pollution is controlled, the number, movement, and activities of persons in the area can create adverse environmental impacts

Other key purposes of the law were to encourage the preservation of tidal and nontidal wetlands within the critical area in order to preserve their essential functions of flood protection, nursery for fish, plants, and wildlife, and water quality improvement; to mitigate impacts on submerged aquatic vegetation that had been shown to be essential to shellfish and finfish; and to preserve the natural circulation of the bay's estuarine waters. Simply put, the commission's challenge was to devise a means of accommodating some additional growth around the bay while protecting habitat, water quality, and the valuable resources of the near-shore land areas.

The passage of the Chesapeake Bay Critical Area Law and the appointment of the commission were only the first steps in a complex, fast-moving process. The commission was given until December 1, 1985, to develop the criteria and submit them to the legislature for ratification. The commission was then to work with local jurisdictions as they developed their implementing programs and to establish approved local programs by June 1988.

The Planning Process: The Commission Goes to Work

In the process of taking the new law from its passage to the actual functioning of local programs, the commission obtained input from interest groups and the general public, drafted criteria for the legislature's ratification, worked with the various local governments to develop implementation plans, and finally began to oversee the on-the-ground implementation of the criteria. The commission's chairman, retired state judge Solomon Liss, emerged as a key figure who kept the process moving forward.

The Commission

As required by the law, the commission members included the chairman, 11 members representing affected local governments, eight members representing diverse interests affected by the legislation, and five cabinet-level state officials. Their experience, divergent views, and commitment to the work of the commission would be major factors in its success. The active participation of the various secretaries of state agencies, for example, demonstrated the importance that the state's political leadership placed on the success of the commission. Their participation also helped ensure the assistance of their departments' staff in the work of the commission and its staff.

Chairman Solomon Liss was commended by all parties for fair, tough leadership during the development of the criteria and through to the review and approval of the local programs. He engendered respect not only among the commission members but also in the legislature and among the many attendees of the commission's hearings. An excellent arbitrator, Judge Liss promoted progress by negotiating concessions from each side on important issues in the commission's deliberations. After Judge Liss's death in 1988, Robert Price, Jr., was named acting chairman for the balance of 1988 and Judge John North II was appointed chairman by Governor Schaefer in 1989.

Other Key Parties

A skilled, professional staff played an important, supportive role in working with the commission members throughout the process of criteria development and local program review and approval. State agencies, including the departments of natural resources, health and mental hygiene, state planning, and agriculture, supplied key data, reports, and staff expertise. The Chesapeake Bay Commission, the Chesapeake Bay Foundation, county planning staffs, and others played important parts in developing the criteria.

Federal agencies such as EPA, the U.S. Army Corps of Engineers, and U.S. Fish and Wildlife Service were not heavily involved in development of the criteria. However, federal regulatory programs and data were an important backdrop to the commission's work. For example, the lack of protection afforded Maryland's nontidal wetlands by the Corps of Engineers under its Section 404 Clean Water Act program was a determining factor in the commission's decision to include nontidal wetlands as a specific resource area to be protected through the critical area program. The Corps, EPA, and the U.S. Fish and Wildlife Service helped prepare a guidance paper for the commission on non-tidal wetlands.

Federal agencies also contributed in other ways. EPA's massive seven-year Chesapeake Bay research project and subsequent report[2] issued in 1983 had stimulated Maryland's actions, including the critical area law, to "Save the Bay." The U.S. Fish and Wildlife Service had produced important data about the state's wetland resources as well as identifying endangered and threatened plant and animal species in the state. The Service's National Wetlands Inventory maps were consulted in delimiting the critical area with regard to tidal wetlands and in identifying known nontidal wetlands within the zone. The Service also assisted in developing two guidance papers with the commission staff.

Finally, the National Oceanic and Atmospheric Administration (NOAA), as the agency responsible for the federal Coastal Zone Management Act, reviewed and ultimately approved Maryland's amendment of the critical areas law and the criteria in considering the amendment of its 1978 coastal zone management (CZM) plan. The approved CZM plan requires federal agency actions, including those on permit applications and licenses, to be consistent with the critical area program and the Maryland CZM plan, absent narrow reasons of national security or projects located entirely on federal lands. Even in the latter instances, the Chesapeake Bay Agreement commits federal agencies to conduct their activities within the criteria to the maximum feasible extent. Maryland's Tidewater Administration within the Department of Natural Resources monitors federal consistency with the state's CZM plan.

Private institutions played important roles in both supporting and opposing the work of the commission. The Chesapeake Bay Foundation was an avid partner in the critical area program. The Foundation coordinated a number of citizen information workshops, established a network of citizens from all walks of life throughout the state who spoke in favor of the new law in commission hearings, and managed various public information mailings. The Smithsonian Institution, University of Maryland, and The Nature Conservancy provided expertise on a range of scientific and technical issues. Groups representing watermen, other environmentalists (such as the Maryland Conservation Council), and marinas supported the criteria; groups representing homebuilders (the Maryland Homebuilders Association), realtors, farming, and forestry interests were generally opposed to the law and the resulting criteria. During development of local implementation programs, the Maryland Municipal League and private consultants became important forces in shaping and guiding local responses and, in many cases, worked directly with commission staff to secure local implementation.

Developing the Criteria

The commission had its first meeting in October 1984. The commission's staff was not completely in place until January 1985. Although the commission had until December 1, 1985, to issue local program criteria, its schedule was greatly accelerated by other constraints. First, the commission had to gather public comment obtained from eight public hearings about the new law that were conducted around the state. The hearings were completed by December 1984 and generated more than 1,000 letters to the commission. Second, the combination of public hearing requirements in the new law and the publication schedule of the *Maryland Register,* the official state publication, meant that the commission had only a few short months—until mid-May 1985—to develop the initial criteria.

To kick off its work and become educated about similar efforts in other states, the commission met with the staff for a two-day workshop in late January 1985. Experts from around the nation with experience in sensitive area/critical lands protection programs were invited to present their ideas. In this workshop, commission members were able to obtain information about the work of the California Coastal Conservancy, New Jersey's Pinelands Commission, North Carolina's Coastal Resources Program, programs in Florida, Oregon, Washington, and New York's Adirondack Park, plus a roundup of experience in state wetland programs. Representatives from various Maryland agencies and the governor's office also participated.

At the end of the session, three subcommittees met to agree on general guidelines for criteria preparation and to set a work and meeting schedule. Each subcommittee focused on specific types of criteria:

- *Development*   Focusing on development and growth generally and how future development could be managed to have the least adverse environmental impact

- *Resource utilization activities*   Focusing on agricultural, forestry, surface mining (including sand and gravel), and aquacultural activities

- *Resource protection*   Focusing on sensitive habitats, plant and animal life, and natural features

The subcommittees began their work in early February and continued on a weekly or more frequent basis through May. A total of 52 separate subcommittee hearings were conducted during the three and one-half month period, plus 16 meetings of the full commission. The subcommittees requested input from state and federal agencies, affected interest groups, business, and other institutions. Citizens were able to participate in any or all sessions. The staff drafted criteria for subcommittee consideration and modification. As subcommittees drafted reports, the chairman, staff, and the state's assistant attorney general assigned to the commission reviewed them to ensure consistency among the subcommittees and compliance with the requirements of the law.

Following the completion of the commission subcommittees' work, draft criteria were approved on May 22, 1985, and published in the *Maryland Register* in June 1985. The commission continued to refine the draft criteria during the summer of 1985. Comments from various interest groups and the public at large, plus suggested changes from commission members, the governor's office, and commission staff, resulted in a number of revisions to the draft criteria, which were republished in September. Following second draft publication, additional public comments and the commission's self-initiated clarification led to publication of the final draft criteria in November 1985.[3]

The November draft criteria were then submitted for joint Senate and General Assembly approval during the 1986 legislative session. At that time, nine additional public hearings were conducted by the commission and, as an adjunct educational effort, the Chesapeake Bay Foundation convened 35 citizen workshops on the criteria.

The law had been structured in such a way as to permit only an "up" or "down" vote on the criteria in the general assembly. The legislators could enact amendments to the law itself, however, that could have the effect of changing the criteria. Governor Hughes sent an unmistakable message that he would veto any significant change to the critical area law but indicated that he would be open to minor changes. While a number of amendments were proposed, only four minor changes made it into the law as the criteria were approved in May 1986 on the final day of the legislative session.

The stage was set for development of local implementation plans, and the commission and its staff lost no time gearing up for another race at the deadlines. Local governments had 270 days to prepare a proposed program. Upon request, the commission could extend the time period another 180 days. The law stated that within 760 days after the criteria became effective, programs approved or adopted by the commission would go into effect. The development of the local programs is discussed in the "Implementation" section later in this chapter.

The Critical Area Criteria

The commission developed criteria that sought to focus growth and development in already developed areas and to increase protection for special habitats or resources such as nontidal wetlands by placing strict limits on growth in undeveloped areas. The first step was to delineate three categories of lands in the critical area based upon current residential and other land use densities: intensely developed areas, limited development areas, and resource conservation areas. Each category was assigned a density limit and incorporated performance criteria that were directed to protecting water quality. These land classifications are the heart of the critical areas program.

Area Classifications

Intensely developed areas (IDAs) are defined as "areas where residential, commercial, and/or industrial developed land uses predominate, and where relatively little natural habitat occurs." The specified density is four units per acre or higher or a predominance of industrial, commercial, or institutional uses in an area of at least 20 contiguous acres. In order to improve water quality, local plans for IDAs should improve the quality of runoff water, encourage use of retrofitting to improve stormwater management, conserve and enhance fish and wildlife habitats to the extent possible, accommodate additional development that does not impair water quality, and avoid expansion into "habitat protection areas," a term which includes nontidal wetlands, various bird, wildlife, and plant habitats, and riparian areas (all of which would or might include wetlands). Local governments must adopt strategies to reduce current levels of water pollution in IDAs by setting standards to lower pollution loadings from new or redeveloped uses.

Limited development areas (LDAs) are defined as "areas which are currently developed in low- or moderate-intensity uses." LDAs also include areas in which natural plant and animal habitats are relatively undisturbed and water runoff is not substantially polluted. The standards for LDAs include housing densities of more than one unit per five acres up to four units per acre; areas that are not predominantly agricultural, open space, forest, wetland, or surface water; and areas "having public sewer or public water or both." (Local interpretation of this last characteristic engendered one of the major tests of wills between some local governments and the commission, as explained in the section on implementation.)

Environmentally sensitive lands in LDAs were to receive substantially higher levels of protection than those in IDAs. Habitat protection areas were to be preserved (not, as in IDA, merely minimizing adverse impacts). Roads, utilities, and bridges could not cross habitat protection areas unless no feasible alternative existed. Wildlife corridor systems must be preserved or created, and wooded areas must be preserved to the extent possible (and mandated in certain areas, such as in buffers along streams or wetlands and other surface waters). No more than 20 percent of an existing forested area could be removed from forest use. The amount of impervious surface area in LDAs was limited to 15 percent of a developed site, and cluster development for housing projects was encouraged. Soil erosion and stormwater controls must be given more attention.

The criteria for the third type of area, *resource conservation areas* (RCAs), provided the greatest environmental protection. RCAs were defined as "areas characterized by nature-dominated environments (that is, wetlands, forests, abandoned fields) and resource utilization activities (that is, agriculture, forestry, fisheries activities or aquaculture)." Standards for RCA established densities below one unit per five acres and dominant land uses in wetlands, open space, agriculture, forest, surface water, or barren lands. The local implementation programs are urged to preserve existing uses to the extent possible, and compliance with the habitat protection area criteria is mandated. Further development for housing could occur at densities no higher than one unit per 20 acres, but local governments could set minimum lot sizes within this overall density limit. Generally, no development of new industrial or commercial areas was permitted within RCA-classified lands.

Intense pressure from rural jurisdictions and some developers secured an option for development on RCA lands. A maximum of 5 percent of an existing RCA area could be developed according to IDA or LDA criteria, provided that new development was adjacent to existing LDA or IDA development, habitat protection areas were avoided to the extent possible, and water quality was preserved or improved. In addition, development permitted through this "growth allocation," as the 5 percent development option was termed, must be located at least 300 feet from tidal wetlands or other tidal waters.

The criteria also included "grandfathering" provisions to accommodate existing development projects and plans that had advanced substantially toward development. Within RCA lands, intrafamily transfers were permitted provided that the "1-in-20" acre density standard was maintained. As will be discussed later, the interpretation and provisions for growth allocation, grandfathering, and the 1-in-20 standard generated the most controversy and friction between the local governments and the commission, as well as in the state legislature and among the public at large.

Other Criteria

Cross-cutting criteria were developed for various activities and for uses of land other than building in all three land areas, and for protection of specific special features or aspects of the critical area. Special criteria were spelled out for shore erosion works (to favor nonstructural means whenever possible); forest and woodland protection (setting detailed standards for tree cutting in certain areas and of certain species); agriculture (mandating best management practices [BMPs] to minimize water pollution); and for surface mining and natural parks. In addition, criteria for habitat protection identified several special habitats, such as riparian areas, nontidal wetlands, and those for threatened, endangered, and other species "in need of conservation," as well as habitats for other plants and wildlife and anadromous fish.

For buffer areas, the criteria required local governments to permit intrusion on the shoreline only by water-dependent activities and facilities. This provision also generated controversy and led to local attempts to ease interpretions of water dependency.

Criteria Relating to Wetlands

Viewed solely from a wetlands perspective—and certainly the program and objectives were much broader and more diverse than wetlands protection alone—the new critical area criteria established a number of protective requirements for tidal and nontidal wetlands. The major wetlands protection measures in the critical area law and criteria include:

1. Protection of all tidal wetlands in the critical area.

2. Protection of nontidal wetlands "of importance to plant, fish, and wildlife, and water quality"; and all areas of one acre or more are to be mapped.

3. Buffers at least 25 feet in width are required for tidal and nontidal wetlands; for tidal wetlands, required widths may extend to over 100 feet depending upon the contemplated activity, steepness of the upland slope, soil erodability, surface mining operations (including sand and gravel extraction), and other factors; some activities (e.g., water-dependent uses, fishing facilities, grazing, selective tree cutting, and shoreline erosion control) are permitted in the buffer as exceptions and may be limited if they have measurable impacts on wetlands and other affected waters.

4. Local governments are required to adopt a wetlands mitigation plan to compensate for unavoidable impacts from water-dependent activities or other problems in nontidal wetlands.

5. Local governments must identify and designate protection areas around habitats of "threatened and endangered species, and species in need of conservation" in wetlands or wherever found (unless evidence of no impacts can be shown); and they must develop protection plans that could include acquisition, conservation easements, cooperative agreements with private landholders, forest management provisions, soil conservation plan provisions, and special subdivision or zoning ordinances.

6. Projects permitted in wetland areas otherwise protected from adverse effects must be "water-dependent," defined as "structures or work associated

with industrial, maritime recreational, educational, or fisheries activities that require location at or near the shoreline within the buffer" set by criteria; even for those uses, the criteria place limits on the amount of disturbance to the natural aquatic environment.

Wetlands are also benefitted indirectly by criteria for shore erosion works; stormwater controls; best management practices on agricultural lands to minimize sediment, nutrient, and pesticide runoff impacts on receiving waters; prohibition of grazing on stream banks and on tidal shorelines (although grazing is permitted by the criteria in nontidal wetlands); maintenance of a minimum 25-foot vegetated filter strip between agricultural activities and tidal waters, tributary streams, and tidal wetlands; protection for anadramous fish habitat areas; and mapping of wetlands and other habitats, resources, and other natural conditions identified by the criteria.

Major Issues in Drafting the Criteria

A number of specific points that were debated thoroughly in the public meetings and in comments on the draft criteria remain controversial in the implementation stage.

RCA MINIMUM DENSITY

The RCA density limitation of one housing unit per 20 acres caused substantial controversy. Commission staff developed a "white paper" that examined other special-area protection programs and evaluated the situation in Maryland. While some areas had decided on requirements for even lower densities, others had approved higher densities. The commission adopted a 1-in-20 standard amid opposition from real estate interests and farmers (who claimed it would devalue property) and builders represented by the Maryland Homebuilders Association.

The interests opposing the 1-in-20 standard for RCA were successful in securing some modifications of the criteria during legislative review and approval in 1986. The modifications allowed clustering of new residential development at a maximum density of one unit per eight acres, and landowners can count their unusable wetland acreage toward allowable density on upland areas in some counties. The legislature's oversight committee for the commission initially suggested the one-to-eight figure. The homebuilders' group proposed a one-to-three standard. However, Department of State Planning forecasts and Chesapeake Bay Foundation research demonstrated that growth trends over the next few decades could be accommodated easily by planned growth capacity in rural areas with a 1-in-20 standard.

GROWTH ALLOCATION

Rural local governments were upset with the amount of their jurisdictions' land area that would fall into RCA classification. They saw themselves as being barred from further economic development and restrained from growth while their more urbanized neighbors could continue to grow and prosper (since more of their land areas would be designated as LDA or IDA). The proposal for a growth allocation initially provided that, within RCA lands, a percentage of existing LDA and IDA areas could for be used for future expansion and growth. The rural counties remained strongly opposed, and at the direction of the commission chairman the staff prepared an alternative. The new approach based the growth allocation on the current amount of RCA-designated land; it allowed up to 5 percent of this area to be added to LDA or IDA lands. The expansion was subject to two caveats: redesignated lands must be contiguous to current LDA or IDA areas, and only half the acreage could be applied to convert RCA land into LDA or IDA land. The other half must be used to convert LDA lands to IDA lands.

GRANDFATHERING

In order to be fair to existing landowners and to developers with projects under way at the time the criteria were adopted, the commission came up with a number of provisions to preserve a project's right to be completed even when it would not comply completely with the new criteria. Any landowner in the critical area was permitted to build a single dwelling on a single parcel of land on which there was no current house, even if in RCA-designated areas. In addition, projects that had advanced to the stage of constructing foundations could proceed. Other provisions enabled recorded subdivision plans or building lot plans to proceed, provided the projects complied with the criteria or were counted by the locality against its growth allocation. Grandfathering issues arose less in the criteria drafting stage than in the implementation phase, when many environmentalists and others were surprised by the amount of grandfathered development permitted.

Implementation[4]

The commission's procedure called for local governments to prepare plans adhering to the approved criteria and to submit them for commission approval. Over a period of one and one-half years, the commission worked with counties, cities, and towns to secure approved plans. Understanding the massive effort involved, the commission assisted local governments in many ways.

Funds to support local planning were included in the commission's state appropriation. The commission also made available, to the extent possible, technical staff to assist local planners or their consultants in preparing plans. In early 1986, even before the criteria went into effect, the commission held a workshop for local officials and their staffs to ascertain problems and issues in implementing the criteria. The commission also asked various state agencies to focus on assisting localities in carrying out their responsibilities for preparation of adequate plans.

In addition, the commission staff asked and received permission to develop nontechnical guidelines to aid local governments in understanding the criteria and what they required of local plans. The staff produced five "guidance papers," including one on nontidal wetlands. Neither the guidelines nor the guidance papers had the force or effect of law or regulation, but they helped local planners understand the commission's interpretation of the criteria and requirements and, consequently, the commission's likely reactions to local plan proposals.

The relationship between the commission and the various local governments varied considerably. On the whole, urbanized jurisdictions found compliance with the criteria easier than did their more rural counterparts. This result can be ascribed partly to attitudes of local officials and partly to resources and experience. Some rural Eastern Shore communities displayed marked antipathy for the critical area law and the criteria; their lack of enthusiasm for the program led to delays in responding. In addition, many smaller jurisdictions lacked a planning department, or even a single planning staff member, and consequently did not have much experience in land use planning.

Seven jurisdictions responded within the initial time period (270 days from the date the criteria went into effect), and most of the others did so within the 180-day extension period (ending in August 1988). All jurisdictions (except four that were granted exemptions from the program in accordance with the law and commission procedures) eventually submitted plans, although the commission required changes in several of them before approval. Some communities waited until late in the game to develop plans, and they did so, it appears, only to avoid a greater role by the commission in the determination of future development. Some submitted plans did not respond to the criteria, which caused delays as they were returned for revisions. In about a dozen instances, the commission began to prepare criteria implementation plans for jurisdictions that were late in submitting plans. However, in all these cases the local governments kept working on their own plans and managed to retain planning responsibility.

While some observers criticized the commission for not moving more quickly to implement local programs for the laggard jurisdictions, the commission believed that the public notice and hearing procedures mandated by the law would cause further delay in implementation for a commission-initiated local program.

Once local plans were submitted, the commission had 30 days in which a five-member review panel conducted a public hearing in the affected jurisdiction. Within 90 days after the local program was submitted, the commission had to approve the plan or notify the local government of specific changes needed. (Failure to act was deemed approval in the law.) Revised plans were to be resubmitted by the locality within 40 days, at which point they were automatically approved unless the commission again (within 40 days) returned them with written reasons for disapproval. After approval was obtained from the commission, the local government had to hold hearings and adopt the program as an ordinance.

Each local plan went to the commission staff for analysis to ensure compliance with the criteria. A staff of 11 technically trained professionals kept a heavy volume of work moving through the process in the relatively short time frame available.

Issues that emerged in the implementation/local plan drafting stage included mapping, definition of "having water and sewer," expanding the critical area to upland areas, growth allocation distribution, and grandfathering. A mapping question arose over the minimum size of an RCA or LDA area. Most counties settled on a 20-acre minimum, but the commission set no general standard. Another question arose about interpretation of "having water or sewer" for LDA designation; in response to one county draft plan (Anne Arundel), the commission clarified the term to require close proximity to existing water or sewer lines and would neither allow inclusion of planned but not existing services nor extend it to include areas distant from current service lines.

Many localities wanted guidance on utilizing the growth allocation amount, such as allocating by year, in phases, through bidding contests, or among larger versus smaller development projects. Additionally, a question emerged over whether the lot area or the paved and developed "footprint" of the structure should be measured in determining the allocation amount. The commission decided that the entire lot, not just the area of the structure on it, should be counted.

Although the criteria encouraged local jurisdictions to expand their critical areas beyond the boundary mandated in the law, expansion was sometimes controversial. The RCA criteria allowed a locality to increase the amount of possible shoreline development by expanding the critical area inland. This particular situation occurred in Kent County and provoked strong reaction. However, the commission concluded that such expansion is permitted by the law and criteria. After securing additional on-site protections for habitat values, the commission decided that the net benefit of this project accrued to the public.

As more grandfathered projects began to emerge, members of the public and the environmental community were vocal in their dissatisfaction. The Chesapeake Bay Foundation issued a critical report on the implementation of the law, finding that grandfathered exceptions (and transfers within families as permitted by the law) would significantly reduce the program's potential benefits. While little empirical data exists, a survey carried out in one Eastern Shore county (Talbot) found over 1,600 grandfathered lots in the critical area. If this situation were repeated in other jurisdictions, the grandfathering provisions could substantially weaken the protection program.

Conclusions[5]

Maryland's Chesapeake Bay Critical Area Program is a model for other jurisdictions contemplating special area management for sensitive bodies of water. Criticisms of its limitations appear, on the whole, to focus on relatively minor points. For example, despite criticism of the narrowness of the 1,000-foot protected band, the critical area law established a precedent for the scope and reach of its provisions. The criteria take technically supportable steps toward reining in unsustainable growth in areas that are acutely sensitive to pollution and human alterations.

On Maryland's sparsely populated Eastern Shore, the mandates of the act forced many of the local jurisdictions to account for environmental factors in their land use planning. This new environmental focus has tended to become a permanent and lasting part of these local jurisdictions' land planning, even outside of the critical area. Similarly, industry is now more apt to focus on environmental issues—wetlands, wildlife and bird habitat, runoff, vegetation— in the course of operating existing facilities or building new ones.

The process of drafting the criteria and developing local plans was an extremely intricate, work-intensive effort. Some observers complained of a lack of meaningful public input in the development of the criteria, yet the commission maintained an open door policy at all of its subcommittee hearings; held multiple public meetings, hearings, and workshops throughout the state; and made sure all affected interests had their day in court. On balance, given the short time lines mandated by the law, the commission received a substantial amount of public comment. This process could only work given a clear mandate (i.e., broad support from the general public and from the state's chief executive), an adequate budget, statutory "hammers" to compel compliance, and leadership and expertise on the commission and its staff. The commission's continued active oversight and implementation role gives the criteria, as implemented through the local programs, continuing vitality.

While federal agency representatives were not formally involved as members of the commission, the commission received substantial input from state and federal officials and staff experts. By amending its coastal zone management program to include the critical area law and criteria, Maryland sought to assure that federal actions would be consistent with the bay program.

With respect to wetlands, the critical area program provides strong protection criteria, disincentives to alterations, and requires replacement for areas lost or adversely affected. Traditionally exempted activities such as agriculture and forestry are specifically included, and protection from their potentially adverse impacts is mandated. Importantly, the program's scale allows development to proceed in more environmentally compatible areas while protecting wetlands. This factor—the existence of adjacent areas to accommodate growth and development—may in the final analysis be the most important element in the success of the Chesapeake Bay critical area program.

However, some criticisms of the program are valid. Perhaps the most worrisome problem is that the legislature and commission did not foresee the extent of grandfathering of pre-critical area development rights. In 1994, ten years after the enactment of the critical area program, even knowledgeable experts are surprised at the amount of grandfathered development. Literally thousands of lots are involved, despite the act's requirement that even grandfathered development meet performance criteria and comply with habitat protection area criteria.

In addition, as of 1994, the growth allocation allowance in rural jurisdictions has not been exhausted, a fact that, when linked with the large amount of grandfathered development, means that the limits on growth have not prevented absorption of growth pressures within the critical area.

However, surprisingly little information is readily available on how much development has occurred in the critical area since the program's implementation. Despite the fact that the act was controversial from its inception, and repeated attempts were made in the legislature to cut it back or otherwise hamper its effectiveness, no systematic data collection has been established. Thus the actual impact of post-critical area development is a matter of considerable conjecture.

In 1994 environmental groups in the state are focusing on other issues and programs; little attention is being paid to the critical area program. The commission relies in large part upon citizen and local jurisdiction complaints for enforcement, and only one assistant state attorney general is assigned to the commission to handle its caseload. Future efforts by the commission are focused on greater public education.

Generally, the critical area program is given credit for making a difference in the bay's water quality. A recent University of Maryland study examined the watershed of one bay tributary to estimate water quality impacts associated with the critical area program. The study concluded, based upon a predictive modeling technique, that the critical area act potentially will reduce non-point source nutrient and sediment pollution in the bay. In the absence of a critical area act, the study model predicted loadings in the watershed under study would be from 200 to 1000 percent higher.[6] In recent years, the bay's water quality has improved but, since so many factors are involved, it is difficult to isolate the effect of the critical area act. Nonetheless, anecdotal evidence supports the conclusion that the critical area law is a beneficial program for the environment and has not had an unduly negative impact on business and economic development.

ACKNOWLEDGMENTS

The authors wish to acknowledge the support and assistance of a project advisory committee, including Michael Bean, Environmental Defense Fund; David Davis, U.S. EPA; John DeGrove, Florida Atlantic University; Ralph Morgenweck, U.S. Fish and Wildlife Service; Glenn Eugster, National Park Service; Bernard Goode, U.S. Army Corps of Engineers; Lindell Marsh, Siemon, Larsen & Marsh; Ann Louise Strong, University of Pennsylvania; James Webb, The Wilderness Society; John Wilson, U.S. EPA; and Fred Worstell, Melvin Simon & Associates, Inc.

NOTES

1. This chapter is based upon a similarly titled study prepared under the supervision of and copyrighted in 1989 by the Environmental Law Institute, Washington, D.C., and which was funded in part by the U.S. Environmental Protection Agency through EPA contract number 68-01-7378. It is reprinted in edited form with permission of the Institute and the authors. The authors are grateful for the extensive background information provided through interviews with Steve Bunker and Saunders Hillyer of the Chesapeake Bay Foundation; David Burke, Department of Natural Resources; William Eichbaum, Department of Health and Mental Hygiene; James Gutman, Robert Price, Jr., and Wally Miller, commission members; Ann Swanson, Chesapeake Bay Commission; Josephy Altrich,

Rodney Brooks, Eileen Peiffer, and Penny Chalkley of the Anne Arundel County Planning Office; Gail Owens, Kent County Planning Director; Alexander Raisen, Kent County Planning Director; Joe Stevens, Queen Anne's County Planning Director; Joe Mangenie, Rock Hall Planning Inspector; James C. Simpson, Maryland State Senator; and Kay Bienen, Maryland Homebuilders Association. Special thanks go to Kevin Sullivan and Dr. Sarah Taylor of the Chesapeake Bay Commission staff for their help and guidance.

2. *Chesapeake Bay Program: Findings and Recommendations,* Philadelphia: U.S. Environmental Protection Agency, 1983.

3. *Subtitle 15 Chesapeake Bay Critical Area Commission Criteria for Local Critical Area Program Development: Final Regulations,* COMAR 14.15.1 et seq., November 1985.

4. The description and evaluation of the implementation program draws on a number of publications, including Charles S. Davis, "A Strategy to Save the Chesapeake Shoreline," *Journal of Soil and Water Conservation,* Vol. 42, No. 2, March-April 1987; Ralph W. Tiner, Jr., *Mid-Atlantic Wetlands: A Disappearing Natural Treasure,* Newton Corner, Massachusetts: U.S. Fish and Wildlife Service and U.S. Environmental Protection Agency, 1987; Saunders Hillyer, "The Maryland Critical Area Program: Time to De-Mythologize and Move Forward," paper by the Chesapeake Bay Foundation, Annapolis, Maryland, June 1988; and Steven Bunker, "The Maryland Critical Area "Program: A Comprehensive Land Management Approach," *National Wetlands Newsletter,* Vol. 9, No. 1, January-February 1989.

5. To update conclusions of the earlier study, several knowledgeable experts were interviewed by Erik Meyers in 1994, including the commission's director, a leading environmentalist familiar with the bay's history, and a senior manager of one of the largest businesses in the state.

6. John Houlahan, et al. "Estimating Maryland Critical Area Act's Impact on Future Nonpoint Pollution Along the Rhode River Estuary," *Water Resources Bulletin,* Vol. 28, No. 3, June 1992.

CHAPTER 10

Anchorage, Alaska's Wetlands Management Plan

David A. Salvesen

EDITORS' SUMMARY

Anchorage, Alaska, like the rest of the state, is rich in wetlands. By one estimate, over 30 percent of the remaining developable land within the city contains wetlands, leading to frequent conflicts involving development versus preservation of wetlands.

In 1982 the Anchorage Assembly enacted the Anchorage Wetlands Management Plan—one of the first comprehensive wetland plans adopted in the country. The plan marked the culmination of a two-year planning process that involved state and federal resource agencies, representatives from development and environmental groups, and city officials. Salvesen notes that the process included one of the first advance identification programs for wetlands.

The plan designated four categories of wetlands: preservation, conservation, developable, and special study. In general, private development was off limits in preservation wetlands, allowed in both conservation and developable wetlands, and temporarily prohibited in special study wetlands. Based on the plan, the U.S. Army Corps of Engineers issued a general permit in 1983 for activities in the developable wetlands. Other wetlands were governed by the individual permit process.

While one of the goals of the plan was to balance development with protection of wetlands, the plan suffered from inaccuracies and inappropriate wetland designations, many of which were based more on land ownership than wetland values. In 1993 the plan was revised, following field inspections that were carried out to ensure that the designations more accurately reflected wetland values. The categories of preservation, conservation, and developable of the 1982 plan were changed to A, B, and C, respectively.

A draft plan was approved by the Anchorage Assembly in late 1993 and forwarded to the state coastal policy council and the National Oceanic and Atmospheric Administration for approval. In early 1994, the Corps issued draft general permits, incorporating the wetland designations of the wetlands management plan, that would apply to activities in category C wetlands. If approved, the new plan should bring the city closer to protecting most high-value wetlands while allowing lower value wetlands to be developed more readily.

Background[1]

Alaska contains an estimated 170 million acres of wetlands, most of which owe their existence to a layer of impermeable, frozen soil, called permafrost, lying beneath the surface. The permafrost acts like a clay liner to prevent water from penetrating the soil, and Alaska's cold weather keeps evapotranspiration to a minimum. Thus, even in areas that receive less rainfall than many deserts, wetlands predominate.

Anchorage, the largest city in Alaska, covers nearly 2,000 square miles and contains over half the state's population. A coastal city, Anchorage sits on a triangular peninsula bounded on two sides by the Knik and Turnagain Arms of Cook Inlet, which is an extension of the Gulf of Alaska, and on the third side by the Chugach Mountains (Figure 10.1). The city consists of three discrete geographic regions: the Anchorage Bowl, Eagle River, and Turnagain Arm. Most of Anchorage's approximately 215,000 residents live in the Bowl and Eagle River regions. These two regions lie on a glacial plain which slopes north and west from the Chugach Mountains. The plain is generally less than 400 feet in elevation, with very low topographic relief. Turnagain Arm is a steep-sided fjord where buildable land is scarce. It experiences extreme fluctuations in tides, second only to those of the Bay of Fundy. Apparently, it was named by Captain Cook who, while searching for the elusive Northwest Passage, reached yet another dead end at the end of the arm of Cook Inlet and had to turn around again. A large portion of the municipal land base is taken up by tidelands, a state park, a national forest, and two military bases that lie to the north and east of the Bowl and comprise approximately 120 square miles.

The city is rich in wetlands. Over 15,000 acres of wetlands lie within its borders. Wetlands occur in the troughs and depressions of the glacial moraines and terraces that formed during the last glacial period, in the bottom of stream valleys, in areas overlying clay, and, in a few areas, above permafrost, which forms an impenetrable barrier to water. Eight different wetland types occur in the Anchorage area. Bogs and wet meadows occur most frequently, although marshes and swamps are also common. With peat deposits up to 30 feet thick, wetlands in Anchorage are typical of northern bogs, or muskegs, as they are sometimes called. One typical wetland type is called "patterned ground wetlands," so called because they form a characteristic pattern across the landscape when viewed from the air. These wetlands are bogs containing shrubs and other low-lying plants, separated by a series of swales.

The Alaskan economy depends heavily on oil. Anchorage's economy, like those of Houston, Denver, and other oil-dependent cities, historically has been vulnerable to fluctuations in oil prices and therefore has experienced periodic cycles of boom and bust. In the late 1970s and early 1980s the economy

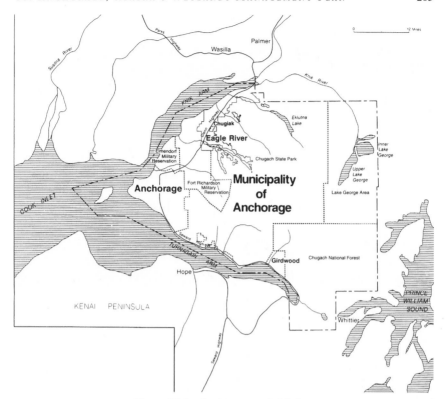

Figure 10.1 Anchorage and vicinity.

was booming as a result of high oil prices and the construction of the Trans-Alaska Pipeline. State oil revenues fueled explosive growth and investment in Alaskan cities and towns, including Anchorage. The robust economy fostered development throughout the city and placed enormous pressure on its wetlands, many of which were in areas zoned for development.

With the city squeezed between the mountains on one side and Knik and Turnagain Arms on the other, development is limited to existing vacant land within the city limits. Most of the good sites have already been developed and what is left often contains wetlands. Thus, development in or near wetlands is often unavoidable. According to one estimate, roughly 30 percent of the remaining developable land in Anchorage contains wetlands. The city's 1982 comprehensive plan for the Anchorage Bowl zoned the remaining undeveloped land in the Bowl as follows: 13,900 acres residential, 1,140 acres commercial, 2,400 industrial, and about 7,500 acres unrestricted.

As development pressure on wetlands increased during the most recent boom years, so did efforts to preserve them. In the late 1970s and early 1980s, federal agencies such as the U.S. Fish and Wildlife Service (FWS) and the U.S.

Anchorage is rich in wetlands such as Potter's Marsh, a brackish marsh along Turnagain Arm.

Environmental Protection Agency (EPA) began pushing for greater wetland protection. At the same time, the Corps became active in Anchorage, expanding its jurisdiction and asserting federal regulatory control over the city's wetlands.

Before a developer may fill a wetland to prepare for construction, he or she must obtain a Section 404 permit from the Corps. In the late 1970s, several Corps permit decisions, some denying and some approving development in wetlands, were controversial. The controversy led to delays in processing other Section 404 permit applications. Obtaining a Section 404 permit took anywhere from three months to over a year, and developers complained that the permit process was time-consuming and, more important, unpredictable.

Predictability is critical for developers, especially in Alaska, where long, cold, and dark winters often make for a short building season. Long-term planning where wetlands were involved—and they often were—was difficult because developers never knew in advance whether or not they would get a permit. Thus, while the city planning office encouraged a high level of growth and development, federal wetland regulations slowed the pace.

The Anchorage Department of Community Planning and Development foresaw additional conflicts over wetland use and sought to establish a more comprehensive planning and permitting approach to guide development and preservation of the city's remaining wetlands. In 1979, faced with mounting pressure to develop and preserve its remaining wetlands, the department began the process of developing a wetlands management plan.

Residential development encroaches on wetlands in Anchorage.

In developing the plan, the department sought to strike a balance between preserving and developing wetlands in Anchorage—to protect critical wetlands without hindering economic growth—and to develop a plan consistent with federal wetland regulatory programs; that is, a plan that did not encourage development in areas where developers would have trouble obtaining a Section 404 permit. In general, the goals of the planning effort were to

- Identify and classify wetlands
- Develop a management strategy to protect most high-value wetlands and to identify wetland areas where development could occur
- Link wetlands planning efforts with other municipal planning processes
- Develop a mitigation strategy for wetlands losses

Although the planning process involved state, federal, and local agencies, it was strictly a local plan, implemented by Anchorage.

The Planning Process

The Anchorage Wetlands Management Plan (WMP) was not developed in a vacuum. While the plan was being developed, the city also was completing its coastal management plan (CMP) and its comprehensive plan. The WMP became part of the CMP, which in turn was incorporated into the comprehensive plan. The Anchorage Department of Community Planning and Development tried to make the three plans consistent. Thus, the WMP addresses wetlands not covered by the CMP, although there is some overlap between the two plans, and the comprehensive plan reflects some of the goals of the wetlands management plan. For example, the comprehensive plan states, "Wetlands shall be preserved in their natural state as identified in the Wetlands Management Plan if they perform essential hydrologic, habitat, or stormwater detention functions. Likewise, wetlands "shall be allowed to be developed . . . if they do not perform essential natural functions and are required for urban uses and activities."

The thrust of the coastal management plan is to devise and implement a rational process for resolving conflicts between development and preservation of coastal resources. The CMP allocates land in the coastal area to three land use categories: preservation, conservation, and utilization. Preservation includes areas that are valuable in their undisturbed or natural condition and which should be essentially free from development. Conservation includes certain natural areas that should be protected, but not at the total exclusion of human activities such as recreation and forest management. The goal is not to maintain such conservation areas in their pristine state, as in the preservation areas, but to regulate or prohibit, if necessary, any uses that would destroy or degrade coastal resources.

Both preservation and conservation lands include restrictions on development in floodplains, coastal wetlands, and certain areas subject to seismic activity. Utilization includes areas in the coastal area suitable for development. This category contains the fewest development restrictions.

According to officials of the Department of Community Planning and Development, the wetlands management planning process was relatively straightforward. It consisted of an inventory phase, an analysis phase, and a development of alternatives phase. It contained the following sequential steps: (1) identify and map wetlands, (2) assess resource values, (3) develop and evaluate alternative levels of wetland protection and development, (4) select the preferred alternative and develop a management strategy, and (5) formulate a plan.

With principal funding from EPA and the National Oceanic and Atmospheric Administration's (NOAA) coastal zone management office, the city hired a consultant to identify and classify its wetlands according to their physical and biological characteristics. The study did not include tidal wetlands because the city's coastal management plan already covers these areas. Only vegetated freshwater wetlands, including nontidal wetlands in the coastal area, were included. Such wetlands include bogs, marshes, swamps, and wet meadows but exclude coastal, marine, and estuarine wetlands, unvegetated wetlands, and deepwater habitats.

Two review committees were established to guide the planning effort, a technical committee and a policy committee. The technical committee, comprising representatives of municipal agencies, the Corps, FWS, and state agencies such as the Department of Fish and Game and the Department of Environmental Conservation, reviewed the consultant's study. The policy committee included the mayor, an Anchorage Assembly member, plus members of the development and conservation communities.

Wetland resources were identified and evaluated based on a number of criteria, such as their value for wildlife habitat, flood control, or recreation. Most of the evaluations were based on a review of existing plans and maps, analysis of aerial photos, and site inspection of selected wetlands. Anchorage's Department of Community Planning and Development did not have the resources to conduct detailed on-site evaluations of every wetland in the municipality. It did, however, conduct a detailed analysis of two large wetlands, Connors Bog and Klatt Bog, because these relatively undisturbed bogs are in many ways typical of Anchorage wetlands threatened by urbanization.

The lack of detailed field studies was viewed as one of the weaknesses of the plan. Many of those involved in the planning process agreed that the wetland assessments were completed without adequate information. As a result, many of the wetland evaluations and delineations were inaccurate, although subsequent informal field inspections by the Corps revealed that most of the initial evaluations and delineations were generally accurate, in the Corps' opinion. Some groups, however, questioned the Corps' findings.

Despite a paucity of verifiable field data, the city's consultant classified wetlands into eight broad types. The predominant wetland types in Anchorage are "nonpatterned elongated complex" (a series of shallow elongated ponds intersected by ridges of upland vegetation) and "forested closed basin swamp" (a black spruce and scrub-shrub bog). Each wetland type was rated as having either high, medium, or low value. For example, a black spruce bog with no water flowing through it was considered low value, but an emergent marsh near the coast which provides critical wildlife habitat was considered high value. The plan laid out a specific management strategy for each wetland type and that strategy helped guide the department when it reviewed permit applications.

Three management alternatives (low, medium, and high) were developed to represent different degrees of trade-offs among development and preservation, the level of regulatory control, and cost. The low-management option would allow extensive development in wetlands and rely on mitigation to reduce adverse impacts. Few development controls, such as new ordinances or changes in subdivision regulations, would be required. The medium option would protect critical wetlands but would allow development in noncritical or low-value wetlands. Mitigation would be used to reduce adverse impacts of development. Finally, under the high option, nearly all remaining wetlands in Anchorage would be protected. This option would provide the greatest protection for wetlands but would likely be the most costly, since the city might have to acquire many of the wetlands on private lands to avoid takings claims. Regardless of the alternative chosen, most wetlands still would fall under the Corps' jurisdiction.

The alternatives were evaluated based on their ability to meet objectives such as administrative and regulatory burden, cost, resource protection, compliance with other laws and programs (such as the municipality's coastal management program), and whether the alternative is consistent with the city's planning objectives. For example, the municipality's comprehensive plan projected a demand for an additional 70,000 new dwelling units over the next 20 to 30 years. Under the high-management level, there would not be enough buildable land within the Anchorage bowl to accommodate this expected growth in population and housing. In contrast, the low-management option would not adequately implement the city's environmental goals, policies, and objectives.

Not surprisingly, the city selected the middle option, which represented a balance between preservation and development. According to the 1982 Wetlands Management Plan, the moderate management level "meets the basic legal requirements for wetland protection under municipal, federal, and state laws and regulations. But it avoided the restrictions on municipal growth and the high acquisition costs associated with a greater degree of wetland protection." Under this approach, the city could focus on preserving wetlands that are critical to stream hydrology, water quality, and stormwater management; that provide important biological, recreational, or scientific functions; and that could be especially difficult to develop. Not all such wetlands, however, were preserved.

Throughout the two-year planning effort, the public was provided ample opportunity to participate. In addition to the numerous committee meetings, over 40 public hearings and public meetings were held. The city also met informally with landowners, developers, environmental groups, and resource agencies. According to one official, Anchorage is a small community, and it would be impossible to develop a plan, especially one which touched so many residents, without extensive community involvement.

The 1982 Plan

Similar to its coastal management plan, the city's wetlands management plan designated most wetlands in one of four categories: preservation, conservation, developable, and special study. In general, wetlands classified as preservation were off-limits to development, with exceptions granted for small fills for utility lines, road crossings, etc. Wetlands classified as developable were slated for fill or other alteration for development. The middle category, conservation, maintained the status quo. That is, developers still had to obtain an individual 404 permit from the Corps before filling could occur. The special study category was established for wetlands that needed further study before they could be placed into one of the other three categories.

According to the wetlands management plan, special study wetlands were those for which there were "insufficiently detailed land use policies and information and a lack of sufficient environmental data to determine wetland status." In effect, a decision on these wetlands was postponed, and in the meantime the Corps decided, on a case-by-case basis, what activities were permitted.

The approximate amount of land in each category in the Anchorage Bowl was as follows:

- Developable—3,950 acres
- Preservation—3,790 acres
- Conservation—1,065 acres
- Special study—600 acres

The plan was adopted unanimously by the Anchorage Assembly in April 1982 and approved by the Alaska Coastal Policy Council and NOAA. One year later, the Corps issued general permits for developable wetlands in Anchorage and designated the municipality as the administering body for the permits.

A general permit is a generic permit issued by the Corps for a category of fills that are similar in nature and that cause only minimal individual and cumulative adverse impacts. General permits, which may be issued on a nationwide, regional, or local basis, greatly simplify the permit process. Once the Corps issues a general permit, individual projects falling within a certain category will not require an individual permit from the Corps unless it decides, on a case-by-case basis, that the more elaborate individual federal permit process is in the public interest.

While the general permits simplified the permit process for projects in developable wetlands, the development restrictions for conservation and preservation wetlands were unclear. To clarify its policy on issuing permits for dredge and fill in conservation and preservation wetlands in Anchorage, the Corps issued a special public notice in early 1986 which stated that:

- Individual permits for the placement of dredged and/or fill material into Preservation wetlands will not be issued, unless a proposed activity would enhance, restore, or preserve the natural character of a wetland, or if the Corps determines that the project is "overwhelmingly in the public interest."

- Before the Corps issues an individual permit for development in Conservation wetlands, an applicant must clearly identify the qualitative and quantitative wetland values that would be affected by the project and the on-site mitigation measures proposed to lessen, compensate, or restore the wetland values that would be adversely affected.

The public notice stated, in essence, that the Corps recognized the local plan as controlling over development and that it would view wetlands in the preservation category as unsuitable for development. Only projects that the Corps determined were "overwhelmingly in the public interest" would be permitted in preservation wetlands. For conservation wetlands, the Corps did not necessarily deny a permit application outright for development in these areas, but it held them to a higher standard of review, for example, by requiring a more rigorous alternatives analysis.

Under Section 230.80 of the EPA 404(b)(1) guidelines, EPA and the Corps may designate certain wetlands as suitable or unsuitable for disposal of dredged or fill material in advance, before development plans are imminent. This advance identification tells developers that EPA (and the Corps) will look unfavorably on any proposal to fill wetlands designated as unsuitable for fill. Although the WMP classified wetlands in advance as, in essence, either off-limits to development or developable, no formal EPA/Corps advance identification process was involved. According to an EPA official, EPA did not conduct an advance identification process of Anchorage's wetlands because (1) advance identification was still a fairly new concept when the Anchorage plan was initiated and EPA was just beginning to initiate advance identification efforts nationwide, and (2) the process is very resource intensive and EPA had minimal staff for Anchorage at the time. Anchorage's venture into advance identification of wetlands was a purely local effort, and one of the first in the nation.

Main Conflicts

The biggest issues during the planning process were (1) whether wetlands should be protected in the first place and (2) which ones would be protected and which ones developed. At the time the process began, many Anchorage residents still viewed wetlands as nuisances: as something to be filled and put to more productive uses. Moreover, many felt that the thousands of acres of wetlands lying outside Anchorage, still relatively undisturbed, should be protected and that those in Anchorage should be developed. In their view all of Anchorage should be zoned for development, and wetland areas outside the city, which were perceived as considerably more beautiful and pristine, should be preserved.

Others countered that the city's wetlands provided innumerable and irreplaceable values, such as open space and wildlife habitat, and that they should be protected precisely because they are easily accessible by its residents. Anchorage is probably the only large city in the United States where residents on their way to work can see moose feeding in wetlands.

The city staff moderated and facilitated the discussions and kept the process moving toward a consensus. Eventually, those initially opposed to wetland preservation admitted that wetlands have intrinsic values and that some are worth saving. The next step was to decide where to draw the lines to divide wetlands into those that would be developed and those that would be preserved. As one participant put it, it was time to decide "whose ox would get gored." Apparently, no elaborate conflict resolution techniques were used. According to one participant, all parties simply sat around the table and "hashed it out until a consensus was reached."

Ideally, Anchorage wetlands would have been classified based solely on their functional values: high-value wetlands preserved, low-value wetlands developed, and in-between wetlands put in the conservation category. In reality this was impossible. As the boundary lines were being drawn, it became apparent that many of the designations were based entirely on property ownership. The WMP wetlands delineation map placed many of the boundary lines separating one wetland category from another exactly along property lines with no particular relationship to the values of particular wetlands.

Of course, this was a politically expedient approach. Most landowners did not want any restrictions placed on their land and they vehemently argued for their wetlands to receive the developable designation. In order for the plan to be accepted, many wetlands found on private property were designated as conservation or developable, and most of the wetlands on city land were designated as preservation, regardless of their resource value. Thus, some high value wetlands were put in the developable category, and likewise, some low-value wetlands were designated as preservation. A fair number of high value wetlands lying on private property in the Anchorage Bowl and Eagle River, however, were classified as preservation.

Officials at the Department of Community Planning and Development pointed out that environmental factors were not the only considerations in classifying wetlands. For example, certain wetlands were located in areas that were designated in the comprehensive plan as parks and open space and were therefore classified as preservation, regardless of their value. Similarly, some high-value wetlands were classified as developable simply because they fell in areas identified in the comprehensive plan as future growth areas. Like the Corps, the city endeavored to balance competing interests in managing its wetlands, and that balance was reflected in both the WMP and the comprehensive plan.

The city relied on a number of different techniques, such as cluster zoning, easements, buffers and setbacks, and land swaps to protect its wetlands. For example, one land swap allowed the city to protect 104 acres of valuable wetlands in Connors Bog. It also offered to buy private lands that were put in the preservation category in order to prevent possible takings claims. Thus far, it has selectively purchased about 115 acres of wetlands at a total cost of about $3.5 million.

Interestingly, some landowners preferred to have their land placed in the preservation category and tried to get the city to buy their property. During the early 1980s, property values were increasing and the city seemingly had plenty of money to make land purchases. But when the local economy declined in the mid to late1980s, property values dropped 30 to 50 percent and many landowners hoped the city would buy them out.

Implementation

Anchorage was one of the first cities to get a general Section 404 permit from the Corps. The permit was issued for the developable wetlands, while the preservation and conservation categories were still subject to the Corps' case-by-case individual permit review under Section 404. The plan really only changed the permit process for wetlands designated as developable but brought long-awaited regulatory relief for developers in those areas. Instead of waiting five months or more for an individual 404 permit to build in wetlands, developers could get approval under the general permits within a day or two. And according to some developers, a prompt approval process is what made the long, drawn-out wetland planning process worthwhile.

Developers were less likely to submit applications for activities in preservation wetlands but were not similarly deterred from the conservation wetlands.

In addition, the Corps permitted fill in several preservation wetlands for public recreational uses. According to one official, the community strongly supported filling some preservation wetlands for softball fields; in balancing competing interests, the Corps responded to this public interest by issuing a permit. These were not, according to the Corps, high-value wetlands but were placed in the preservation category because they were owned by the municipality.

To compensate for the wetland loss, the municipality placed restrictive covenants on similar-sized, city-owned, developable wetlands to prohibit development. While construction of the new fields may have pleased the community, it irked EPA officials and others who believed that if "a deal is a deal," then no fill should be allowed for nonwater-dependent uses in preservation wetlands. EPA also contended that wetlands used for compensation were not economically developable, so the new restrictions gained nothing in compensation.

Mitigation

The Anchorage Department of Community Planning and Development has no formal mitigation policy. Although mitigation was discussed and identified as a goal of the 1982 plan, city officials felt the concept of mitigation was not fully developed at the time the plan was prepared. The city further argued that mitigation requirements for development in the preservation wetlands were unnecessary since development would generally not occur there, and mitigation would not be required for the developable wetlands either since the city wanted to reduce the regulatory burdens on developers. The city did recommend, however, that developers minimize the amount of fill, for example, by clustering buildings or by avoiding construction during bird or fish breeding seasons.

The Corps generally required in-kind mitigation for the few projects permitted in preservation wetlands. Thus, when a wetland was destroyed, a wetland of the same type and value was supposed to be created or preserved to compensate for the loss, although this seldom occurred. EPA was not enamored with this policy, which, the agency asserted, resulted in a gradual degradation in wetland quality and quantity. For example, wetland values can change over time: a high-value wetland can lose many of its most precious attributes when development occurs nearby.

The preservation category contains many low-value wetlands, either because they were designated as preservation in the original WMP or because they have gradually become degraded. When such low-value, preservation wetlands are filled, the Corps will only require that a low-value wetland be created as in-kind compensation, whereas EPA argues that the Corps should at least account for the wetlands diminished quality caused by development and require that they be replaced with high-value wetlands. To the Corps, however, the past is irrelevent. It bases mitigation requirements only on a wetland's current values or condition.

Since its adoption in 1982, the wetlands management plan steered development toward developable wetlands and away from preservation wetlands. A 1993 FWS study of wetlands permitting and wetlands losses in Anchorage revealed that, from 1982 to 1990, some 618 acres of developable wetlands, 220 of conservation wetlands, and about 30 acres of preservation wetlands were filled.[2] Overall, the city had lost about 10,000 acres of wetlands in the Anchorage Bowl since 1950.[3] Most (80 percent) of the wetlands losses occurred before the expansion of the Corps jurisdiction beyond navigable waters. The most extensive filling of preservation wetlands occurred as the result of widening a highway: 110 acres of preservation wetlands were filled. To offset the losses, approximately 211 acres of wetlands were flooded to increase their value for wildlife.

Revision of the Plan

Although most participants initially were satisfied with the plan, disagreements between the Corps and federal resource agencies such as EPA and FWS over the proper course of action on particular wetlands gradually grew more common. For example, in the late 1980s, a developer planned to fill 25 acres of wetlands that EPA considered prime wetlands. According to EPA, the wetlands were classified as developable but, because of their high resource values, should have been classified as preservation. Wetlands in the developable category were governed by a general permit, which generally presents no opportunity for public review. At its discretion, however, the Corps can require that a developer obtain an individual permit instead, which EPA and others unsuccessfully petitioned the Corps to do. After reviewing the project, the Corps determined that an individual permit was not warranted.

In a similar case, a developer, fearful that his land would be reclassified from developable to preservation, filled a portion of a wetland that was popular with the local community. No prospective buyers were identified; according to EPA, the development prospects were purely speculative. Located in the middle of the city, the wetland received a tremendous amount of public use and the developer's activity raised considerable public outcry. However, despite the vigorous objections of EPA and others, the Corps did not object to the fill since this wetland fill was covered by the general permit.

A common criticism among the plan's detractors was that although it provided speedier permit processing for developable wetlands, the plan provided no long-term protection for wetlands in the preservation category.

One of the biggest problems with the plan, however, was the conservation designation; nobody really approved of it. Some local observers claimed that it was too vague. It became a catch-all category for wetlands in which agreement could not be reached on whether to place them in the preservation or development categories. An official at the Department of Community Planning and Development remarked that the conservation category was created for wetlands about which the city did not have enough information or where there was no strong public consensus to either preserve or develop the wetlands.

Perhaps this problem reflects the uncertainty and lack of consensus over the fate of wetlands throughout the United States. Environmental groups claimed that the conservation category was just another license to develop, while developers asserted that the lack of certainty on permits in these areas was not improved by the designation. Both groups recommended abolishing the category entirely and making the hard decisions up front by classifying all wetlands as either developable or preservation. According to one official, if any single issue would have prompted revision of the WMP, it was the general dissatisfaction with the conservation category.

The 1982 Wetlands Management Plan required a reevaluation after five years and a full revision at least once every ten years. In early 1987, then-Mayor Tony Knowles set up a task force to review the plan and recommend possible changes. Specifically, the group was directed to reevaluate the wetland classifications and determine whether, based on new or better information on the city's wetland values, certain wetlands should be reclassified.

The task force included representatives from the real estate community, conservation groups, federal resource agencies, the Corps, and city officials. According to one member of the task force, there was a remarkably high level of cooperation and mutual understanding between the real estate community and the environmental community. Environmental representatives acknowledged that the city needed to make room for future growth and that some development would have to occur in wetlands. Likewise, developers were willing to support wetlands preservation; they just wanted to know, with some degree of certainty, where they could and could not build.

The task force met regularly and began the long, slow process of revising the plan. It collected additional information on the value of different wetlands covered by the plan, investigated various mitigation options for each wetland category, and evaluated best management practices for construction in wetlands.

Mayor Tony Knowles pressed the task force to complete the revised plan before the new administration took office. His administration had invested considerable time and effort in the plan, and Knowles and many task force members also believed that the incoming mayor would not support revisions of the plan. According to one task force member, as the Knowles administration was drawing to a close, the feeling among task force members was that if Tom Fink was elected, they could "kiss the task force good-bye."

The tight schedule imposed on the task force caused the draft of the revised plan to be completed hastily and, according to some members, inadequately. Some site visits were conducted, but many of the revised wetland assessments were based on a relatively small number of field evaluations. As a result, the task force did not unanimously support the draft revised plan, which was aired at a Planning and Zoning Commission public hearing. But the plan stalled following the election of the new mayor, Tom Fink. Shortly after he took office in 1988, Mayor Fink, as expected, effectively disbanded the task force by never asking it to reconvene. The momentum that had built up for revising the Anchorage wetlands plan quickly died shortly after his election.

The Corps was reluctant to make major revisions to the WMP unilaterally. It believed that any attempt to change the agreements made back in 1982 could upset the tenuous balance of interests. As one Corps official concisely summed up the agency's position, "a deal is a deal." According to another Corps official, "the integrity of the plan is its balanced approach."

The impending June 1993 expiration of the Corps' general permits for Anchorage finally prompted the city (in mid-1991) to begin revising the plan. The city already had missed its deadline for revising the wetlands management plan in 1992, but it did not want to lose its general permits, which greatly facilitated development in developable wetlands. But by 1991, the shortcomings of the 1982 plan, in particular the wetland designations, were impossible to ignore.

Even the Corps had finally been persuaded that the wetlands designations should be reevaluated prior to reauthorization of the general permits. It agreed to extend the general permits for six months, but, in deference to resource agencies, it removed many high value or contentious wetlands from the general permits and established more stringent conditions for development in developable wetlands. Development could still occur in the wetlands no longer covered by the general permits, but landowners would have to obtain an individual Section 404 permit.

The city began plan revisions by inspecting and evaluating over 200 wetlands using a wetlands assessment methodology developed the previous year in conjunction with state and federal resource agencies. The methodology evaluates four wetland functions: hydrology, habitat, species occurrence, and recreation/heritage. All wetlands were reevaluated in the summer of 1991 and classified as either high, medium, or low value, with the preservation, conservation, and developable categories replaced with A, B, and C, respectively. The special study category of the 1982 plan was abolished.

Wetlands receiving high marks for more than one of the four specified functions generally were classified as A; those receiving low scores for more than one function were classified as C; while B wetlands fell somewhere in between (see Figure 10.2). The city developed site-specific management strategies to accompany each wetland designation in order to protect some of the remaining values of each wetland. For example, some B or C wetlands contained pockets of valuable wildlife habitat. These pockets would be protected somewhat through buffer zones or setbacks where no development could occur.

Despite state and federal resource agency participation in developing the assessment methodology, the agencies found many faults with the final wetlands designations. The Alaska Department of Fish and Game, for example, observed that the designations are not mutually exclusive: a wetland that exhibits values of greater than C but lower than A in more than one category can also score higher than A and lower than C in more than one category. Thus, a wetland classified as B in this instance could also be classified as A or C.[4] Moreover, some of the categories were modified based on the city's "best professional judgment." Table 10.1 shows the number of acres of wetlands in each category (A, B, and C) for the three main regions of Anchorage.

Initially, the criteria for upgrading or downgrading a particular wetland was neither clearly described nor made available for public review. This made the entire assessment methodology seem arbitrary in the eyes of the environmental community as well as state and federal resource agencies. According to the Corps, people expected too much from the assessment methodology. "The scores are only the beginning of the assessment, not the end," explained a Corps official. On closer inspection, some changes were necessary. Also, some wetlands received high marks because of their value for open space and recreation, but the Corps must focus on water quality and navigability. Thus, some wetlands with a high recreational value were downgraded from A to B or C. In late 1993, the city released a report justifying its changes to the categories.

The draft revised wetlands management plan must clear numerous hurdles before it is adopted as a final plan and incorporated into the Corps' general permit. Having been approved by the city's Planning and Zoning Commission in September 1993 and the Anchorage Assembly in December 1993, the draft plan also must be approved by both the state Coastal Policy Council and the National Oceanic and Atmospheric Administration, since the WMP is part of Anchorage's coastal zone management plan. The lengthy approval process, which began in mid-1993, will likely stretch until the end of 1994 and could easily extend to mid-1995 if complications arise.

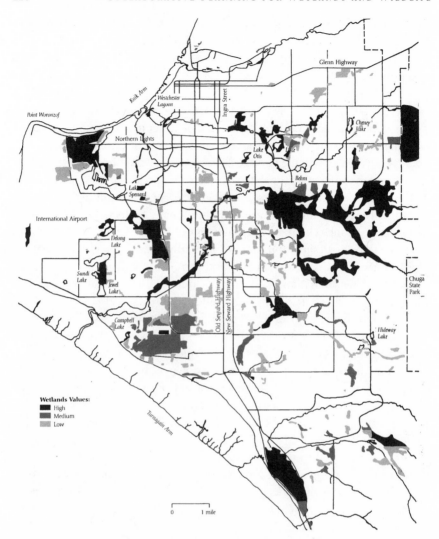

Figure 10.2 Distribution of wetlands and associated wetland types in the Anchorage area.

By itself, the Anchorage wetlands management plan is only a planning tool; it carries no regulatory teeth. The real prize for the city is the general permit from the Corps, which would authorize the municipality of Anchorage to act as the permitting agency for development in C wetlands, thus greatly speeding the permit process. Only when the plan is codified in the Corps' general permit will the true value of the plan be realized.

Recognizing this, the city worked to make the plan consistent with the Corps' proposed general permit. Despite pressure from some landowners, the

Table 10.1   1993 Draft Wetlands Management Plan:
Wetland Acres by Category

Location	A	B	C
Anchorage Bowl	3,597	1,288	1,842
Eagle River	1,790	944	573
Turnagain Arm	469	113	135[a]
Totals	5,856	2,345	2,550

Source: Figures from personal communication with Mary Lee Plumb-Mentjes, Senior Project Manager, U.S. Army Corps of Engineers, Alaska District, December 23, 1993.

[a] The Corps' proposed general permit lists 75 acres of wetlands in Turnagain Arm.

city refused to tamper with individual wetland designations. According to the Corps, general permits already have enough problems obtaining approval. One Corps official remarked, "If the [Anchorage] Assembly made this a political process by playing around with individual sites, it would encumber the review process." In any case, the Corps would retain final review and authority to determine compliance of a given activitity with the general permits.

The proposed general permit is actually five separate permits that would apply to different types of activities in C wetlands: (1) residential fill pads for driveways; (2) roads and other linear developments; (3) commercial and community development and parking lots; (4) industrial developments; and (5) wetlands or habitat enhancement. As proposed, the draft general permits will cover excavation, mechanized land clearing, and filling of wetlands designated as C in the revised (October 1993) Anchorage wetlands management plan. They would not apply to estuaries or anadromous riverine wetlands, protective greenbelts, or any other wetland not designated C. Also, the permits would not apply to speculative fills.

Numerous provisions were incorporated into the general permits to reduce adverse environmental impacts to wetlands. They include, for example, requirements that applicants design their projects to minimize the area of wetlands to be filled, establish a minimum setback of 66 feet from all streams and water bodies, and include measures to reduce adverse impacts on "fish, wildlife, and natural environmental values." Moreover, equipment must not be stored or operated in adjacent wetlands.

In addition, the general permits incorporate site-specific conditions modeled after the management strategies of the Anchorage wetlands management plan. The conditions specify actions that must be taken, for example, to protect adjacent properties from flooding, to buffer adjacent wetlands from adverse impacts, and to avoid draining adjacent wetlands. For instance, for wetlands along Baxter Lake, the proposed general permit states that "A hydrological analysis shall be done . . . to prevent flooding, maintain both surface and subsurface cross drainage and prevent drainage of adjacent wetlands."[5]

Not all wetlands are covered by such site-specific conditions. For some wetlands of low value, the Corps decided that no specific conditions were necessary.

Conclusions

A number of politically expedient compromises were made in order to bring the 1982 Anchorage wetlands plan to fruition. In particular, the classification of many wetlands was based more on land ownership than on the relative value of wetlands. Wetlands on private or public property were generally classified as developable or preservation, respectively, regardless of their values. This approach resulted in some high-value wetlands being designated as developable simply because they were located on private land; similarly, some low-value wetlands were classified as preservation because they occurred on city-owned land. But the Department of Community Planning and Development never intended the classifications to be based entirely on environmental values; other factors and considerations were incorporated into the original wetlands management plan, which became part of Anchorage's comprehensive plan.

Initially, the compromises generally provided something for everybody. Environmentalists were assured that, at least in the short run, the vast majority of wetlands in the preservation category would not be developed, while the development community could count on more predictable and expedited permit process for projects in developable wetlands.

Given the time of its development and what it was intended to do—balance economic development with wetland preservation, provide greater predictability, and increase general awareness of wetland values—the plan is remarkable in its achievements. Most of the agreements were kept. The city asserted that, overall, it protected most of those wetlands it had committed to protect and allowed development to occur only where it said it would. The plan provided the basis for the Corps to issue general permits for wetlands designated as developable, so the city, the Corps, and developers got what they wanted. Except for some relatively minor fills for utility lines, roads, and ball fields, most of the wetlands in the preservation category have been preserved, which generally pleased conservation groups.

By 1987, however, when the Corps' general permits (usually issued for five years) were about to expire, state and federal resource agencies began pushing for reclassification of wetlands in Anchorage. With development slowed to a near standstill and land prices depressed, the late 1980s was an ideal time to reevaluate the plan, reclassify wetlands based primarily on resource values, and make other necessary revisions.

Unfortunately, the mayor, assembly, and the Corps remained apprehensive about making any major revisions to the plan. It was not until the general permits were about to expire in 1993 that the revision process began in earnest.

Insofar as the new designations are based more on relative wetland values and not on property ownership, the 1993 draft plan improved considerably on the 1982 plan. The difficulty, however, lies in protecting high-value (A) wetlands on private land. With funds scarce, the city cannot afford to buy such wetlands. Neither can it completely restrict development in them without risking a lawsuit challenging that such action constitutes a taking of private property without compensation. Yet without assurances that A wetlands will be protected, many participants believe that the plan is neither balanced nor fair, given that over one-third of Anchorage's wetlands will likely be covered by a general permit. According to an official at the State Department of Fish and Game, "If you are going to create a general permit for some wetlands then you need to protect others."

With many hoops left to jump through, revision of the plan remains uncertain. Some believe that the plan, with its general permits, provides less protection for wetlands than under the individual permitting process. In fact, the National Wildlife Federation has threatened to sue the Corps if it reauthorizes the general permits for Anchorage. Others assert that the plan does not adequately address cumulative wetland losses.

One thing is certain, however: the planning and revision process has raised considerably the awareness of wetland issues and wetland values in Anchorage. Virtually all wetlands in Anchorage have been studied, inspected, and evaluated. According to the Corps, "We've really worked these sites over." Such detailed knowledge of most wetlands will enable the agencies, in theory, to protect the most valuable wetlands and allow some development to occur in others.

ACKNOWLEDGMENTS

The author wishes to thank the following people for their assistance in providing information for this chapter: Cliff Eames, Alaska Center for the Environment; Mary Lee Plumb-Mentjes, Alaska District, U.S. Army Corps of Engineers; Glenn Seaman, Alaska Department of Fish and Game; Sandy Tucker,

U.S. Fish and Wildlife Service; and Thede Tobish, Anchorage Department of Planning and Community Development.

NOTES

1. This chapter is based upon a similarly titled study prepared under the supervision of and copyrighted in 1989 by The Environmental Law Institute, Washington, D.C., and which was funded in part by The U.S. Environmental Protection Agency under EPA contract number 68-01-7378. It is represented in edited form with the permission of the Institute and the authors.
2. "Anchorage Wetlands Trends Study: 1950 to 1990," U.S. Fish and Wildlife Service, Anchorage Field Office, 1993, p. 3. Note that, from 1982 to 1990, 260 acres of preservation wetlands, 316 acres of conservation wetlands, and 1,492 acres of development wetlands were authorized for fill.
3. In 1950 the Anchorage Bowl contained about 18,900 acres of wetlands. By 1990 about 9,960 had been destroyed as a result of commercial and industrial development. See Clayton D. Robison, Jr., "Alaska Wetlands Are Not Different," *National Wetlands Newsletter,* September/October 1993, p. 14.
4. Personal communication from Lance L. Transky, Regional Supervisor, Alaska Department of Fish and Game to Michael J. Meehan, Director, Department of Community Planning and Development, September 20, 1993, p. 2.
5. "Draft Public Notice, Proposed General Permits 93-10, 93-11, 93-12, 93-13, 93-14, Anchorage Wetlands Management Plan," U.S. Army Corps of Engineers, Alaska District, December 23, 1993.

The East Everglades Planning Study

Kathleen Shea Abrams, with
Hugh Gladwin, Mary Jean Matthews,
and Barbara C. McCabe

E D I T O R S '   S U M M A R Y

The East Everglades, a 242-square-mile region lying between Everglades National Park and the urbanized areas of Dade County, Florida, is a study in continuing change and complexity and, in planning terms, in alternating conflict and consensus.

Conflicts among management objectives and competing uses in the East Everglades initiated two related planning efforts. The first, at the end of the 1970s, produced a scientific data base and a regulatory strategy that allowed continued, though restricted, development. The second effort, in the mid-1980s, built on the first plan by adopting strategies for incremental water management changes, residential flood protection, and land acquisition. This second planning effort, conducted under the auspices of the Everglades National Park/East Everglades Resource Planning and Management Committee (RPMC, or the ENP/EE Committee) is the focus of this chapter.

The challenge for the committee was to find a balance among competing objectives, such as plentiful water supply and adequate flood protection for agriculture, industry, and the public in the Miami/Dade County area; a more natural water delivery that would also provide high-quality (and timely) water for fish and wildlife in Everglades National Park; an inexpensive natural water purification system for nutrient-laden agricultural runoff; and recreational opportunities.

The committee has been effective in informing the general public and interest groups about the area's complex problems and possible solutions, and in adopting a process for adjusting resource management decisions as new knowledge is gained. In addition, the committee built broad public support for land acquisition and flood protection, both vital to the success of wetland protection and restoration. However, two key issues—flood protection for agriculture and the Park's water quality—remain controversial and not fully resolved, although significant steps have been taken in each case.

Environmental Significance of the East Everglades[1]

The East Everglades, encompassing some 153,600 acres or roughly 242 square miles, was a largely privately owned and undeveloped wetland lying between Everglades National Park (the Park) and the urban/rural limits of Dade County, Florida (see Figure 11.1). This remnant of the historic Everglades is neither park nor city but is home to both wildlife and people, exhibiting the complex relationships of aquifer and surface-water systems and of critical habitat and permanently altered wetland areas.

The central floor of the vast Everglades marsh is relatively impermeable, as it is composed of peat, marl, and clay; while highly porous limestone, constituting the very productive 3,200-square-mile Biscayne aquifer, underlies the marsh's edges.[2] The Biscayne acquifer, a federally designated sole-source aquifer, is the principal source of drinking water and irrigation for south Florida. The permeability of this aquifer makes it one of the most productive potable water supplies in the world.

The East Everglades contains the headwaters of two major natural water courses, the Northeast Shark River Slough (NESRS) and Taylor Slough. The Shark River Slough, some 25 miles wide, flows through 80 square miles of the southern end of the Everglades, including the Park; Taylor Slough drains approximately 40 square miles south and east of the Shark River Slough. Hardwood hammocks, or tree islands, dominate higher elevations, while a mosaic of sawgrass marshlands, sloughs, and flatlands covers lower elevations.

Sawgrass marshlands in the southern reaches of the East Everglades are subject to a saline influence that gradually increases in a north/south gradient toward Florida Bay. During the past several decades, both ground- and surface-water salinities have increased because of drainage and other water manipulation by humans.

The East Everglades area is an integral part of the entire south Florida region's agricultural, urban, and natural subsystems. According to Dade County's planning department, the area encompasses roughly half the land potentially available for agricultural development in the county. Urban uses rely on the East Everglades to supply drinking water and control flooding by retaining large quantities of water.

Although the East Everglades lies outside the boundaries of Everglades National Park, it is critical to maintaining valuable resources in the Park and the southern Everglades ecosystem, including Florida Bay. The timing, quality, and quantity of surface flows through the East Everglades into the Park and on to Florida Bay are critical not only to freshwater ecosystems within the Park and the East Everglades but also to fisheries in the Gulf of Mexico and Atlantic Ocean. These fisheries rely on the Everglades marsh for nursery grounds and

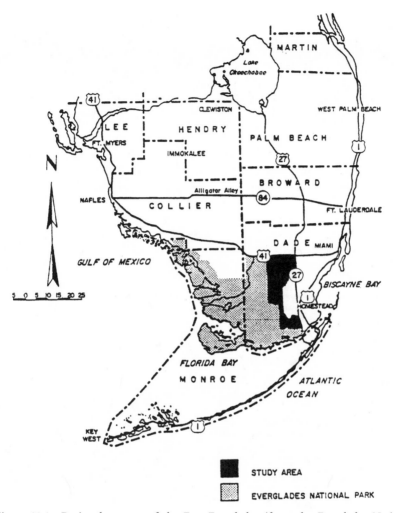

Figure 11.1 Regional context of the East Everglades (from the Everglades National Park/East Everglades RPN Implementation Plan).

on Florida Bay for feeding grounds. Freshwater volume is an important factor in preventing saltwater intrusion along the extensive coastline shared by the Park and Dade County.

Numerous plant and animal species have adapted to this special environment. For example, vegetative communities, which respond to very minor changes in slope, consist of

- Aquatic plants that grow in the ponds and sloughs formed by shallow depressions

Dwarf cypress stand out against a backdrop of sawgrass prairie. (Photo courtesy of Helen Longest-Slaughter.)

Deer pose for a photo amid the sawgrass prairie of the Everglades. (Photo courtesy of Helen Longest-Slaughter.)

- Sawgrass, a heavy type of sedge plant that dominates the wet prairie, forming layer upon layer of rich muck soil as it dies

- Hammocks, or tree islands, and willows that thrive where substrates deposited by the slow-moving water have raised the elevation above the prairie floor

Tree islands are home to tropical hardwoods, cabbage palms, royal palms, bromeliads, and orchids, and to tree snails with patterns unique to each hammock. Alligator holes create pockets of water where fish and amphibians can survive during prolonged dry periods. Wood storks and other aquatic birds take advantage of the high concentrations of fish found in these holes by producing young in the dry season.

Human alteration of the area's hydrology has adversely affected other ecosystem processes, such as soil formation and fire incidence, that in turn affect the Park's natural resources. For example, high water levels flood alligator nests and disperse food sources of wading birds during critical nesting periods. Low water levels cause conditions conducive to severe fires, which consume organic soils and enable nonnative (exotic) woody plant species, including Australian pine (*Casuarina* sp.) and punk trees (*Melaleuca quinquenervia*), to displace native plant communities.

In addition, many wildlife species rely on undeveloped lands within the East Everglades for nesting, feeding, foraging, and cover. The region supports over 350 species of amphibians, birds, reptiles, fishes, and mammals that include federal- or state-listed endangered species such as the Florida panther, Everglades snail kite, peregrine falcon, wood stork, bald eagle, Cape Sable seaside sparrow, and American crocodile. At one time the area provided 35 percent of South Florida's wood stork feeding grounds, but now the area is no longer suitable for feeding wood storks during the crucial nesting period because of the water level manipulation. The reduction in incidence of 12 rare, endemic plant species that provide supplemental gene pools to protected Park species has had a detrimental effect on the biological diversity and productivity of the area. Moreover, yearly fish densities and aquatic productivity have declined, and the aquatic trophic-level food chain has been altered.

The South Florida Water Management System

After Florida was granted statehood in 1845, the earliest public policy for the state's vast wetlands was, in a nutshell, "ditch and drain." In particular, after 1900 an influx of settlers was attracted to the region by promises of cheap land. State and private interests, such as railroad companies, altered wetlands for navigation, agriculture, and urban settlements.[3]

Following two hurricanes in the fall of 1947, Congress adopted a plan for flood control called the Central and Southern Florida Flood Control Project, which was developed by the U.S. Army Corps of Engineers (Corps). By 1949 the state legislature created the Central and Southern Florida Flood Control District (FCD), which became the local sponsor for the Corps' project, to operate and maintain the newly proposed works upon completion by the Corps.

Severe droughts from 1961 to 1965 changed the Corps' emphasis from flood control to water storage. The Corps and the FCD had successfully established three water conservation areas (WCAs), totaling some 1,344 square miles in parts of Dade, Broward, and Palm Beach counties, that supplemented the water storage capability provided by Hoover Dike in Lake Okeechobee. In total, the Corps built 780 miles of levees and 492 miles of canals.[4] Water storage in the lake and the water conservation areas is controlled by water release schedules agreed to by the Corps and the FCD that reflect the agencies' shared goal of balancing competing needs such as flood control, water supply, and wildlife habitat maintenance.

In the mid-1960s disagreements began to surface between the National Park Service (NPS), representing Everglades National Park, and the FCD over

A complex web of water-control structures has permanently altered the natural water flow of the Everglades. (Photo courtesy of Everglades National Park.)

the schedule of water releases from WCA-3 into the Shark River Slough and from there to the Park. Although historically the Park received more than half its water from rainfall, the rest originated from overland flow coming from the Everglades to the north and the Big Cypress Swamp to the northwest. Completion of the eastern perimeter levee system, however, and the canals and levees surrounding the water conservation areas, significantly altered historic water flow through the southern Everglades. During drought conditions in the 1960s, the water level in WCA-3A never reached the level specified for release to the Park, thus cutting the Park off from the overland flow. In 1967, a 9.5-mile canal extension was dug from WCA-3A into the heart of the Park's section of the Shark River Slough in an effort to deliver additional water when the rest of the Everglades was dry.

In 1970, responding to Park water problems, the U.S. Congress enacted the River Basin Monetary Authorization and Miscellaneous Civil Works Amendments Act (PL 91-282) that mandated a minimum water delivery schedule to the Park. Requirements for regulatory releases from WCA-3A through the water control structures along Tamiami Trail would supply all external water for the eastern portion of the Park.

Continued problems in the Park from a protracted drought in south Florida in 1971 prompted then-governor Reubin Askew to convene a key policy conference on water management. Policy recommendations from the conference formed the basis for the Florida Water Resources Act of 1972, which broadened the authority of the Flood Control District. In 1976, the FCD became the South Florida Water Management District (the District), an agency with taxing power over a region encompassing 17,000 square miles in 16 counties with 40 percent of the population and 31 percent of the land area of the state.

The state has delegated increasing responsibility for water quality regulation and water management to the five water management districts in Florida because of their independent taxing powers. The Florida Department of Environmental Protection (DEP) has retained authority for dredge-and-fill permitting and for establishing and enforcing water quality criteria for discharges to wetlands.

The 1980 Management Plan

Until the 1970s there was little development pressure in the East Everglades. Midway through the decade, however, residential and agricultural development west of the East Everglades flood protection levee grew rapidly.[5] Development at nearly urban densities was permitted without requiring public water supply and flood-proof roads. Dade County, which had issued the land use permits, became concerned about flood risks to development and the inevitable demands for roads, drainage, and other governmental services.[6] At the same time, the public began to recognize the East Everglades' value as a primary recharge area for the Biscayne Aquifer and the area's critical value to the adjacent Park and Florida Bay.

In 1978, in response to these concerns, Dade County initiated the East Everglades Resource Planning Project, which evaluated growth and resource management problems in the area and made recommendations for addressing them in the 1980 Management Plan for the East Everglades. Major funding for this research was provided by the U.S. Environmental Protection Agency (EPA). The project was guided by an interagency steering committee composed of representatives from the county, Florida Department of Environmental Protection, the District, the National Park Service, and a citizen's advisory committee that included environmentalists and East Everglades homeowners and farmers.

According to its statement of purpose, the study sought to obtain scientific data and to analyze, synthesize, and project the effects of various land and water uses on the ecosystems of the East Everglades.[7] The plan contained an inventory and assessment of the area's hydrology, land uses, and natural features in an effort to estimate its capacity for agricultural and residential development and wildlife habitat. The management plan also called for managing the area primarily for its hydrological and wetlands values, while allowing "seasonal agriculture" and low-density residential development to continue.

The management plan and its plan of study recognized conflicts between use of private property and public interests in the East Everglades. The plan sought to resolve the complex environmental, economic, and social issues that surround the future supply of water for Dade County and the Everglades National Park. The preface to the plan of study asserted the county's intention to continue to accommodate "the national and international demand for the products of Dade County agriculture and the desire of property owners to use their East Everglades land holdings," although at the same time giving precedence to "the long-term health of the water supply. . . ." In fact, the plan stated that "the land of the East Everglades is . . . held in private ownership and, subsequently, the use of such property commensurate with its natural character must be allowed." The preface to the plan, however, recognized the potentially high costs to taxpayers at large of low-density rural development in floodplains and wetlands.

The Dade County Commission formally adopted the management plan in January 1981. It also adopted ordinances for its implementation. A zoning overlay ordinance down-zoned the area by a factor of eight, from one unit per five acres to one unit per 40 acres, and established environmental performance standards for the area's development. Although the one-unit-per-40-acre density could be boosted to the previous density (one unit per five acres) in existing residential areas, the flood control measures required to permit the increase in density were never provided.

A severable use rights (SURs) ordinance (similar to a transfer of development rights program) allowed density to be transferred from parts of the East Everglades into areas within the 1990 urban growth boundary on the county's land use map.

The 1980 plan accomplished much. It built a valuable data base concerning the area's hydrology, soils, vegetation, wildlife, land use patterns, and water quality impacts. It defined three primary management areas based on their wetlands characteristics. It formulated a set of regulatory recommendations that lowered allowable residential densities in all areas; specified which areas were suitable for seasonal farming; and encouraged recreational uses, including recreational facility development and seasonal and permanent wetlands.

The management plan, however, fell short of its goal of resolving the complex environmental, economic, and social issues of the East Everglades.

Seasonal agriculture and residential development were permitted uses in seasonal wetlands, and some residential development was allowed even in permanent wetlands. While the plan called for protection of wetlands and preservation of critical wildlife habitat, it did not foresee that a solely regulatory approach to wetlands protection would be insufficient.

Meanwhile, residential and agricultural development continued, despite occasional incidents of flooding. Notwithstanding the newly adopted plan and ordinances, the county continued its practice of granting density variance increases in urban Dade County without requiring purchase of SURs. Hence, any potential market for the SURs allocated to East Everglades property owners was negated, an occurrence that caused property owners to accuse the county of acting in bad faith.[8]

Additionally, farming interests interpreted the term *seasonal agriculture* to mean assured farming during each year's winter season, even if District action were needed to draw down groundwater levels in wetter-than-usual years. Farmers began to plant year-round crops as farmland elsewhere in the county became scarcer and costlier.

Emerging Centers of Conflict

The inevitable problems engendered by these practices became apparent in 1981 when the governor ordered state assistance to evacuate residents following severe flooding that lasted for weeks in the wake of tropical storm Dennis. But flooding in the residential area was only one part of a complex set of problems in the East Everglades. These problems centered on four areas: the 8.5-square-mile residential area; the Frog Pond agricultural area; another agricultural area along the western bank of the L-31N canal, and the Aerojet industrial complex.

The 8.5-Square-Mile Residential Area

The 8.5-square-mile area (see Figure 11.2) contains several hundred single-family residences and agricultural structures, a large number of plant nurseries and farms, and an estimated population of between 700 and 900 persons. Few roads are built to floodproof elevations. Outside of the 8.5-square-mile area, another 8,300 estimated ownership tracts have been laid out, varying in size from 1.25-acre lots to 640-acre lots. Most tracts are smaller than 40 acres and most are vacant and unimproved, in fact not posted, fenced, or marked in any way.

Perhaps the droughts of the 1970s had given a false sense of security that widespread development could proceed in the 8.5-square-mile area. Even the

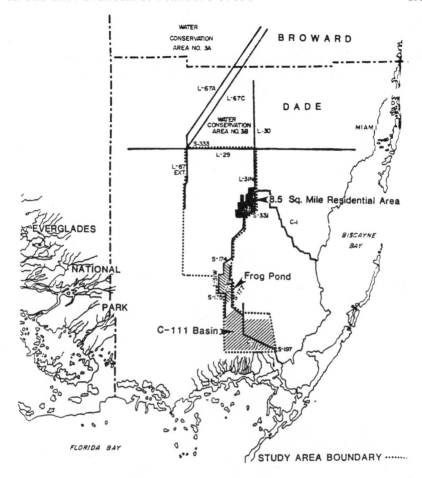

Figure 11.2 Major areas of concern (from the Everglades National Park/East Everglades RPN Implementation Plan).

stringent performance criteria in the county's zoning ordinances may have created false expectations of security from flooding among those seeking to build in the East Everglades. The intense rainfall that accompanied the tropical storm was statistically a one-in-200-year event, but U.S. Geological Survey records show that the resulting 7.8-foot flooding had been equalled or exceeded four times from 1965 to 1969. In the 8.5-square-mile residential area, prolonged surface flooding occurred an average of once every five to seven years.

Flooding was not the only problem in this area. Residents and property owners were convinced that Dade County was purposefully holding down property values in the expectation of public purchase. Buildable lots of less than 40 acres were permitted only if protected against floods. The lack of flood protection made building permits difficult to obtain, even though an influx of Hispanic buyers had purchased many lots (some advertised as "waterfront property") and had often paid many times the appraised value. Property owners thus continued to press for flood protection facilities.

Agricultural Areas

The L-31N and Frog Pond agricultural areas are located within former wetlands lying close to existing canals. Year-round groves of avocados, limes, and mangoes, and seasonal row crops of malanga (taro) and tomatoes are the dominant agricultural use. Even though the canals, which fostered agricultural expansion, provide some drainage, a high risk of flooding remains.

Still, development for agriculture continued for many years. Most permit applications for this area, however, were withdrawn or denied by the Corps of Engineers. Denials were based on environmental protection requirements, including the availability of alternative unfarmed sites in the 8.5-square-mile area and of upland sites east of L-31. However, all permits for Frog Pond area farming had been issued several years ago. With the exception of several tree island preserves, the Frog Pond had been rock plowed to clear the land and prepare the limestone for planting. Frog Pond farmers have been particularly resistant to any attempts to acquire their properties or to reduce the value of their land for farming.

Aerojet General Corporation Site

Aerojet General owned a large amount of land in the East Everglades and operated an industrial complex for manufacturing rockets. In the early 1960s the Aerojet General Corporation had planned to barge rocket motors through the C-111 canal from the company's testing area in south Dade County to the Intracoastal Waterway and then to Kennedy Space Center. The National Audubon Society filed suit against the Corps of Engineers, which had built the canal, claiming that saltwater intrusion from the canal would cause major ecological changes in the Park. As a result of the lawsuit, the Corps agreed to block C-111 at its lower end with an earthen plug. NASA rejected the proposed rocket booster program, however, and the complex was later deactivated.[9]

C-111 is still used, however, to provide flood control for southern Dade County. In times of heavy rain, the earthen plug has been removed to offer immediate flood relief to farms and residents. This was done twice in 1981, once in 1982, once in 1985, and again in August 1988. The 1988 removal caused massive freshwater discharges over an eight-day period, resulting in dramatic die-offs of fish and other saltwater aquatic life.

Rock plowing continues to pit agricultural interests against conservation interests in the East Everglades. (Photo courtesy of Everglades National Park.)

Litigation and Negotiation

In the early 1980s conflicts between the District, the Corps, the Park, and local farmers and homeowners heated up. The water conservation areas in the East Everglades began to deteriorate noticeably due to high levels of nitrates and phosphates contained in runoff from agricultural areas south of Lake Okeechobee. The WCAs were being choked by cattail, an indicator of poor water quality, and nonnative pest trees were displacing native vegetation and altering the habitat value for native species, such as the Everglades snail kite and its source of food, the apple snail.[10]

Since the Park is the primary flood outlet for the WCAs, the National Park Service called for dramatic improvement in water quality for the benefit of the Park. In March 1983, Park officials submitted a seven-point proposal to the South Florida Water Management District, which, in response, issued its own "Seven-Point Plan." The plan called for a new water delivery schedule and studies with the Corps on potential impacts of modifying structures and canals in WCA-3 and the Shark River Slough.

By August of that year, then-Governor Bob Graham announced the Save Our Everglades program. The program established an overall mission for improving the Everglades system and provided a framework for addressing problems systematically. The program's goal was to enable the Everglades by the year 2000 to look and function more as they did in 1900 than they did in 1983.[11]

Meanwhile, litigation erupted over flooding. In 1978 a water control structure known as Structure-333 was built to allow releases into the Northeast Shark River Slough. Property owners and farmers, worried about potential high groundwater levels that might result from such releases, persuaded the Corps and the District to postpone releases.

In 1983, however, in response to the Park's and District's concerns over water quality, the Corps announced a plan to begin water releases. The U.S. Congress also stepped in with legislation that authorized experimental water releases for a two-year period, and it had promised that homeowners and farmers would be compensated if adversely affected by the releases. (The legislation also authorized $10 million to provide flood protection to the 8.5-square-mile residential area and to purchase up to 6,000 acres of farmland, but the money was never appropriated.)[12]

Farmers and homeowners brought a lawsuit against the District and the Corps to stop the planned releases. The farmers also wanted the Corps to continue its annual fall drawdowns of water levels to assist fall planting. The advent of the lawsuit intensified negotiations that were then taking place between the District and representatives of the farmers and homeowners. Also, in late 1983 and early 1984 the District formed an internal task force to devise a conflict management strategy for the East Everglades; the task force analyzed the interests and concerns of the various parties involved in the ongoing disputes, and it evaluated water management options for achieving multiple objectives. The next year, the Park, anxious to avoid lengthy legal battles over plans for restoration of the Northeast Shark River Slough and Taylor Slough, reached an agreement with the farmers that allowed the experimental water releases to go forward with stringent measures to prevent groundwater rises in developed areas. The Park agreed not to object to seasonal drawdowns for two years if, in turn, the farmers promised not to object to the releases. (The provisions of this agreement were incorporated into the subsequent deliberations of the Everglades National Park/East Everglades [ENP/EE] Committee.)

The turmoil between government agencies and local interests in the early 1980s, only partly sketched here, called for a decisive effort to resolve differences and to structure a strategy for future actions in the East Everglades. That came with Governor Graham's establishment of a Resource Planning and Management Committee in February 1984.

The Resource Planning and Management Committee

Florida's program of Areas of Critical State Concern was established in 1975 (Chapter 380.05, Florida Statutes). An Area of Critical State Concern is a delineated geographical area in which conservation and development issues are considered of statewide importance. Once an area is designated, local governments must draft land use plans and implementing ordinances that reflect state-developed principles for guiding development. Actual implementation of the land use plans and regulations rests with the local governments. The state, however, retains oversight for each local development order within the area's boundaries.

In 1979 the legislature amended the act to require establishment of a Resource Planning and Management Committee (RMPC) when the state is considering designation of an Area of Critical State Concern. The governor appoints a voluntary, multiple-interest group to meet over the course of one year to address resource protection and development issues within a delineated planning area. Its recommendations are submitted to the governor and cabinet for approval. Local governments within the area can modify their land use plans and implementing ordinances to reflect the RPMC's approved recommendations. If they do not, however, the state may designate the area as an Area of Critical State Concern, with continued state involvement and oversight of the development process within the area.

From the standpoint of some local governments within the RPMC area, the process is a combination of steel fist and velvet glove, but participation on the RPMC assures local governments that their perspectives will be a part of the RPMC process.

According to Section 380.0045(4), state and regional agencies are directed to "cooperate to the maximum extent possible in ensuring that the program is given full effect." There is no requirement for state agencies, however, to adopt different standards or to designate staff resources for an RPMC area, except in the case of the lead agency, the Department of Community Affairs (DCA). Federal agencies are invited to participate with the hope that subsequent federal actions will conform with the RPMC plan. To address the complex set of issues that had been emerging over several decades, Governor Bob Graham established the ENP/EE Committee on February 7, 1984, as a Resource Planning and Management Committee for the East Everglades.

Objectives of the Committee

Water was the central issue before the committee, which was directed to devise a plan aimed at achieving environmental restoration of wetlands and saltwater bodies, water quality protection, adequate flood protection for residential and agricultural landowners, and Park protection by means of land acquisition and other methods. The committee's objectives were to

1. Restore, as much as practicable, the natural sheet flow of water into the Park through the Shark River Slough

2. Ensure that the quality of the water flowing into the Park and the Biscayne aquifer is not degraded due to development practices in the East Everglades

3. Ensure that the quality and quantity of water entering Florida Bay will allow rejuvenation of the estuarine systems and restoration of their productivity

4. Coordinate with local, regional, and state governments and property owners in the area to develop recommendations for adequate flood protection measures for residential and agricultural areas within the East Everglades

5. Ensure that future development in Dade County does not affect the vitality of the natural ecosystems in the East Everglades and the Park

6. Establish priorities for land acquisition and land acquisition alternatives to protect the Park[13]

The governor's directive called for a comprehensive strategy that would protect water quality, acquire and manage land, and manage water for multiple purposes.

Participants and Key Stakeholders

Chapter 380 of the Florida statutes establishes the mandated, minimum membership for committees and also enables the governor to make additional committee appointments beyond the designated state, regional, and local government agencies. The state land planning agency, DCA, is the lead agency. The statute directs DCA to provide committees with administrative and technical support to the greatest possible extent. In addition, within six months of its formation, a committee must make an initial report to the secretary of the Department of Community Affairs.

Besides DCA, Florida state agencies participating in the committee included the Department of Environmental Regulation (DER), the Game and Freshwater Fish Commission (FGFWFC), the Department of Natural Resources (DNR), and the Florida Department of Agriculture (DOAg). DER is responsible for protecting water quality and wetland habitat values. The FGFWFC and DNR are responsible for acquiring and/or managing public lands for wildlife and recreation. (In 1992, DER and DNR were combined into a single agency, The Department of Environmental Protection.) The DOAg regulates agricultural chemicals and promotes farming and farm products. The South Florida Water Management District, a regional agency, is charged with supplying drinking and irrigation water and flood control to public and commercial interests and, with DER, protecting water quality and wetland values.

Local agencies included the Dade County Planning Department and the Department of Environmental Resources Management (DERM), which are responsible for planning for or regulating local growth and development and for assuring an adequate supply of potable water for present and future multiple uses.

Governor Graham exercised his authority to expand membership of the RPMC beyond a representative group of relevant public agencies to a microcosm of the area's array of competing interests. These interests ranged from improved flood protection for agricultural and residential property to assuring an adequate urban water supply to wetlands restoration and critical habitat preservation. The ENP/EE Committee included environmentalists, Dade County businessmen, East Everglades residents, farmers, and Miccosukee Tribe representatives. Federal agencies involved were the National Park Service, the Corps of Engineers, and the Department of Agriculture (USDA).[14]

The governor appointed as chairman a vice-president of a large, local homebuilding corporation who had served as Dade County manager during the late 1970s.

Despite the breadth of interests represented on this committee, two key federal agencies, the Environmental Protection Agency and the U.S. Fish and Wildlife Service, were not among the participants, even though both agencies have authority to affect the conservation and development agreement hammered out by the committee. Interviews with state officials suggest that these agencies were not invited to participate because it was believed their interests would be adequately represented by their state counterparts, the Department of Environmental Regulation and the Florida Game and Freshwater Fish Commission.

Other stakeholders not represented on the committee were residential property owners outside the 8.5-square-mile area and Aerojet General Corporation. Residential property owners outside the 8.5-square-mile area had no property owners association nor official spokesperson to represent them on the committee. Aerojet, although a major landowner in the area, was in the process of negotiating sale of much of its East Everglades land holdings to the state.

Conduct of the Study

Deliberations of the East Everglades Committee were conducted in the manner of the state's prior resource planning and management committees: DCA staff members prepared issue papers; the committee chairman appointed subcommittees and assigned specific issue areas; the subcommittees developed recommendations concerning these issue areas; and the recommendations were reported to the full committee, where a majority vote of those present and eligible was needed to accept, modify, or reject recommendations for the plan.

DCA staff members drafted much of the committee's plan and the committee revised substantial sections line by line during meetings. Recommendations with majority support formed the basis for the committee's plan, which was submitted to the DCA for adoption by the governor and cabinet. Six months after the formal adoption of the plan by the governor and cabinet, the ENP/EE Committee met to review agency reports of plan implementation, to determine progress, and to form action recommendations for DCA. Then the committee was disbanded.

The RPMC process relies on participant cooperation. No agency except the DCA is specifically funded for participating in the RPMC process. However, the Corps of Engineers, National Park Service, Soil Conservation Service, DCA, DER, the District, and Dade County's departments of planning and environmental resource management not only participated in the RPMC process but also contributed staff expertise to a technical advisory committee. The technical committee also included a hydrologist employed by a group of East Everglades agricultural interests.

The ENP/EE Committee differed from other Florida RPMCs in that the chairman, rather than a government agency, was usually the most active member. But since most controversies in the resource planning and management area centered on water and water management, the District played a major role in focusing issues and building consensus throughout the process. The District sponsored an American Assembly, a consensus-building policy development process among key decisionmakers and interests on overall water management goals for the RPMC area, especially Florida Bay. The goals and recommendations of the conference, which advocated a balance of habitat protection and wetlands restoration with enhanced flood control and assured water supply, were brought back to the full committee for adoption.[15] The District also designed the iterative testing and conflict resolution strategies that the committee adopted as integral parts of its plan.

Obstacles to Consensus

Economic and philosophical differences permeated the RPMC process. Agricultural interests and residents both wanted flood protection. In addition, area farmers wanted earlier drawdowns of groundwater levels to make the soil drier at greater depths, allowing cultivation of more lucrative crops earlier in the season.

The importance of agriculture in southern Dade County cannot be overlooked: it is a multimillion-dollar business that accounts for half the winter crop of tomatoes and winter vegetables produced in the United States, although the total acreage planted in tomatoes has been shrinking.[16] In the East Everglades, over 26,000 acres were potentially available for agriculture—more than half the land in south Dade County suitable for agriculture.[17]

Metro-Dade County, the combined city/county agency, was particularly concerned about assuring a local water supply for a proposed large well field to be located in or near the East Everglades. In a 1984 District board meeting, representatives of the county's planning and environmental permitting departments objected to proposed drawdowns for farming operations in the East Everglades. The Corps of Engineers decided in 1988 to stop them altogether, but Frog Pond agricultural interests continued to demand reinstatement of the practice or construction of permanent flood protection works.

Environmental interests, including representatives of Everglades National Park, pointed to the changed water regime as the primary cause of deteriorating conditions in the Everglades. Wood stork colonies in the Park are but one example. In the 1930s 3,000 to 5,000 pairs of wood storks were reported in the East Everglades. Between 1948 and 1960 the average number of breeding pairs was just over 2,000. But counts for 1970 to 1987 found that the mean annual breeding population of wood stork had plummeted to 374.[18]

Government agencies with different missions disagreed with one another regarding the priorities of restoration activities. For example, DER asserted that long-term comprehensive monitoring of agricultural operations was essential, whereas the District pointed to prior studies that had found no evidence of aquifer pollution from East Everglades farming. (These studies had monitored a narrow range of pollutants for short periods.) The District and DER agreed to a two-year monitoring study, but the interagency disagreement arose again after initial monitoring results showed negligible amounts of herbicides and pesticides in the East Everglades water column. Although the study continued to find minimal evidence of pollution at the test sites, DER and DERM remained skeptical of the results because of the location of test wells and other aspects of testing.[19]

Philosophical differences could also be found *within* some of the participating public agencies, especially the District. Among other things, the District is charged with providing flood control, protecting wetlands, assuring water supply, and regulating water use for consumption. The District attempted to resolve the issues raised by its competing responsibilities by forming an intradepartmental task force on the East Everglades in late 1983 to develop a comprehensive water management strategy. This task force was instrumental in analyzing data and devising water management recommendations in response to the District's and the committee's needs.

Distrust in the District's ability to address competing needs was evident in the views of various factions: the Park, the county, the farmers, and the home-

A tranquil sunset over a sawgrass slough belies the rancorous debates over the future of the East Everglades. (Photo courtesy of Helen Longest-Slaughter.)

owners all believed that water was not being managed properly. In short, the RPMC process began in a climate in which each group felt its interests had been damaged by public agency action.

Insufficient and patchy understanding of the area's complex hydrology and the potential impacts of proposed operational and structural changes had a substantial impact on the final shape of the special area plan. Large-scale, irreversible changes in the hydrology of the Everglades, including the timing, quantity, and quality of water releases, had continued for approximately 80 years. Relationships among built structures—the canals, roads, and levees that traverse them—and the natural systems were not fully understood. As a result, sweeping changes to the existing system were considered inadvisable. What developed from the RPMC process was an incremental approach, where hypotheses could be tested while risks were minimized.

The ENP/EE Committee's Plan and Implementation Program

To address the breadth of the governor's charge to the ENP/EE Committee, nearly 70 policies or actions were articulated in the plan's recommendations, which included separate actions for different geographic areas (e.g., Northeast Shark River Slough) and issue areas (e.g., streamlining the permitting process). The recommendations were made within the context of an overt strategy to deal with the insufficiency of information about the workings of the natural systems in the Everglades. A summary of the problems faced by the ENP/EE Committee (along with their methods of resolution) is presented in Table 11.1.

The three-part strategy included the establishment of an iterative testing process (ITP), the formation of the Southern Everglades Technical Committee (SETEC), and the development of a conflict resolution process. The ITP provides an approach to determining the best water management by making incremental changes to existing systems, structures, and operating procedures and then testing their results. Once the best method of implementation was defined, it would be adopted as standard policy. The process of modifying water management practices for various parts of the natural system and testing their system-wide impacts on the Everglades ecology and hydrology has demanded close coordination among the Corps of Engineers, the Park, and the District.

The second part of the strategy was established by SETEC, the forum for informing and coordinating the iterative testing process. Membership in SETEC was open to any group or agency conducting hydrological or ecological research about water delivery or quality in the southern Everglades.

TABLE 11.1 Important East Everglades Problems with
ENP/EE Committee Methods for Resolution

Problems	Resolution mechanisms
Multiple decisionmakers	• Local, state, and federal government plus private interest representation on the ENP/EE Committee
Potential impacts on various stakeholders of proposed changes; e.g., in water delivery to Everglades National Park or in new agricultural operations	• Various stakeholders represented on the ENP/EE Committee • Governor's charge to devise plan for multiple objectives • Iterative testing process (ITP) • Land-acquisition recommendations • Flood-protection recommendations
Multiple interrelationships among environmental, economic, social, and technological variables	• Issue papers, briefings, and field trips to inform all members • ITP evaluation of interrelationships • C-111 conference examining problems and recommending action plan for C-111 Basin
Unforeseen problems that can be created by poorly informed actions	• ITP • SETEC • Interim regulatory guidelines for rock plowing during water quality monitoring program • Use of data from 1980 Management Plan
Risk, uncertainty, and ambiguity that can result from dramatic changes in resource management	• ITP • Ongoing conflict resolution • SETEC

The third part of the strategy recognized that recommendations of the implementing committee could lead to controversy and conflict. The ENP/EE Committee recommended the establishment of a structured, three-step conflict resolution process to undertake cooperative problem solving, negotiation, and, if necessary, mediation to resolve disputes over data or policy. Together, the overall implementation strategy allowed actions to be modified as new information became available.

Two examples of specific actions recommended by the plan illustrate the complexity of the issues and the level of cooperation required of the participants.

Land Acquisition Program

First, the committee agreed that land acquisition, because it provided compensation to private landowners, was the best means of protecting the public and private interests in the East Everglades. During the Reagan administration, however, and particularly under James Watt (who served as Secretary of the U.S. Department of the Interior during the ENP/EE Committee's tenure), the U.S. Department of Interior's land acquisition budget was slashed dramatically. Even funds authorized by Congress had been left unappropriated. Consequently, the committee recommended acquisition and management by the state and the District.

The inholdings to be purchased included part of the Aerojet complex, for which acquisition efforts were under way when the ENP/EE Committee was established. The Trust for Public Land bought 50,200 acres of Aerojet's property, which was then jointly acquired by DNR and the District. The total purchase price exceeded $17 million.[20] The committee also gave top acquisition priority to land with the greatest development potential, specifically lands west of the 8.5-square-mile residential area and undeveloped lands in Management Area 3.

For some time the remaining East Everglades lands were given low priority for state acquisition; the East Everglades was number 46 on the 60-item priority list of the state Conservation and Recreation Lands program. On June 13, 1989, however, the governor and the cabinet voted to include the area within the Save Our Everglades program. This action, in effect, authorized the state to negotiate the land acquisition.[21] Soon after, however, in December 1989, the U.S. Congress enacted the Everglades National Park Protection and Expansion Act, PL 101-229, which authorized the acquisition of 107,600 acres to expand Everglades National Park. The land acquired by the state through The Trust for Public Land was transferred to the Park as part of this acquisition program.[22]

Flood Protection Policies

A second recommendation of the plan concerned the issue of flood protection for the 8.5-square-mile residential area, which addressed concerns over development densities, land acquisition, and restored sheet flow. The plan recommended the following actions:

- Provide flood protection to the 8.5-square-mile residential area for a 1-in-10-year storm without regard to possible impacts from Northeast Shark River Slough

- Develop an environmentally sound design for flood protection, consistent with the restoration of sheet flow to Everglades National Park and acceptable to local, state, and federal regulatory agencies

- Obtain guarantees from the county and the District, prior to design of flood protection, that density will not exceed one unit per five acres and that flood protection would not set a precedent for further development beyond the 8.5-square-mile residential area

- Develop local cost-sharing methods for flood control measures that are acceptable to all substantially affected interests, including the county, landowners, the federal government, and the District

- Arrange with property owners within the 8.5-square-mile residential area that in return for an agreed funding program for flood control, they would withdraw their objections to restoring the Northeast Shark River Slough

- Acquire the priority lands adjacent to the 8.5-square-mile residential area before construction of the flood protection system is completed.

By calling for development restrictions, these commitments harked back to the 1980 Management Plan for the East Everglades. Unlike the 1980 plan, however, committee policies made commitments for public land acquisition and flood protection and identified the entities responsible for carrying them out.

Implementation Program

The plan was to be implemented by assigning primary responsibility for each recommended action to one or more agencies, identified as the lead agencies, and assigning secondary responsibility to other agencies, called contributing agencies. As is the case with all of Florida's RPMCs, the DCA has overall responsibility for coordinating, monitoring, and reporting plan implementation actions. Lead and contributing agencies are expected to submit regular reports to DCA on the status of implementation actions assigned to them.

DCA is responsible for reviewing and compiling those reports into implementation status reports for distribution to the governor, lead and contributing agencies, and other members of the committee.

Responsibility was assigned to a variety of agencies. For some actions, it was allotted to the Southern Everglades Technical Committee, comprising technical and scientific representatives of the various interests represented on the ENP/EE Committee.

1989 Status Evaluation

In 1989 the study authors evaluated the implementation of the ENP/EE plan. Officials of local, regional, state, and federal agencies were interviewed; members of the ENP/EE Committee were surveyed; and agency reports and memorandums since 1985 were analyzed. Interviews with state, regional, and federal officials also sought information about the RPMC process in general.

Analysis of Implementation Efforts

Table 11.2 shows the results of the analysis of plan implementation status overall and for each issue area. Two-thirds of all of the proposed actions were reported as complete; 17 percent were reported as incomplete; 12 percent had no reported implementation; and the fate of the remaining 5 percent of actions was unknown. Completed actions varied widely according to the issues involved. Of the eight water management actions outside the C-111 basin, six were judged complete and two were reported as incomplete. For the five C-111 basin items, however, one was complete, three were incomplete, and one was unknown. For the total of 11 water quality actions, five were complete, four had no action, and two were incomplete or unknown. Of the 17 land planning and management actions, 15 were complete and the other two either were incomplete or had no action taken. Follow through was least for C-111 basin actions and for water quality actions.

The lack of completion on C-111 actions in large part stemmed from the status of the Corps of Engineers' general design memorandum (GDM), which at the time of the evaluation was still being prepared. The severe impacts of "pulling the C-111 plug" in August 1988 and subsequent public response to that action, described earlier, apparently delayed the GDM while the Corps and the District discussed the adoption of interim measures.

Also, land acquisition was slowed by staunch resistance from farmers and residents to selling their properties. When Aerojet Corporation indicated interest in selling its remaining land in the Frog Pond area, the District at-

TABLE 11.2   Analysis of Implementation Status of Plan Actions

Action items	Complete	Incomplete	No action	Unknown
Overall	27 (66%)	7 (17%)	5 (12%)	2 (5%)
Water management				
C-111 Basin	1 (20%)	3 (60%)	—	1 (20%)
Other	6 (75%)	2 (25%)	—	—
Water quality	5 (45%)	1 (9%)	4 (36%)	1 (9%)
Land planning/				
management	15 (88%)	1 (6%)	1 (6%)	—

tempted to acquire it and eliminate farming in that area. Instead, Aerojet sold the land to farmers, thus continuing the conflict over flood protection for the Frog Pond area.

Three of the water quality implementation actions were to be implemented only if the recommended two-year monitoring program revealed evidence of degradation from East Everglades agricultural operations. Since monitoring results showed negligible amounts of pollutants from East Everglades farming operations, no action was taken on these items.

Results of the Interviews and Survey

A majority of the respondents believed that the plan had a positive impact on water management and land use practices but that wildlife habitat and water quality had shown little or no improvement. As for implementation efforts, one-quarter of the survey respondents believed them to be quite successful, two-fifths rated implementation as moderate, and one-third—mostly state agency staff—thought implementation was not meeting objectives well. These perceptions of the plan's relative impacts are generally consistent with the analysis of implementation efforts.

State agency officials indicated a general lack of awareness of the plan and their agency's implementation responsibilities, reflecting several agencies' lack of involvement since approximately 1986 (when the last DCA status report on the ENP/EE plan was issued). Apparently, many agency staff members with East Everglades responsibilities at the time of plan adoption were no longer with the agency or had been assigned other responsibilities.

An exception to this general rule concerns the land acquisition action items, where implementation was being carried forward by joint state/federal action. Many of the government agencies represented on the ENP/EE Committee subsequently served on Governor Bob Martinez's Land Acquisition Task Force.

Representatives of regional agencies believed that implementation was a general weakness of resource planning and management committees. They claimed that more effective implementation could be achieved if federal agency participation were broader and more binding. Though federal respondents thought that the Environmental Protection Agency and U.S. Fish and Wildlife Service should have been members of the committee, some state respondents thought that federal agencies withheld participation in order to act on their own if they disagreed with plan recommendations.

Local government respondents expressed a generally positive view concerning the adequacy of the plan itself and its implementation. The plan provided "the database for decisions to be made" and made the permit process "more efficient and predictable." According to these respondents, the most significant results of plan implementation were the land acquisition initiatives by the District, state, and federal government. One local government respondent declared that the main benefit of the committee was educating regional, state, and federal agencies about the East Everglades. This respondent also felt the ENP/EE plan accomplished little beyond what was already contained in the 1980 Management Plan.

Many respondents expressed concern about the high level of nutrients flowing into the water conservation areas and about evidence of mercury pollution. Some federal respondents criticized the plan's recommended water quality actions as falling short of federal wetland protection requirements, specifically with reference to agricultural rock plowing and its impacts on habitat.

Some respondents who had local or state regulatory responsibility at the time of the committee's tenure revealed that, although they had serious concerns during plan development that the plan might be "giving away more than the state's (water quality) law would allow," in retrospect they believed the plan was sound. By contrast, a state agency executive who was not involved in state government during the committee's tenure expressed concern about potential water quality deterioration that could result from implementing flood protection recommendations for the 8.5-square-mile residential area.

The Metro-Dade County comprehensive plan forms the planning framework for land use decisions in the East Everglades. Half the survey respondents reported that they or other representatives of their agencies or organizations assisted Metro-Dade County during 1987–1988 in preparing components of the county's local comprehensive plan for the East Everglades area. However, only one survey respondent from regional, state, or federal agencies or from the private sector was aware that the Metro-Dade plan and its zoning laws had incorporated any of the ENP/EE Committee plan's recommended actions.

Some affected private-sector interests represented on the committee objected to the process as inherently unbalanced and unfair to minority views because representatives of government interests on RPMCs typically outnumber and out vote private-sector representatives. State and regional agency respondents underscored the importance of having a balanced membership on RPMCs, though their reference was to a state/local government balance. In the opinion of these respondents, more local representation was needed.

Status of the Plan and Implementation in 1994

According to local participants in the implementation process, the plan's primary recommendations have been carried out.[23] The iterative testing process has become a regular part of state and federal activities in the East Everglades. The District has continually adjusted its water management techniques and facilities affecting Northeast Shark River Slough and Taylor Slough to provide a more stable water flow. Since 1992 actions by the Corps of Engineers and the District have been guided by the General Design Memorandum prepared by the Corps for modifying water delivery to the Park. The memorandum contains hundreds of pages of detailed designs and drawings for changes in the Everglades facilities; it is now being expanded by detailed engineering designs that will not be completed until 1998 or 1999.

Implementation assignments made by the plan have been supplanted by the absorption of much of the land into the Park, where the National Park Service has jurisdiction, and the advent of the Corps' memorandum, which essentially transferred much of the administrative leadership for implementation to the District and the Corps. At the state and local levels, however, many of the agencies and staff formerly involved in the RMCP planning effort are continuing to assist in resolving planning and implementation issues.

In some ways, the intricate implementation devices recommended in the plan have given way to a broader, more decisive strategy to acquire the remaining private lands in the East Everglades. Over the past few years, federal, state, and local officials have concluded that acquisition is the one sure method of dealing with the basic conservation issues at stake in the East Everglades. One federal and two state legislative initiatives are presently being considered to authorize funding for acquisition of two-thirds of the remaining private tracts in the area. A task force is expected to be appointed soon to deliberate the future of the 8.5-square-mile area, with expectations that the outcome will be either more stringent enforcement of existing controls or acquisition of those properties.

Still, the acquisition process takes time. The 1989 federal acquisition program is proceeding slowly, with only a few thousand additional acres purchased. The program is being held back by a lack of staff and by landowners insisting on condemnation actions to obtain prices similar to those they paid for the properties. The future promises continued resistance from property owners and thus a lengthy acquisition process.

Conclusions about the Planning Process

Several lessons can be drawn from the ENP/EE Committee experience for similar collaborative planning efforts in other areas:

• An informed constituency should be continued after completion of plans. Either the ENP/EE Committee or an ad hoc group should have been assigned responsibility for supporting implementation efforts. Long-term actions such as wetlands restoration and flood protection need consistent follow through by informed government and private interests. Partly due to the lack of such a group, C-111 basin issues and water quality considerations in the water conservation areas are still incomplete.

• Plans should provide a means for implementing agencies to bridge changes in administration and personnel. A strategy for such bridging at all levels of government was not an explicit part of the plan developed by the ENP/EE Committee and adopted by the governor and the cabinet, but it should have been. Agency lapses regarding coordination, monitoring, and reporting followed the committee's demise. SETEC, for example, was established as a monitoring and coordinating entity but ceased meeting in 1988. As another illustration, the ENP/EE plan called for use of conflict resolution for disputes arising among affected interests during plan implementation. The committee helped to fill that function during its tenure, and SETEC did so for some disputes on technical issues. When these committees disbanded, their conflict resolution functions were not continued.

• Private sector participation was vital for an area such as the East Everglades, where most of the land was privately owned. The appointment of private-sector interests to Florida's resource planning and management committees has provided a potentially powerful way for encouraging private–public collaboration in creating solutions. More private-sector representation might have improved plan implementation.

• Such a process might not lead to total consensus. When parties to a dispute have inflexible positions on central issues, a jointly devised and accepted plan is unlikely. In the case of the ENP/EE Committee, the issue of flood protection for East Everglades agricultural land could not be resolved for this reason; several members opposed flood protection for agricultural operations under all circumstances, and farmers opposed public acquisition or withdrawal of their lands from agriculture.

• Federal agency participation in the planning and implementation process is critical to its success. All affected federal interests should be invited to participate. At a minimum, federal agency representatives to a consensus-building committee should have policy positions of authority so they can fully participate in plan formation and implementation.

- The issue of "binding" federal agencies in a plan jointly devised with state, local, and private interests needs to be addressed. The Environmental Protection Agency already has undertaken negotiated rulemaking in some circumstances. Area-wide planning and regulation may present additional opportunities for this negotiated approach.

- Consistency of plan recommendations with state and federal wetlands regulations requires careful attention. An RPMC plan should acknowledge and accommodate existing federal, state, and local law and regulations. Where existing rules appear inappropriate, the plan should offer a sound rationale for recommendations to establish specific area-wide standards derived from an area-wide database.

In summary, the RPMC process has the capability, if appropriately used, to develop the rationale and political constituency for solutions to wetlands conflicts. The ENP/EE Committee helped to do so during its tenure. The subsequent appointment of a land acquisition task force, which carried forward what the committee had begun three years earlier, underscores the need for continuation and follow through of plan implementation. If RPMCs continued their tenure, or if an ad hoc group were appointed to monitor and support plan implementation, greater assurance of agency follow through and of continued political interest would result. The practice (in Florida and elsewhere) of disbanding a planning advisory committee when a plan has been adopted should be revised.

Notwithstanding its drawbacks, the ENP/EE Committee was effective in informing diverse public and private stakeholders about the area's complex problems and benefits, in promoting the iterative testing process for adjusting resource management decisions as new knowledge was gained, in establishing the Southern Everglades Technical Committee as an ongoing mechanism for technical coordination, and in calling for continued conflict resolution. Finally, the committee built a political constituency for land acquisition and flood protection—a constituency omitted from previous plans but vital to the success of wetlands protection and restoration in the East Everglades and in Everglades National Park.

According to a September 1994 news release of the South Florida Water Management District, the District and the Corps of Engineers signed an agreement that clears the way for construction, operation, and maintenance of a project that will provide more natural water flows in the Everglades National Park. The Everglades National Park Expansion and Protection Act of

1989 authorized the Corps of Engineers to modify the Park's water management system to restore more natural hydrologic conditions and to acquire 107,600 acres of land in the East Everglades for incorporation into the Park. The $101 million construction project will implement many of the recommendations that the RMPC made in the mid-1980s. The federal government will pay for the construction and 75 percent of the operation and maintenance of the facilities, with the District paying for the remaining 25 percent of operation and maintenance.

NOTES

1. This chapter is based upon a similarly titled study prepared under the supervision and copyrighted in 1989 by The Environmental Law Institute, Washington, D.C., which was funded in part by The U.S. Environmental Protection Agency under EPA contract number 68-01-7378. It is reprinted in edited form with the permission of The Institute and the authors.

2. Information in this section is drawn largely from *Water Resources Atlas of Florida,* edited by Edward A. Fernald, Tallahassee: Florida State University, 1984; the *Proposed Management Plan for the East Everglades,* prepared by the Dade Planning Project, October 1980, especially pp. 1–14; and *A Report to Governor Bob Martinez,* prepared by the East Everglades Land Acquisition Task Force, published in Tallahassee, October 1988.

3. Much of the information in this section is drawn from the *Water Resources Atlas,* op. cit. note 2 and from Kathleen Shea Abrams and M. J. Marvin, "Water Management in the Everglades Ecosystem," unpublished paper for the FAU/FIU Joint Center for Environmental and Urban Problems at Florida Atlantic University, Fort Lauderdale, Florida, 1989.

4. Nelson H. Blake, *Land into Water—Water into Land: A History of Water Management in Florida,* Tallahassee: University Presses of Florida, 1980, p. 178.

5. Report of the Land Acquisition Task Force.

6. Information about events leading to the 1980 plan was obtained from Reginald Walters, Director, Dade County Planning Department, July 21, 1989.

7. *Plan of Study for the East Everglades Resource Planning Project,* prepared by the Dade County Planning Department, February 7, 1978.

8. Abrams and Marvin, op. cit. note 3.

9. Luther J. Carter, *The Florida Experience: Land and Water Policy in a Growth State,* Baltimore: Johns Hopkins University Press, 1974, p. 181.

10. Abrams and Marvin, op cit. note 3.

11. Barbara C. Brumback and Richard A. Brumback, "A Strategic Plan to

Restore the Everglades," in *Restoring the Earth,* Washington, D.C.: Island Press, 1989.

12. "U.S. Panel Approves Glades Flood Safety," *The Miami Herald,* November 16, 1983.

13. Everglades National Park/East Everglades Resource Planning and Management Committee, *Implementation Plan,* prepared by the Florida Department of Community Affairs, Tallahassee, 1985.

14. John M. DeGrove, "Critical Area Programs in Florida: Creative Balancing of Growth and the Environment," *Journal of Urban and Contemporary Law,* Vol. 34, pp. 51–97 (1988).

15. Stephen S. Light, "Restoring Water Deliveries to the Southern Everglades: Lessons Learned," an unpublished paper presented to the Urban Land Institute Federal Permits Working Group in Washington, D.C., in 1989.

16. Personal communication from Chris Meline, University of Florida Cooperative Extension for Dade County, July 25, 1989.

17. Dade County Planning Department, "Potentially Available Land Suitable for Farming Outside the 1985 Comprehensive Development Master Plan Boundary," unpublished working paper, 1987.

18. Light, op. cit. note 15.

19. Personal communication from Dennis Howard, Metro-Dade Department of Environmental Resources Management, August, 27, 1989.

20. "Issue Paper: Save Our Everglades," prepared by the Office of the Governor, Tallahassee, 1983.

21. Personal communication from Mollie Palmer, Department of Natural Resources, July 19, 1989.

22. Personal communication to the editors from Frank Bernardino, Assistant to the Director, Dade County Department of Environmental Resources Management; and Pat Tolle, Chief Information Officer for the Everglades National Park, February 1994.

23. Information to update the case study was obtained by the editors from Frank Bernardino and Pat Tolle, op. cit. note 22, and from Jean Evoy, principal planner with the Metro-Dade Planning Department, February 14, 1994.

Collaborative Planning for Development in Bolsa Chica, California's Wetlands

David A. Salvesen

E D I T O R S '   S U M M A R Y

Perhaps nowhere else in California has a battle between real estate development and wetlands protection endured for so long as over the coastal site known as Bolsa Chica. The 1,600-acre site along the Southern California coast contains a mix of upland and lowland areas, including over 900 acres of wetlands, most of which have undergone numerous alterations over the years. Salvesen points out that this is no pristine wetland. In addition to dikes and roads that criss-cross the site, over 150 oil rigs continue to pump oil from beneath the lowlands. Nonetheless, many of the remaining wetlands provide critical habitat for a host of shorebirds, several of which are endangered.

Treasured for its wildlife habitat, the site is also valued highly for its real estate potential, being one of the largest remaining undeveloped tracts of land along the Southern California coast. Bluffs overlooking the wetlands and the coast offer million-dollar views. Yet, opposition has stalled development proposals for over a decade.

Finally, in 1988 a coalition was formed that included as members the two primary adversaries, the developer and a local environmental group. Salvesen traces the development of a plan to restore and protect wetlands while allowing some development to occur. One year later, the group released the plan, which called for a limitation of development to one-quarter of the site and restoration and preservation of most of the wetlands.

Background

Along the coast of Southern California, surrounded on three sides by the city of Huntington Beach, lies a 1,600-acre site called Bolsa Chica. The site

Bolsa Chica remains an active oil-producing area, with over 150 rigs pumping oil.

contains a mix of upland and lowland areas; the latter once comprised an extensive estuarine area at the mouth of the Santa Ana River. Since the turn of the century, however, the lowland part of the site has been severely altered—first by a gun club that diked the wetlands to create duck ponds and later by oil companies that installed dikes and access roads that criss-cross the site to serve the numerous oil wells still in operation today. Over 150 rigs continue to pump oil from what was once one of the largest oil producing areas in California. Service roads and drilling pads divide the lowlands into numerous wetland cells where water ponds during the brief rainy season. In addition, a flood control channel cuts through the northern portion of the site, and two World War II bunkers with 16-inch thick reinforced concrete walls lie buried in one of the bluffs, called the Bolsa Mesa, overlooking the wetlands.

The Huntington and Bolsa Chica mesas form the southeastern and northwestern borders of the property, respectively, while the Pacific Coast Highway forms the southwestern boundary (Figure 12.1). Yet, despite decades of alterations that permanently changed the site, several hundred acres of wetlands remain that, according to the U.S. Fish and Wildlife Service, provide critical habitat for a number of endangered birds.

Bolsa Chica (meaning "little purse" in Spanish) is valued not only for wildlife habitat and oil reserves but also for its development potential. As one

Figure 12.1 Location of Bolsa Chica study area (courtesy of Koll Real Estate Group).

of the few remaining large, privately owned, undeveloped tracts of land along the Southern California coast, the property is extremely valuable for real estate development. For nearly 20 years Signal Landmark, which subsequently became the Koll Real Estate Group, has been trying to develop the site.[1] But strong opposition, primarily from a local environmental group, the Amigos de Bolsa Chica, effectively blocked all development efforts.

In 1988, after nearly two decades of conflict, the Koll Real Estate Group and Amigos agreed to settle their differences and, working as part of a coalition with Orange County, the city of Huntington Beach, and the California State Lands Commission, to develop a compromise plan for the site that, if permitted, would allow some development to occur but would also preserve most of the remaining wetlands. In May 1989 the coalition agreed on a concept plan that calls for residential development on 412 acres, including 82 acres of wetlands, while creating, restoring, or preserving over 1,000 acres of wetlands, open space, and wildlife habitat.

The Koll Real Estate Group owns the largest share of property at Bolsa

Chica. Several public and private entities also own substantial parcels: the Metropolitan Water District of Southern California owns about 83 acres (which Koll Real Estate has agreed to purchase); The Fieldstone Company owns approximately 42 acres; the Huntington Beach Company owns nearly 24 acres; and the State Lands Commission owns 337 acres, including 31 acres under Pacific Coast Highway (Table 12.1). In addition, Shell Oil Company operates the oil field under an agreement with Koll, but the mineral rights are owned by successors to the original gun club members—the Bolsa Tenants in Common. Any proposal for the site will have to take into account the multiple ownerships, past and present alterations, and the often-competing goals of preservation and development.

In 1989 EPA determined that the site contained 918 acres of wetlands. Although historically dominated by salt marsh vegetation, the site today features a variety of aquatic habitats such as salt marsh, brackish marsh, open water, unvegetated seasonal ponds, and salt flats.

The change in habitats has brought about a change in the number and types of animals, particularly birds, that use the site. Wading birds have benefited from the creation of seasonal ponds, while birds that depend on salt marshes have suffered. Bolsa Chica supports four federally listed endangered birds: the California least tern, the light-footed clapper rail, the peregrine falcon, and the California brown pelican, as well as one state-listed endangered bird, Belding's savannah sparrow. It also serves as a vital stopover for birds migrating along the Pacific flyway. The roughly 300-acre parcel owned by the State Lands Commission is managed as the Bolsa Chica Ecological Reserve by the California Department of Fish and Game, although only 170 acres have been restored with funds provided by Koll.

TABLE 12.1   Acreage by Ownership

Owner	Acres
Koll Real Estate Group	1,190
State of California	337[a]
Metropolitan Water District (MWD)	83
City of Huntington Beach	43
Fieldstone Company	43
Huntington Beach Company	24
Ocean View School District	15
D.E. Goodell	6
Total	1,741

[a]Not including 232.5 acres owned by the state at Bolsa Chica State Beach.

Some wildlife has managed to coexist with oil production.

Many types of shorebirds depend on the unique marsh habitats of Bolsa Chica for food and shelter.

The Bolsa Chica Ecological Reserve was once a 300-acre tract of degraded wetlands. About 170 acres have been restored to provide habitat for a number of endangered birds.

Initial Development Proposal

When California was admitted to the Union in 1850, it acquired, with certain exceptions, all the submerged lands and tidelands within its borders. In that same year Congress, under the Swamp Lands Act, granted states the swamp and overflowed lands within their borders. Over the years, much of this land was sold or given away by the state, but some remains in state hands. In California, the submerged lands and tidelands are held in the public trust by the State Lands Commission.

In 1970 uncertainty over the state's legal interest in the tidal and submerged lands at Bolsa Chica held up Koll's proposal for residential and commercial development. To develop the property, Koll first had to establish clear title to its holdings. To settle the issue, Koll met with the State Lands Commission, which then set up an interagency task force comprising state resource agencies to work with Koll and develop a plan for the site. The task force's plan, which culminated in a formal agreement between Koll and the State Lands Commission in 1973, called for exchanging about 527 acres of state land for some 325 acres of Koll's land—a measure that allowed each to consolidate its holdings. The plan also envisioned residential and commercial development and a marina that would be accessible by a new ocean entrance to be constructed at Bolsa Chica.

The 1973 agreement seemingly offered something for everybody: commercial and residential development for Koll; recreational boating and fishing for the public; and, for state resource agencies, restoration of over 450 acres of wetlands. Orange County, in particular, strongly supported the proposal and later used it as the basis for its Local Coastal Program (LCP). The county sought to expand the commercial and recreational role of Bolsa Chica to provide an additional source of county revenue—much like its nearby marina at Dana Point, where the county leases the project to private operators.

But around 1977 the agreement ran into stiff opposition from a local neighborhood group that objected to the increased noise and traffic the project could bring; surfers who feared that the new ocean entrance would have an adverse effect on surfing; and, most notably, the Amigos de Bolsa Chica, who believed that the state should have received and protected a greater share of the wetlands at Bolsa Chica. In fact, in 1979 Amigos sued Koll and the state of California, and later launched a plan of its own for Bolsa Chica. Amigos' plan called for restoring 1,200 acres of wetlands, restoring tidal flows to the site, and allowing modest development on the upland areas.

The Planning Process

Under the California Coastal Act of 1976, the Coastal Commission regulates a broad range of activities, including real estate development within the coastal zone—generally, a 1000-foot-wide strip of land that extends the length of the California Coast. (The coastal zone is defined as "that land and water area. . .specified on the maps. . .[that] extends inland to the first major ridgeline paralleling the sea, or five miles from the mean high tide line of the sea, whichever is less." The commission retains authority over development in the coastal zone until local governments adopt a local coastal program (LCP) and ordinances consistent with the act. Once the commission certifies an LCP, the local government can assume its own permitting responsibilities.

In 1980 Orange County began preparing an LCP for Bolsa Chica. In 1986 the land use plan portion of the LCP was certified conditionally by the Coastal Commission pending further study on several issues, including the effects of the proposed navigable ocean entrance on the adjacent shoreline and beaches. While the city of Huntington Beach tentatively supported the plan, it was also concerned that a new ocean entrance could lead to erosion of its prized beaches.

As evidence the city cited the continual beach erosion at the nearby Seal Beach naval weapons station on Anaheim Bay north of the city. Breakwaters constructed for the station during World War II had disrupted the flow of sand that normally migrated south along the coast from the mouth of the San Gabriel River in Anaheim Bay (Seal Beach) to Newport Beach. That migrating sand replaced what was lost naturally to the erosional forces of wind, waves, and currents; it kept the beaches intact in a relatively balanced state of erosion and replenishment. Since the naval weapons station was constructed, over $18 million has been spent by the U.S. Army Corps of Engineers to replenish sand south of the entrance to Anaheim Bay. The city was concerned that another artificial sand replenishment program would be needed for its beaches if another navigable ocean entrance was built at Bolsa Chica.

In the early 1980s, at the request of Huntington Beach and Orange County, the U.S. Army Corps of Engineers Waterways Experiment Station in Vicksburg, Mississippi, under contract with the State Lands Commission, built a working scale model of the proposed Bolsa Chica marina, including the proposed navigable ocean entrance, to analyze the effect of the entrance on the city's beaches. The Corps' model demonstrated that the beach erosion caused by the ocean entrance could be mitigated, but mitigation would be very expensive. As a result of growing citizen opposition and the city's concern over how to fund the mitigation, in 1987 the city withdrew its support for the navigable ocean entrance, adding yet another setback to Signal's proposal and the county's LCP.

The Coalition Plan

After nearly a decade of fighting over the future of Bolsa Chica, with little progress by either side, both Amigos and Koll appeared ready to negotiate. City and county government officials and political leaders were exasperated by the endless public conflicts and confrontations. In 1988 Orange County supervisor Harriet Weider, then mayor of Huntington Beach John Erskine, and former city administrator Paul Cook urged the competing interests to come together to see if they could reach a compromise on development and preservation of Bolsa Chica. Meanwhile, Peter Denniston, then president of Signal (Koll's predecessor), having sensed a change of political and public opinion, decided to take a fresh look at development of the site and to obtain greater input from groups such as the Amigos.

Thus, representatives from Koll, the Amigos de Bolsa Chica, Orange County, Huntington Beach, and the State Lands Commission formed the Bolsa Chica Planning Coalition in October 1988 to try to hammer out a compromise plan for the site. These five representatives comprised the executive, voting board of the coalition, while a second, larger group was formed to provide technical support. The executive board operated under a consensus-based decision-making process. The support group consisted of representatives from both state and federal resource agencies as well as a number of local groups. Federal agencies such as EPA, FWS, and the Corps were invited to participate in the support group but, primarily because of budget constraints, their participation has been spotty. According to an official at EPA's regional office in San Francisco, federal regional staffs simply do not have the travel budget to attend the meetings. A few years later, state officials stopped attending the meetings, citing budget constraints.

After a slow start, the coalition began tackling some of the issues that had blocked development of the site for nearly two decades, such as the marina, commercial development, ocean inlet, and the fate of the remaining wetlands. Former adversaries worked together to break the impasse: to develop a plan that would protect the most sensitive environmental areas of the site while allowing for reasonable development to occur. With the help of a mediator, the coalition reached agreement on the areas designated for development or restoration and on May 22, 1989, released its draft concept plan for Bolsa Chica (see Figure 12.2). The draft plan eliminated the proposed marina as well as the hotel and related commercial development, and lowered the cap on the number of homes from the proposed 7,200 to 5,700.

Roughly three-fourths of the site (about 1,100 acres) would be set aside as wetlands, endangered species habitats, and open space (see Table 12.2). Residential development would be concentrated on the mesas and in the inland or easternmost portion of the site, adjacent to an existing residential area (see Figure 12.3). In 1991 Koll reduced the number of homes to 4,884, consistent with the coalition's cap but sensitive to and compatible with surrounding land uses.

Koll hopes to create a master-planned "American coastal town" featuring

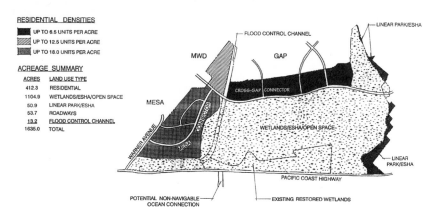

Figure 12.2 Bolsa Chica Coalition Plan (courtesy of the Bolsa Chica Planning Coalition).

TABLE 12.2   Acreage by Land Use Type

Land use type	Acres
Wetlands/habitats/open space	1,104.9
Residential	412.3
Linear park/habitats	50.9
Roads	53.7
Flood control channel	13.2
Total	1,635

Source: Bolsa Chica Planning Coalition Concept Plan, May 1989.

nearly 5,000 cottages and townhomes built around New England-style commons. It will include both single-family detached homes and multifamily housing, with densities ranging from 3.5 to over 36 units per acre.[1] Houses will range in price from about $180,000 to over $1 million. In addition, the project will include 22 acres of new community parks, 15 miles of new pedestrian, equestrian, and bicycle trails, and completion of a 106-acre linear park, called the Bolsa Chica Regional Park.

Restoration Plans

In August 1989, at the request of the coalition, the California Coastal Conservancy engaged Dr. Michael Josselyn, biologist at San Francisco State University's Tiburon Center for Environmental Studies, to develop a series of restoration plan alternatives for Bolsa Chica. The proposed restoration plan calls for creating a mix of coastal wetland habitat types, enhancing habitat for endangered species, establishing buffer areas between developed areas and wetlands, modifying and removing existing roads and drill pads, and phasing out and removing oil production facilities and operations. Specifically, 228 acres of wetlands would be created, primarily to mitigate impacts of development in the lowlands, and 620 acres of degraded wetlands would be restored. In addition, about 66 acres of environmentally sensitive habitat areas and approximately 36 acres of coastal wetland buffers or open space would be established, for a total of 1,106 acres of coastal wetland ecosystem.[3]

Restoration will be phased in with development over a period of about 10–20 years. The Bolsa Chica Mesa will be developed first and the lowland area last. Koll expects that three-fourths of the restoration will be completed in 13 years.

The restoration plan calls for enhancing the tidal prism at the site by increasing the flow of water through the existing tide gates and by constructing a new, nonnavigable tidal inlet. Currently, tidal water reaches Bolsa Chica via

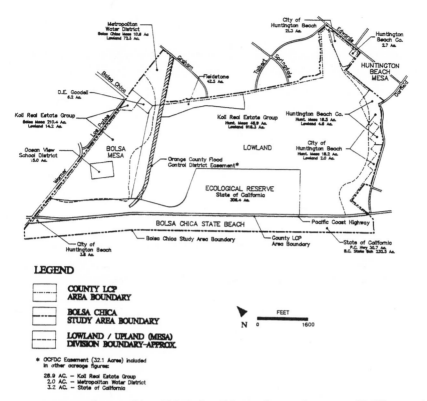

Figure 12.3 Land ownership within Bolsa Chica study area (courtesy of Williamson & Schmid).

a channel that extends six miles north to the Anaheim Bay. But tide gates limit the ebb and flow of water to the marsh. As a result, according to the USFWS, several tidal zones are squeezed into a very narrow range, which limits the diversity of birds found at the site. The proposed tidal inlet would improve circulation of water from the ocean through the restored tidal wetlands. Since much of the site lies about four feet below sea level, however, the depth and reach of the tidal waters must be controlled to prevent roads and buildings from being flooded.

Koll originally estimated that the restoration would cost around $100 million. It publicly pledged to contribute roughly $48 million and assumed that the rest of the money would come from other sources, primarily the Port of Long Beach. A substantial portion of the money would be used to pay for oil that would be left in the ground if Shell Oil was asked to close its wells prematurely to make way for restoration and development of the site.

In September 1993 the Koll Real Estate Group scaled back plans for restoring degraded wetlands at the site, citing financial and regulatory barriers. Due to delays in flood control improvements by the Corps, it seeks to delay for three years the removal of some 100 oil wells from the site, thus postponing the start of the restoration as well.[4] To further cut costs, and in response to public and agency criticisms, Koll also plans to shorten the length of the proposed jetties, build a smaller tidal inlet, and excavate the proposed deepwater habitat to only five feet instead of ten.

The pullback was announced after the Port of Long Beach decided that it was no longer interested in contributing to the cost of restoring wetlands at Bolsa Chica. Earlier, the port sought to participate in the restoration in order to compensate for wetlands it planned to fill as part of a planned port expansion. In mid-1993, however, the port announced that it will pursue a less ambitious expansion that involves building primarily on upland areas it had recently purchased, rather than in adjacent wetlands, thus substantially reducing its need for (off-site) mitigation.

As expected, some chemical contamination has occurred at the site as a result of years of oil production. As owner of the oil, Shell Oil Company is responsible for the cleanup, which is already under way.

Permitting

Although Bolsa Chica lies on unincorporated land, which normally would give regulatory oversight to the county, the city of Huntington Beach became the lead regulatory body in 1990 due to its interest in annexing the site and Koll's willingness to allow the annexation to occur. Both a state environmental impact report (EIR) and a federal environmental impact statement (EIS) were required for the development proposal. A draft EIR, prepared under the direction of the city of Huntington Beach, was released for public comment in mid-1992. The document, unfortunately, was found wanting. According to a county official, the EIR was not very thorough and it posed more questions than it answered.

Meanwhile, elections in 1992 changed the composition of the city council in a way that was unfavorable to Koll—from pro-development to slow growth. This, along with its growing frustration with the lack of progress by the city and the inadequate EIR, prompted Koll to ask the county to oversee the project. Actually, the county had no choice. Koll was no longer interested in having Huntington Beach annex the site, thus the responsibility for the project automatically reverted to the county. In addition, the county had assumed responsibility for wetlands management, a role the city wished to avoid, and it made sense for the entire project approval process to be carried out by the county, including preparation of a new, adequate EIR.

The move angered many city activists and alienated Amigos, who felt that Koll should have worked through the coalition to resolve conflicts. A county official noted, however, that the switch back to the county makes sense, given the county's experience with wetland restoration projects, such as restoration of Talbot marsh, located about five miles from Bolsa Chica, and its experience in working with regional issues. Moreover, the official observed that the city was probably relieved that such a politically heated issue was tossed back to the county. Whatever the reason, a new EIR had to be prepared under the county's oversight.

The draft EIR, about three inches thick, was released in December 1993. It expanded the alternatives section and addressed many of the comments of the first EIR. Table 12.3 briefly summarizes the chronology of events at Bolsa Chica.

In yet another twist of fate, the county released a revised draft EIR in August 1994 that differed substantially from the earlier draft EIR. The county changed both the amount of development that would be allowed at Bolsa Chica and the degree of wetland restoration. For example, the revised EIR reduced the number of housing units from about 4,200 to between 2,500 and 3,200 under two development options:

- *Option 1*   Up to 900 units would be permitted in the lowlands and up to 2,300 units in the Bolsa Mesa. Kohl would be responsible for restoring 1,000 acres of wetlands.

- *Option 2*   Up to 2,500 units would be permitted, all in the Bolsa Mesa. No development would be permitted in the lowlands, and Kohl would not be responsible for any wetland restoration.

According to the county, the public response to the 1993 draft EIR was overwhelming. Many comments expressed opposition to any development in the wetlands and pressured the county to limit development to the mesa while requiring Kohl to foot the bill for restoring the wetlands. The revised EIR makes it perfectly clear that "people can't have their cake and eat it too."[5] There will be either development in wetlands with restoration paid for by Kohl or development in the uplands only and no restoration by Kohl.

Significantly, the revised draft omitted the creation of a new tidal inlet. According to the Corps, most biologists favored the construction of the inlet.[6] Apparently, opposition to the inlet from several groups, such as the Surf Riders Association, who feared that even a small, nonnavigable inlet would exacerbate beach erosion, convinced the county to remove the inlet from consideration.

TABLE 12.3   Chronology of Events at Bolsa Chica

Year	Events
1970	Signal Landmark buys about 2,000 acres at Bolsa Chica from a company formed by gun-club owners.
1973	Signal and the state swap lands. The state ends up with 300 acres of wetlands which, following restoration, later become the Bolsa Chica Ecological Reserve. Signal proposes a mixed-use development that would include a 1,300-slip marina with hotels, restaurants, and 5,700 homes.
1975	Amigos de Bolsa Chica forms.
1979	Amigos sues the state and Signal over the 1973 agreement and the proposed development.
1985	The California Coastal Commission approves Signal's proposed development.
1987	The plan to build the marina unravels as Supervisor Harriet Weider joins neighbors in opposing the project.
1988	Bolsa Chica Planning Coalition forms.
1989	The coalition releases a plan that calls for preserving roughly 75% of the site and limiting development primarily to the upland areas.
1990	Huntington Beach approves a request by Signal for the city to become the lead regulator over the project. The county relinquishes lead-agency authority.
1992	Draft environmental impact report released. The report is sharply criticized by U.S. EPA and U.S. Fish and Wildlife Service.
1992	Henley Properties, parent corporation of Signal Landmark, merges with sister corporation, The Henley Group, which then purchases the Koll Company's real estate holdings and becomes the Koll Real Estate Group.
1993	At the request of the landowner the county rescinds the agreement to let the city regulate the project.
1993	Concurrently with the announcement by the Port of Long Beach that it will no longer pursue restoration of wetlands at Bolsa Chica in exchange for wetlands filled by port expansion, Koll revises its wetland restoration plans and pledges to undertake the entire restoration effort for about $48 million.
1993	Under the county's supervision, a (second) draft environmental impact report is completed.
1994	Revised draft EIR released.

Source: Adapted from Pat Brennan, "Environmentalists Doubt Wetlands Economic Forecast," *Orange County Register,* October 19, 1993.

The county threw everyone a curve with its revised EIR, which brought the permitting process to an impasse. According to the Corps, most resource agencies are in favor of the tidal inlet. And the Corps' EIS, which is expected to be completed in early 1995, still includes an analysis of Kohl's development proposal, which includes building a new ocean entrance. According to the county, however, the ocean entrance is not foreclosed, it just is not part of the EIR. "There are so many complicated issues at Bolsa Chica that we have to whittle them down to a manageable level," notes a county planner.[7]

Both Koll and Orange County must still hurdle a number of legal and regulatory obstacles before the first house is constructed and additional wetlands are restored at Bolsa Chica. For example, Koll must obtain a Clean Water Act Section 404 permit and a Section 10 permit from the Corps of Engineers, and the county must gain approval of its local coastal program. Koll applied in 1993 for a 404 permit to fill about 100 acres of lowlands (part of which may not be wetlands) and has begun its 404(b)(1) alternatives analysis and its biological assessment for USFWS. If all goes well, Koll faces at least another two years of additional processing before the coalition's plan can be approved. Also since construction and restoration will be phased in as oil production is phased out, it will likely be another 10 to 20 years before the plan is fully implemented.

Koll estimates that, since the coalition was formed, it has spent about $20 million on the project—or about half what it pledged for the restoration—for biological studies, market studies, legal and management fees, and the EIR.

Conclusion

In a state that has lost over 90 percent of its wetlands, it is not surprising that a proposal to build on one of the largest remaining coastal wetlands has met with such opposition. Yet, despite the pitched battles fought between Amigos and Koll, the two, along with the city of Huntington Beach, Orange County, and the state, managed to form a workable coalition and hammer out a compromise plan that calls for setting aside 75 percent of the site and limiting development to only 25 percent, most of it in upland areas. Of the estimated 918 acres of wetlands, some of them severely degraded, less than 100 would be filled. Overall, almost 1,100 acres of wetlands will be restored, enhanced, or created. Koll has committed to contributions of $48 million to restore wetlands that have suffered from decades of alterations in the form of dikes and dams. Oil rigs, pipelines, tank farms, and a waste handling site continue to pose threats to the wetlands.

Koll has wisely tied restoration and preservation of the wetlands to development approval: no development, no restoration. Considering the absence of a white knight to step in, buy the property, and pay the estimated $100 million for restoration (the state is in no financial position to contribute much to the project), the compromise plan certainly seems reasonable.

Nonetheless, in mid-1992 the Bolsa Chica Land Trust was formed to acquire (assuming the project would be for sale), restore, preserve, and maintain the entire Bolsa Chica site, both wetlands and uplands. Several hardline members of the trust are former members of the Amigos, which has been accused of forming too close a relationship with Koll.

After it developed the plan in 1989, the coalition slowly began to dissolve, its primary mission accomplished. Meetings were held less frequently, and both the state and federal government officials ceased attending. While the coalition could have continued to act as a vehicle for resolving conflicts, it gradually lost its support. According to a county official, "There's nothing for the coalition to do. Its job was completed when it released the plan in 1989."

In 1993 Koll side-stepped the coalition in deciding to have its permits processed by Orange County, rather than the city of Huntington Beach. The coalition heard about Koll's switch through the newspaper. According to Koll, "the coalition was instrumental in developing the plan. But there is not much to talk about until the EIR is completed."[8] Also, two of the coalition's members, the city and the county, are regulators whose jurisdiction covered or would be affected by development at Bolsa Chica. This puts the regulators in an uncomfortable and sensitive position of helping to shape and possibly advocate a project on which they may later regulate.

The saga of Bolsa Chica will likely continue for several years. Koll does not expect to build the first house until 1997 at best. If nothing else, this case study illustrates just how difficult, time-consuming, and expensive it is to try to balance development and wetlands protection, particularly where there is a history of strong animosity between a developer and environmental groups.

NOTES

1. In mid-1992 Signal Landmark hired the Koll Company to manage the Bolsa Chica property, among other sites. Shortly thereafter, Signal Landmark's parent corporation, Henley, changed its name to the Bolsa Chica Company. In 1993 the Bolsa Chica Company purchased the real estate operations of the Koll Company. The new company, which owns and manages Bolsa Chica, is called the Koll Real Estate Group. To avoid confusion, the latter name will be used throughout the text.

2. "Draft Environmental Impact Report for the Bolsa Chica Project," Orange

County Environmental Management Agency, Orange County, California, December 20, 1993, pp. 1–3.

3. Draft Environmental Impact Report, op. cit. note 2.

4. Shelby Grad, "Builder Announces Budget Cut for Bolsa Chica Restoration," *Los Angeles Times,* September 26, 1993, p. B6.

5. Personal communication with Ron Tippets, Senior Planner, Orange County (California) Planning Department, September 8, 1994.

6. Personal communication with Bruce Henderson, U.S. Army Corps of Engineers, Los Angeles District, September 8, 1994.

7. Ron Tippets, op. cit. note 5.

8. Personal communication with Lucy Dunn, Senior Vice President, Koll Real Estate Group, November 30, 1993.

Conclusion

Douglas R. Porter and David A. Salvesen

The experiences with collaborative planning related in the preceding chapters demonstrate that, for all its promise, collaborative, area-wide planning remains a time-consuming, resource-intensive, and uncertain process. Collaborative planning generally is undertaken in circumstances where concerns have flared into conflicts and attitudes have ripened into mind-sets, virtually guaranteeing a difficult and lengthy consensus-building process. Negotiations take place in regulatory arenas where few guidelines define the players, the process, or preferred outcomes. Plans, once determined, are accorded an uncertain reception within existing regulatory regimes and are indifferently served by established funding and administrative mechanisms.

Several years after completion of the Anchorage wetlands management plan, for example, one of the environmental representatives who participated in the drawn-out and often contentious process observed that the resulting plan may not have provided any greater protection for wetlands than provided by the case-by-case permitting process. Moreover, mistrust and political maneuvering among participants frequently mars the process: in the East Everglades, agricultural interests were simultaneously participating in planning and in lobbying Congress for legislation that would thwart the efforts of the planning group.

Yet, for all its faults, collaborative planning is worth the effort if it succeeds in reconciling otherwise intractable environmental and development issues. Although collaborative planning is proactive in its approach to addressing conflicts between development and conservation, it is seldom employed until developers, conservationists, and regulators have reached a point where virtually every permit application becomes a bitter battle. In those circumstances, when everyone involved has a stake in finding solutions, collaborative planning becomes a welcome alternative to protracted conflict and stalemate.

The Bolsa Chica, California, experience serves as an illustration. What finally brought the Koll Real Estate Group and the Amigos de Bolsa Chica to the negotiating table was sheer exhaustion from a multi-year battle in which neither side gained a positive result. For all their efforts, development in wetland areas was stymied and degraded wetlands were not restored. Joint planning to achieve a workable consensus was the only path left.

The nine planning efforts reported in this publication demonstrate the variety of trade-offs that can bring consensus on issues. Developers find solace in securing designations of developable land and more predictable approval procedures, even while they are required to alter project plans, set aside large tracts for preservation, and fund restoration and management activities. Conservationists obtain sought after reservations of critical wetlands and wildlife habitats and reduction of the piecemeal degradation of ecosystems, although they must accept selective destruction of natural resources. Public agencies, faced with politically charged controversies, find reasonable middle courses that deflate conflicts while achieving public aims.

Beyond the immediate value of working out acceptable solutions in a conflict-ridden climate, however, the collaborative planning process also serves a larger objective: it places conservation needs within the wider context of community growth and change. The process opens up opportunities for integrating programs for protection of wetlands and wildlife with local, regional, and state strategies for future development. Participants in collaborative planning broaden their awareness of the complex interactions of humans and nature, and plans framed in a cooperative climate begin to build a structure of interlocking, mutually supportive, area-wide approaches to preserving a sustainable environment.

Critical Issues in Collaborative, Area-wide Planning

Marsh and Lallas (in Chapter 2), as well as Beatley (in Chapter 3), touch on several concerns that challenge the effectiveness of collaborative planning, including the roles of federal agencies, funding for planning, equity effects of plans, funding for implementation, and enforceable assurances that plans will be carried out.

Federal Agency Roles
Collaborative planning is sparked by the need to obtain federal permits for development in wetland and wildlife areas, and federal agency involvement in collaborative planning is critical to its success. But agency participation often is hampered by policy and budget constraints. EPA, USFWS, and the Corps repeatedly have emphasized their general support for collaborative planning,

and they have worked to employ it in their regulatory processes. However, they have not always followed through with agency participation in, and commitments to, the planning process.

In part, this is due to the lack of resources to conduct more than a handful of such plans each year. In the East Everglades and in Bolsa Chica, federal agencies were only sporadically involved in the planning process due to the agencies' limited travel budgets.

A few observers have accused the agencies of shying away from involvement in planning efforts to avoid possible takings claims from property owners affected by plans. Also, resource agencies like EPA or USFWS that have charters for environmental protection are reluctant to make commitments on plans that classify certain natural areas as expendable.

Another approach, still experimental, is illustrated by the Hackensack Meadowlands planning process, in which EPA and the Corps (along with state agencies) are developing a special area management plan in advance of specific development applications. To facilitate future land use decisions, the plan will identify wetland areas where development should not occur. EPA and the Corps signed a Memorandum of Understanding on August 26, 1988, recognizing this process. They included a safety valve, however, a provision that indicates a limitation on a long-term commitment: "Any party may, upon written notification to the other parties, withdraw from the agreement and proceed independently pursuant to applicable requirements." Such provisions may be useful in gaining consensus on agreements but they undercut the certainty of commitments to the plan.

Funding for Planning

Collaborative planning usually occurs in a regulatory "no man's land," in which no agency possesses clear responsibility for underwriting the process by funding or administrative support. As the examples testify, area-wide planning requires management, staffing, and studies that must be funded from some source or sources. In some cases, a lead local or state agency will assume responsibility for basic staffing, although this may be limited by budget and staff resources. Federal agencies sometimes provide special grant funds to carry out needed studies or demonstrations, as in the Hackensack Meadowlands and in the East Everglades. Most often, however, developers find it necessary to initiate area-wide planning to break a regulatory logjam. In this case, one or more developers may fund initial efforts to organize a collaborative planning process and commission studies to assist the group's deliberations. Participation of federal, state, and local agency staff representatives in the planning efforts depends on cooperation from those agencies.

A major obstacle to engaging in collaborative planning is the lack of a basic funding source for initiating and carrying out a planning process. In effect, collaborative planning processes "fall between the cracks" of governmental budgets, and funding must be arduously pieced together from a variety of sources. This often limits the comprehensiveness of planning efforts and burdens the entire effort, especially as technical studies and data needs become more complex and, at the same time, more essential to decision making.

Equity Issues: Whose Ox Gets Gored?

Most area-wide plans earmark natural resource areas for preservation. Invariably, many of these areas are privately owned. One source at the USFWS, for example, estimated that over 70 percent of wetlands in the United States lie on private lands. Furthermore, a few landowners frequently bear the largest share of the burden of protecting wetlands or wildlife habitat, which makes the task of designating lands to be set aside even more difficult.

Once areas have been designated for acquisition and preservation, the funding question arises. Marsh and Lallas (Chapter 2) discuss the possible funding sources, which include developers, since their activities threaten the resource; the federal government, whose Clean Water and Endangered Species acts restrict uses of private land; nearby landowners who will benefit from increased property values; state, local, and special agencies that require land for facilities and services; and the general public, which desires conservation as a public good.

Usually, participants in area-wide planning attempt to strike a balance between public and private interests. Ideally, land use designations in area-wide plans should attempt to protect wetland and habitat resources. However, they also must recognize political, legal, and economic concerns such as land ownerships and alternative uses, if only to avoid a taking of private property without compensation, a violation of the Fifth Amendment of the Constitution. In Anchorage, Alaska, for example, many of the lines separating preservation from developable wetlands apparently followed property lines rather than natural boundaries. In the political climate in which the plan was prepared, that bow to accommodating property interests was necessary for agreement.

Funding for Implementation: Whose Pockets Are Deepest?

The examples of collaborative planning in this book demonstrate that in most cases compensating landowners for their loss is critical to the success of an area-wide plan, both to avoid stirring up a takings challenge and to garner landowner support for the plan. In the East Everglades, major elements of the plan were not put into effect until substantial funds became available to buy private land for wetlands preservation. The Chiwaukee Prairie project was in jeopardy until the compensation issue was addressed in the plan. The completion of the Balcones Canyonlands project was affected by the lack of acquisition funding.

A variety of compensation mechanisms have been used, including direct acquisition, land swaps, transfer of development rights, or purchase of conservation easements. Acquisition funding may come from a variety of sources, such as federal grants, state and local taxes, and developer fees or contributions. Federal money is scarce, however, and an increasing number of wetland and wildlife areas now compete for available funds.

Developer fees can help foot some of the bill, but alone they will be insufficient. In strong real estate markets, the money raised through impact fees often cannot keep pace with rapidly escalating land values. In Southern California, Riverside County raised funds through a $1,950 per acre development fee to purchase habitat for the endangered Stephens' kangaroo rat. But by the time the money was available, land values had increased 50 percent.

Moreover, reliance on developer fees to pay for preserved areas, as has been proposed for the Balcones Canyonlands and other areas, requires development to proceed. Riverside County has found that fee collections, in the moribund real estate economy of the early 1990s, have dropped to the point that its wildlife habitat program is itself endangered. In addition, conservationists remain unenthusiastic about the notion of allowing some development in order to raise funds for protecting habitat or wetlands from additional development.

Assurances: Sticking to the Plan

Given that area-wide planning is a voluntary process, how does the group ensure that participants will stand by an agreement, with its inevitable compromises? In particular, how can commitments be obtained from government agencies to abide by the plan? The Achilles heel of the East Everglades plan was that EPA was not party to the agreement. After the plan was completed, the agency vetoed rock plowing in the Frog Pond, an activity that the planning committee had agreed to allow as one of a host of difficult compromises. As a result, farmers lost faith in the plan and instead sought relief in the courts.

For a plan to be effective and for it to have some degree of staying power, it must become part of a legally enforceable agreement. Marsh and Lallas (Chapter 2) mention several types of assurance mechanisms. Some area-wide plans have been incorporated in local comprehensive plans or become part of a state coastal zone management plan. The CREST plan is being implemented through the state coastal management and growth management programs in Oregon and Washington. Habitat conservation plans are sanctioned by the USFWS, which establishes what essentially is a development agreement. The Corps officially acknowledges special area management plans. However, the complex process that the Hackensack Meadowlands Commission is using to mesh federal planning procedures and commitments with local and state planning requirements demonstrates how difficult the process can be.

Guidelines for Collaborative Planning

With few established standards or guidelines to follow, and no specific agency to provide support (or write rules), collaborative planning for conservation remains a voluntary, ad hoc, learn-as-you-go process. Each planning effort is unique. A number of common factors, however, drawn from the preceding chapters, appear to be important to the success of a planning effort.

Political Leadership

Leadership from a key public official is vital to endow the planning group with legitimacy, a sense of purpose, and at least a perception of power. A strong leader within the planning group will help the group maintain its focus, keep a reasonable timetable, avoid stalemate, and help parties reach compromises. As an illustration, in drafting the criteria for the Chesapeake Bay Critical Area Program, Judge Solomon Liss's strong guidance helped move the commission members toward consensus. He imparted a sense of fairness and openness to the proceedings that benefited all parties.

After completion of a plan, its successful implementation will depend on leadership from a resourceful political leader or agency. In Anchorage, Alaska, then-Mayor Tony Knowles strongly supported both wetland protection and wetland planning efforts. He made the wetland management plan a top priority of the Department of Planning. The subsequent mayor gave little support to the wetland plan, however, and the city's efforts to revise and improve it halted after his election. In Maryland, then-Governor Harry Hughes and his staff actively encouraged the critical area program to protect the Chesapeake Bay, including creation of a new program to limit development in sensitive areas around the Bay. And in Florida, then-Governor Bob Graham's interest and support helped the East Everglads plan gain early momentum and broad participation.

Participation of All Affected Interests

Collaborative planning efforts must involve all those with a stake in the results. In most cases, this includes regulators, developers, environmentalists, and property owners as a minimum. Permitting agencies with jurisdiction over the planning area must be persuaded to participate actively in the planning process. Although this may present problems in some instances, and agency representatives may not be able to officially bless an agreement, their participation ensures a level of understanding about issues that can be critical to later actions.

The voluntary consortium of federal, state, and local governments that participated in the CREST planning process illustrates the point. Through their joint planning endeavors, local public officials and their constituents became knowledgable about wetland protection issues. In general, member governments supported the CREST plan, which has been incorporated into municipal plans and ordinances. The other planning efforts described in this book provide further examples of the benefits of collaboration and consensus-building in planning for conservation.

Continuity of Planning and Management

Once a plan is developed, some mechanism must be created to fund its implementation and to monitor the plan—tracking commitments, permit approvals, and resource gains and losses. The Chesapeake Bay Critical Area Commission's continued involvement in carrying out the plan for the bay has kept public interest focused on the plan throughout its implementation. The commission continues to ensure implementation of the plan by local governments and to make land use decisions consistent with the state program. In the Hackensack Meadowlands, once the area-wide plan is complete, HMDC will be responsible for implementation and monitoring. By contrast, one of the flaws in both the East Everglades and Anchorage planning efforts was that the advisory committee that prepared the plan was disbanded after its adoption. As a result, the effort lost momentum, implementation was weakened, and when new conflicts arose, as they inevitably do, no group or mediator was responsible for resolving them. Similarly, the CREST staff, which reviews permit applications and assists local government planning efforts, was sharply reduced after the plan was adopted, curtailing its implementation program.

Another administrative requirement is the need to bridge changes in administrations and agency personnel. Establishment of a lead agency with clear responsibilities for follow-up implementation is an important step.

Development Safety Valves

Plans seem to work best where development pressures can be accommodated nearby. Conversely, area-wide planning seems to be most difficult in areas with a preponderance of wetlands or endangered species habitat that are subject to strong development pressures. In such circumstances, finding room for some development is a key to consensus.

In the Chesapeake Bay critical area, the commission focused on preserving valuable natural resource areas but also bowed to reality by designating intensely developed areas to which development can be directed. These areas provide a safety valve for development pressures. Similarly, in addition to its preservation category, the Anchorage wetlands planning committee created a developable land category where wetland filling could occur, and the Corps issued a general permit for those areas. By contrast, the pervasiveness of wetlands in the East Everglades, and the need for preserving the entire ecosystem, practically ensures that development will remain in conflict with conservation objectives. As a result, the East Everglades plan is probably the most complex, controversial, and tenuous of the examples presented in this book.

Anticipating Future Conflicts

Many HCPs address only a particular endangered species, but Beatley (Chapter 3) points out the importance of taking a comprehensive, multi-species approach to include not only currently listed endangered species but also those that are threatened as well as species likely to be listed in the near future. In Southern California, for nearly a decade before the Stephens' kangaroo rat was listed, developers and regulators alike knew that it was a prime candidate for listing but chose to ignore the possibility. Only after the rat was finally listed, precluding several large areas from development, did developers begin to assess the impacts of the listing on their projects. At that point, it became a painful and expensive problem.

As Beatley observes, looking forward to potential listings through a multi-species approach can accomplish development ends while achieving conservation objectives. The multi-species conservation planning being undertaken by Southern California counties, in fact, anticipates that advance planning could mean that some species may never require listing.

Integration of Area-wide Plans with Local Plans

Area-wide conservation plans should be integrated with local comprehensive plans and/or coastal zone management plans. This provides a "reality check" that assures coordination between local and area-wide planning but also establishes an implementation mechanism through the regulations and programs that link to local comprehensive plans. In the Hackensack Meadowlands, the SAMP will form the basis for HMDC's regional plan, thus directing future development away from wetlands and endangered species habitat. The plans for Chiwaukee Prairie, Chesapeake Bay, the Columbia estuary, and the East Everglades anticipate that local government plans and standards will be consistent with conservation plan goals, as well as statewide goals.

Mediation to Resolve Conflicts

In Chesapeake Bay, East Everglades, and Bolsa Chica, mediators were brought in to help the planning groups reach consensus on a number of issues. Although not necessary or practical in many collaborative planning programs—a skillful chairperson or staff may provide sufficient guidance—a mediation or dispute resolution approach is a useful method for overcoming deadlocked discussions.

These issues and guidelines suggest the factors that must be considered in organizing and carrying out a collaborative, area-wide planning process. The examples described in this book, however, clearly suggest that planning programs must be specifically tailored to the particular interests and conditions of the area and the jurisdictions involved. Unfortunately, lacking a recognized source of funding for such planning efforts, each program also will reflect financial pressures that will limit data collection and analysis and the participation of concerned interests and agencies. Nonetheless, the experiences demonstrate the inventiveness and perseverance of stakeholders in structuring collaborative processes and working through them to reconcile environmental objectives with development intentions.

Index

Contributors

KATHLEEN SHEA ABRAMS is director of the Office of Environmental Education for the State Department of Education in Tallahassee, Florida. She prepared the East Everglades study (Chapter 11) when she was an associate director of the Florida Atlantic University/Florida International University Joint Center for Environmental and Urban Problems in North Miami and Fort Lauderdale, Florida.

MARK B. ADAMS is a geographic information systems specialist with the Cape Cod National Seashore Office of the National Park Service. He coauthored the CREST study (Chapter 6) as a consultant to the Environmental Law Institute.

TIMOTHY BEATLEY is associate professor and chair of the Department of Urban and Environmental Planning at the University of Virginia in Charlottesville, Virginia. He holds a Ph.D. in city and regional planning from the University of North Carolina at Chapel Hill and writes extensively on planning and environmental issues.

DAVID BRAUN is director of The Nature Conservancy of Texas in San Antonio, Texas, which has been heavily involved in the Balcones Canyonlands habitat conservation planning process.

EDWIN W. FINDER consults with the Hackensack Meadowlands Development Commission, serving as Special Area Management Plan Coordinator. He is a senior real estate consultant with Parish and Weiner, Inc., in Tarrytown, New York.

ROBERT FISCHMAN was formerly staff attorney and director of the natural resource law program at the Environmental Law Institute in Washington, D.C. Currently, Mr. Fischman is an associate professor of law at Indiana University in Bloomington, Indiana.

T. JAMES FRIES is director of the Texas Hill Country Bioreserve for The Nature Conservancy of Texas in Austin, Texas. He has been responsible for The Nature Conservancy's involvement in the Balcones Canyonlands Conservation Plan since January 1991.

HUGH GLADWIN, who assisted in preparing the East Everglades study (Chapter 11), is an associate professor of sociology and anthropology and associate director of the Institute for Public Opinion Research at Florida International University in North Miami, Florida.

LEAH V. HAYGOOD is director of environmental planning and programs with WMX Technologies, Inc., in Washington, D.C. She prepared the Chiwaukee Prairie study (Chapter 8) while an associate in the environmental dispute resolution program at The Conservation Foundation.

PETER L. LALLAS is an attorney/advisor in the general counsel's office of the Environmental Protection Agency in Washington, D.C. While assisting in preparing the introductory overview of collaborative planning (Chapter 2), he was an attorney with Siemon, Larsen & Marsh in Irvine, California.

ANNE MARSH was formerly the editor of the Environmental Law Institute's *National Wetlands Newsletter*. She is now a doctoral candidate at the Yale Univeristy School of Forestry and Environmental Studies.

LINDELL L. MARSH is a partner with the law firm of Siemon, Larsen & Marsh in Irvine, California, who specializes in collaborative planning to resolve conservation/development issues. He initiated and co-chaired the series of working group discussions convened by the Urban Land Institute and the Environmental Law Institute that led to this book.

MARY JEAN MATTHEWS is a senior research associate and director of publications at the Florida Atlantic University/Florida International University Joint Center for Environmental and Urban Problems in Fort Lauderdale, Florida. She assisted in preparing the East Everglades study (Chapter 6) while a visiting research associate at the center.

BARBARA C. MCCABE is completing coursework toward a doctorate in public administration and policy at Florida State University in Tallahassee. She assisted in preparing the East Everglades study (Chapter 11) when a senior research associate and assistant director of the Florida Atlantic University/Florida International University Joint Center for Environmental and Urban Problems in Fort Lauderdale, Florida.

SCOTT T. MCCREARY is a principal of CONCUR, a facilitation and environmental policy firm in Berkeley, California. His doctorate from the Massachusetts Institute of Technology is in environmental policy and dispute resolution. He coauthored the CREST study (Chapter 6) as a consultant to the Environmental Law Institute.

ERIK MEYERS is general counsel and director of the Wetlands Program for the Environmental Law Institute in Washington, D.C. He is an advisor to ELI's *National Wetlands Newsletter* and has contributed to several books on wetlands.

DOUGLAS R. PORTER is president of The Growth Management Institute and is a planning and development consultant in Chevy Chase, Maryland. While director of public policy research at the Urban Land Institute, he assisted in convening the working group discussions and research studies that led to this book.

DAVID A. SALVESEN is an environmental writer and consultant in Kensington, Maryland. His studies of Anchorage (Chapter 10) and Bolsa Chica (Chapter 12) were prepared while he was senior research associate for the Urban Land Institute, where he also assisted in managing the working group discussions that led to this book.